Nancy Mingus

Alpha
Teach Yourself

Project
Management

in 24 hours

ALPHA

A Pearson Education Company

Alpha Teach Yourself Project Management in 24 Hours

Copyright © 2002 by John A. Woods, CWL Publishing

This is a CWL Publishing Enterprises book developed for Alpha Books by CWL Publishing Enterprises, John A. Woods, President, 3010 Irvington Way, Madison, WI 53713-3414, www.cwlpub.com.

International Standard Book Number: 0-02-864223-6
Library of Congress Catalog Card Number: 2001095333

Printed in the United States of America

First printing: 2002

04   03   02   4   3   2

Trademarks

SENIOR ACQUISITIONS EDITOR
Renee Wilmeth

DEVELOPMENT EDITOR
Nancy D. Warner

SENIOR PRODUCTION EDITOR
Christy Wagner

COPY EDITOR
Jan Zunkel

INDEXER
Brad Herriman

PRODUCTION
Svetlana Dominguez
Gloria Schurick

COVER DESIGNER
Alan Clements

BOOK DESIGNER
Gary Adair

MANAGING EDITOR
Jennifer Chisholm

PRODUCT MANAGER
Phil Kitchel

PUBLISHER
Marie Butler-Knight

Overview

Contents

PART III Executing Your Project

HOUR 13 Doing the Work — 183

HOUR 18 Evaluating Project Status   257

About the Author

Nancy Blumenstalk Mingus is President of Mingus Associates, Inc., a writing, training, and consulting company specializing in project management and historic preservation. Founded in 1989, the company has worked with a wide variety of clients, including the Army Corps of Engineers, Cornell University, M&T Bank, Mark IV Industries, NCR, Ralston Purina, Sundstrand Corporation, and Systemation.

Mingus has been working in or with project management for nearly 25 years. She has written more than 50 articles and has delivered over 500 workshops on a variety of project management, training, computer, and historic preservation topics. She holds a Master's in Education and a Master's in Historic Preservation and received her PMP certification from the Project Management Institute in 1996.

She serves on the board of several organizations, including the Buffalo chapter of the Project Management Institute. She is also chair of the Historic Preservation Commission in the Town of Amherst, New York.

She firmly believes that learning to manage projects more effectively can help people not only in their careers but also in their personal lives. To that end, this book presents the basics of effective project management.

Mingus resides with her husband, daughters, and cat, Max, in Williamsville, New York.

Dedication

This book is dedicated to my husband, Michael Mingus, and to my daughters, Marissa and Paige, for their patience with my crazy work schedule writing this book while also completing a Master's thesis.

Acknowledgments

I wish to thank John Woods of CWL Publishing for selecting me for this book and helping me through the process.

I also wish to thank Michael Tomlan, whose sage editorial help on my Master's thesis inadvertently helped me in writing this book.

Introduction

The number of people functioning as project managers has mushroomed in the past decade. The traditional path to project management had been from best technical person to project manager, but practitioners soon realized project management was not just technical skill. While technical skills may be helpful, planning, general management, and extensive people skills are also required to effectively manage a project.

Unlike in accounting or other professional fields, there is no right or wrong way to manage a project. Still, over the years, project managers have developed a set of best practices to help increase the chance of project success. The material presented in this book represents those best practices, but also includes the author's personal tips and suggestions for what has worked for her and other project managers whom she knows. This will help you learn not just the theories, but the practicalities, too.

Part I, "Learning the Basics," introduces you to the rationale behind project management, discusses the leading project management trade organization and some of its standards. It also discusses the project initiation and planning processes and provides guidelines on important components of a formal project plan.

Part II, "Developing Project Plan Details," delves into more detail on critical planning tools such as Work Breakdown Structures, project estimates, network diagrams, project schedules, Gantt charts, and risk plans.

Part III, "Executing Your Project," covers project execution, that is, doing the work. Topics include setting project baselines, executing your control plans, tracking your project progress, and updating your project plans.

Part IV, "Controlling Your Project," discusses the control aspects of a project that go hand-in-hand with project execution. These include monitoring costs, evaluating project status, getting projects back on track, and reporting on your project's performance.

Part V, "Closing Out Your Project," outlines the steps to follow to wrap up your project. These include turning products over to clients, performing a final evaluation of your project, and applying what you learned on this project to future projects. This part ends with an overview of the capabilities of project management software packages and a brief discussion of some of the more popular packages.

Last but not least, this book has a lot of miscellaneous cross-references, tips, shortcuts, and warning sidebar boxes. Here's how they stack up:

GO TO ▶
This sidebar gives you a cross-reference to another chapter or section in the book to learn more about a particular topic.

JUST A MINUTE

 This sidebar offers advice or teaches an easier way to do things.

STRICTLY DEFINED

Strictly Defined boxes offer definitions of words you may not know.

PROCEED WITH CAUTION

 Proceed with Caution boxes are warnings. They warn you about potential problems and help you steer clear of trouble.

 These sidebars give you tidbits of information that you might want to know.

TIME SAVER

 This sidebar tells you a different way to perform a task to save time.

PART I
Learning the Basics

HOUR 1

Understanding Project Management

CHAPTER SUMMARY

LESSON PLAN:

In this hour you will learn about ...

- The benefits of using a project management process.
- A brief history of project management.
- The Project Management Institute (PMI).
- Project management concepts.
- The five PMI processes.
- Project management methodologies and life cycles.
- The three projects we'll use as case studies.

Before we start talking about the specific tools and techniques that will help you to manage your projects more effectively, it's important to have some background information. The sections in this hour provide the foundation on which the remaining lessons build.

UNDERSTAND PROJECT MANAGEMENT RATIONALE

In this section we'll explore the rationale for using standard project management techniques when working on your projects. We'll review some of the common project management fallacies as well as the realities.

BEWARE OF PROJECT MANAGEMENT FALLACIES

The most common project management fallacies tend to come in opposing pairs.

The first pair relates to using project management techniques. The positive fallacy is that using project management tools and techniques rigorously will guarantee project success. Nothing, however, can guarantee project success. The opposing fallacy is that using project management techniques doesn't help project success—and, in fact, may add such overhead that it causes projects to be less successful. While using project management techniques does add up-front costs, they are minimal, especially when compared with the benefits.

GO TO ▶
See Hour 8, "Developing Project Estimates," where estimating is explained in more detail.

PROCEED WITH CAUTION

If you will be managing projects within a corporate environment, you may find that you need to also educate your colleagues about the project management fallacies and realities.

The second pair of fallacies concerns estimates, with the first saying that estimates are accurate and should be carved in stone. This is not realistic. However, neither is the opposing fallacy, that estimates are always unreasonably inflated and should be ignored and/or cut in half to be closer to reality.

Last are the *project plan* fallacies, the first of which is that if project managers plan correctly, everything will go according to plan. It is unrealistic to think that project managers can anticipate every eventuality. On the other hand, believing that nothing ever goes according to plan is also not true and may be a self-fulfilling prophecy.

STRICTLY DEFINED

A **project plan** is a formal document with many components. It is not just the project schedule as created in a software package.

DEAL WITH PROJECT MANAGEMENT REALITIES

Somewhere in the middle of the pairs of fallacies mentioned in the previous section are the project management realities. Following standard project management techniques *can* significantly increase the chance of project success. Many project managers have success rates nearing 100 percent. The techniques take time to implement, but various studies have shown that for every hour spent in project planning, projects can actually save 20 or more hours in executing and controlling, which also increases the odds of project success.

In regard to estimates, they are just that: guesses at how long something will take and how much it will cost. But several proven techniques will help you estimate more realistically over time. As with everything, estimating more accurately is a learning process, not just for individual project managers, but for their teams and organizations as well.

In terms of proceeding as planned, seasoned project managers understand that they and their teams are human. Tasks are not always defined correctly, estimates are not always accurate, and unanticipated events can change a project drastically. But by applying project control techniques to a project, especially risk management techniques, projects can proceed more closely to plan.

KNOW A LITTLE HISTORY

The project management field is evolving, but many of the tools and techniques have been with us for more than a century. This section explores some of that early history as well as the more recent developments in the field.

GANTT, PERT, AND CPM

The most important techniques we use in project management today have their origins in the work of Henry Gantt in the late 1800s. Gantt developed a system he called "The Task and Bonus System" and implemented it at Bethlehem Steel, where he was working at the time. In this system he introduced and refined several project management concepts, such as breaking down a process into a series of tasks, performing work to standard estimates on those tasks, and tracking progress against those estimates. He created a new type of chart to track this progress so that it could be verified, as he called it, "at a glance." Gantt charts are still the most popular project scheduling and tracking tools.

GO TO ▶
See Hour 11, "Creating a Gantt Chart," for more details on Gantt charts.

In the 1950s, two new project-planning strategies were introduced. Both were intended to help minimize the risk of going over schedule on projects.

One was called the Program Evaluation and Review Technique, or PERT for short. PERT uses a *network diagramming* technique called activity on arrow and an estimating technique called weighted averaging. The estimating portion of this technique is still used, although the Critical Path Method has largely replaced the network-diagramming portion.

STRICTLY DEFINED

A **network diagram** is a special type of chart showing the interrelationships between project tasks.

The Critical Path Method, or CPM, is also a network diagramming and scheduling technique. This technique uses a diagramming method called activity on node and creates the project schedule based on the longest path through the network.

GO TO ▶
Both the PERT and CPM techniques are described in more detail in Hour 9, "Creating a Network Diagram."

THE PROJECT MANAGEMENT INSTITUTE

While there have been project managers for centuries, the recognition of project management as a profession is more recent. During the early industrial age, project managers were the most technically qualified people in their organizations, and the role of project manager tended to be a stepping-stone to a job as a functional manager. But in the 1970s, individuals and organizations began to recognize that project managers needed different skill sets than functional managers. By the end of the 1990s, project management was generally recognized as a profession, especially in large corporations and in corporations specializing in information technology, construction, architecture, and engineering.

Much of this increased recognition of project management as a profession can be traced to the Project Management Institute (PMI), an international trade organization for project managers. Formed in 1969, PMI spent the first few decades of its life as a relatively small group of project managers primarily in the engineering and construction fields. By the mid-1990s, membership had grown to 12,000; less than a decade later, by the end of 2000, membership had exploded to over 70,000 worldwide.

One of the first steps in turning a job into a profession is establishing standards for practice. Just as architects gained professional status in the early 1900s by developing their own standards through the American Institute of Architects, PMI has increased not just the visibility but also the standards of practice for project managers.

They have done this in two ways. First, they distilled the wealth of information on project management and produced a slender volume titled the *A Guide to the Project Management Body of Knowledge*, generally abbreviated as the *PMBOK Guide*. The first widely recognized guide was released in 1987, and it identified the generally accepted practices in project management and organized them by project functional areas. In 1996, this guide was updated and expanded, and in 2000, the guide was updated yet again. In addition to the revisions to the guide, PMI continues to develop standards for several of the typical project management processes, including the creation of *Work Breakdown Structures* (WBS).

STRICTLY DEFINED

A **Work Breakdown Structure**, also known as a **WBS**, is a hierarchical arrangement of a project's tasks in levels similar to a company's organization chart.

The second way in which PMI has promoted the professional status of project managers is through certification. While the success of the certifications in other fields has been spotty at best, Project Management Professional

(PMP) Certification found a recognition, albeit slowly. In the first years of certification, few PMP certifications were issued, yet as of year-end 2000, there were more than 27,000 holders of the PMP certification.

 FYI For more information on the Project Management Institute, visit their Web site at www.pmi.org.

UNDERSTAND PROJECT MANAGEMENT CONCEPTS

Now that we've covered some background information, we're ready to discuss some of the basic project management concepts. We'll start by discussing commonalties in projects and then define some project-related terms and review project success measurements and factors.

DEFINE PROJECT AND PROJECT MANAGEMENT

When someone mentions the term "project," we all have a variety of images and terms popping into our minds. Take a few minutes now to jot down some of those terms.

On most people's lists would be the following: deadlines, start date, end date, schedule, tasks, resources, cost, and sequential. Other terms may include milestones, change, conflict, communication, goal, requirements, and risk. Hundreds of terms might be listed to describe various aspects of a project, which makes it important to have a common definition of the word.

While project has several definitions, a simple and relatively inclusive one is a sequence of tasks performed to achieve a unique goal within a specific time frame. Uniqueness is key here. It's what separates projects from operations and what makes them more difficult to manage. Once you figure out how to perform an operation, you can just repeat the steps, but because every project is unique, the steps vary. The good news is that in most industries, while the specific steps vary in every project, the types of steps are consistent and are generally repeatable.

To standardize further on the definition of the word, the Project Management Institute, in its *PMBOK Guide*, defines a project as follows: "A temporary endeavor undertaken to create a unique project or service."

Traditionally, project management was viewed as the planning, scheduling, and controlling of a project to meet the project's goals. While this is still a valid definition, keep in mind that it doesn't include the critical human relations and project evaluation components that are generally performed after a project is complete. The Project Management Institute uses this definition for project management: "The application of knowledge, skills, tools, and techniques to project activities on order to meet or exceed stakeholder needs and expectations from a project."

MEASURE PROJECT SUCCESS

The two traditional measurements for project success are that the project be …

1. On time.
2. Within budget.

There are, however, three additional measures of success that need to be considered:

3. Were the project goals met? [Scope]
4. Was the client satisfied? [Quality]
5. Were there no casualties, either to the team or to interrelationships? [Resources]

Unfortunately, many people concentrate so much on the first two—time and budget—they fail in the latter three. While this may be good for the project managers and their organizations in the short term, in the long term it has a detrimental effect.

The interrelationships of these five measures of project success can be represented graphically in what is often referred to as the *Project Management Triangle* or *Time, Cost, Scope Triangle* (see the following figure). The *Scope* side represents the agreed-upon project work and requirements, the Cost side represents the total dollar cost of the project, and the Time side represents the project duration. Inside the triangle, Resources refers to the people and equipment in use on the project and Quality to how close the project is to satisfying client expectations.

STRICTLY DEFINED

Scope is the amount of work to be done in a project.

What this figure portrays is that there is a relationship between the scope of a project, how long that project will take, and how much it will cost. If the scope of a project is increased once estimates have been established for time and cost, the only way to maintain the same relationship is to also increase time and/or cost.

If time and cost are kept the same, as shown in the *Scope Creep* version of the triangle (see the following figure), then the other two components suffer. Either resources are overworked, which may lead to casualties, or quality is reduced, which may lead to unsatisfied clients. In some cases, both of these may happen.

STRICTLY DEFINED

Scope Creep is the continual addition of unplanned work to the project.

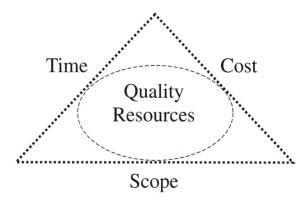

KNOW THE CRITICAL SUCCESS FACTORS

The following factors will help guarantee project success measured by all of these criteria:

1. A clear, written, and agreed to statement of the project's goals and requirements
2. Ongoing participation in the project by the project sponsor, clients, and team
3. Realistic project time and cost estimates
4. Ongoing change and quality control

Taking the time to establish these factors is vital. The mechanisms for doing so are described in the rest of this book.

WORK ON PROJECT PROCESSES

To help project managers meet these success criteria, the Project Management Institute recognizes five categories of project activities generally referred to as *project processes* (see the following figure).

The iterative relationships among the five project management processes.

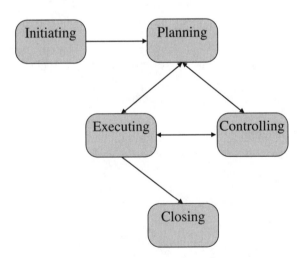

These five processes are introduced here and discussed in more detail in subsequent hours.

- **Initiate a project.** Initiating activities involve both the starting of a project as well as the starting of other phases within the project.

- **Plan.** Planning activities include the creation of the project plan, work breakdown structure, and initial schedule. The planning processes are perhaps the most important in a project because proper planning can significantly reduce the time spent in the execution processes. Various surveys conducted over the past 20 years indicate that for every hour spent in planning, 20 to 100 hours can be saved in execution.

- **Execute.** Executing activities are the activities in which the actual project work is done. In information systems, this would be where software packages are analyzed, designed, developed, and tested. In construction, this would be where concrete foundations are poured, walls are erected, and fixtures are installed.

GO TO ▶
See Hour 2, "Initiating a Project," where the activities to perform in the initiating process are explained in more detail.

- **Control.** Controlling activities measure and monitor the executing activities and help the project manager evaluate project progress in terms of cost, time, and quality.

- **Close.** Closing activities include closing phases and projects as well as holding the important lessons learned session, which helps improve the effectiveness of future projects.

PROJECT MANAGEMENT SKILL AREAS

In the PMBOK Guide, PMI identifies nine skill areas for project managers:

- Integration Management
- Scope Management
- Time Management
- Procurement Management
- Human Resource Management
- Communication Management
- Quality Management
- Cost Management
- Risk Management

In the *PMBOK Guide*, PMI refers to these nine skill sets as Knowledge Areas. Each knowledge area is briefly described here and more completely described in subsequent hours.

Integration Management skills are used to integrate the work in other core areas. The primary focus of integration management is the creation of a cohesive, comprehensive, and well-designed project plan and the execution of that project plan. Another component of this skill is the overseeing of the change control process, both as it is developed in the plan and as it is executed throughout the life of the project.

Scope Management is the skill project managers use to define the work that needs to be done on any given project. This entails making sure that all the work required is included and that no unneeded work is added. It includes formal project and phase initiations, developing the written scope statement (with scope exclusions), and listing major and intermediary project deliverables. It also includes the formal agreement by major players to the scope as defined and scope change control (the ongoing process of evaluating project changes).

PROCEED WITH CAUTION

The Scope Management portion of Project Management is vital, especially in the planning stages, because it sets the client's and the entire team's expectations for the project.

Time Management is the skill that most people associate with project management because it is crucial for keeping on schedule. It includes creating or refining the project work breakdown structure, determining dependency relationships among the project tasks, estimating the effort and duration of the tasks, and creating a project schedule. It also includes the control component of monitoring and updating the project progress and making changes to estimates and schedules. A commonly misunderstood facet of project management is that, by the nature of projects, estimates and schedules will change. As long as the project manager stays on top of these changes, this should not affect the final target completion date.

Procurement Management, also known as *Contract Management*, involves developing, executing, and monitoring contracts with service and product vendors. It also includes deciding what must be procured, soliciting bids for the products or services, selecting the appropriate vendor, and closing the contract once the project has been completed.

Human Resource Management addresses the people involved in a project. It includes the planning components of determining what skills are needed to perform the various project tasks, defining the participants' roles and responsibilities, and selecting potential candidates for those tasks. It also includes acquiring the appropriate resources (either internally, from external departments, or even external companies) and any professional development that the team members may need to improve their project performance.

Communication Management is the often neglected, yet perhaps most important, component of project management. It includes deciding who needs what information, to what level of detail, and in what media and time frames. These needs are documented in the communication plan subsection of the project plan so that parties can review them and then follow them. The communication plan may also specify the format to be used for each communication and turnaround times for each communication. Once the plan is approved, project managers then use their communication management skills to make sure the information is gathered and distributed according to the plan.

Quality Management has three subsets, generally referred to as Quality Planning, Quality Assurance, and Quality Control. In Quality Planning, a project manager defines what represents quality and how quality will be measured. In Quality Assurance, the project manager watches the overall quality of a project to see that standards will be met. In Quality Control, the project manager examines actual project outputs to evaluate their conformance to the standards set in the plan.

GO TO ▶

See Hour 5, "Developing Project Control Plans," for more information on the planning aspects of communication and to Hour 14, "Following Your Control Plans," for more information on the executing aspects.

Cost Management includes determining the project cost categories, estimating the use of each resource in each category, budgeting for that estimated cost and getting it approved, and then controlling the cost as the project progresses. Both fixed costs—such as equipment and software purchases—and variable costs—such as team member time—are included in the planning and estimating and are then monitored and controlled.

Risk Management starts with identifying the potential risks to a project and then determining the likelihood of each risk happening and how that risk would impact the project if it occurred. From this list and ranking, contingencies are developed for the highest risks. As the project is executed, one can use these contingencies to regain control of a project if a potential risk does occur.

By understanding and applying the knowledge in each of these knowledge areas, a project manager can maximize the potential for a successful completion of any project.

Two other tools to help a project manager be more effective are *methodologies* and *life cycles*.

MASTER THE METHODOLOGIES

Project Management methodologies are guidelines for the type of documentation and authorities required to proceed at various points in a project. These guidelines help in two main ways: They provide beginning project managers with a framework within which to work, and they help an organization standardize on procedures and terminology.

Organizations create their project management methodologies in three ways.

- Purchase a methodology from another company. (There are several vendors of methodologies for the various industries as well as vendors who sell generic methodologies.)
- Develop their methodologies from scratch. (Some organizations prefer this.)
- Customize a purchased methodology.

Regardless of how an organization acquires a methodology, it is not uncommon for those methodologies to evolve over time.

KNOW YOUR LIFE CYCLES

Each organization with a Project Management methodology usually has its own Project Management life cycle as well. Simply put, a life cycle helps divide each project into discrete phases or stages, which then dictate the types of activities performed in those phases/stages. Here are three examples of Project Management life cycles:

- Project initiation, planning, construction, project review
- Start-up, planning, implementation, post-implementation
- Initiating, planning, developing, evaluating

Combining methodologies with life cycles can help an organization build repeatable project successes. But even without a formal methodology or life cycle, you can substantially improve your chances of project success by using the tools and techniques described in the remaining 23 lessons.

JUST A MINUTE

If you work in an organization, find out what, if any, project management methodology and life cycle are standard. While the names for each phase and the names for activities and tasks will vary from those discussed here, the work being done will not. This will help you relate the discussion here to what your organization requires.

APPLY WHAT YOU'RE LEARNING

To help you understand how to apply the project management techniques we'll be discussing, we will be working with three projects. The first two will be used to show you how to perform the steps introduced in a section, and the third will give you a chance to practice applying the techniques. The basic premise of each case is given in the following sections.

CORPORATE AWARDS BANQUET AND PURCHASING SYSTEM

You work at the Leetle Toy Company, a small manufacturing company. Peter Leetle founded the Leetle Toy Company in 1956. The business operated on a shoestring for many years, until 1965, when Leetle's sister-in-law, Jackie Jamison, joined the company. During her first year, she designed the company's new logo and created its hallmark toy, the Leetle Bug. For the past 35 years, the Leetle Bug has been the company's best selling and most loved toy, although Leetle Toy Company also sells a line of licensed Disney characters, traditional teddy bears, and other stuffed toys.

Peter Leetle died in 1985 and Jamison retired, leaving the company in the capable hands of its current president, John Leetle. In these past 15 years, the company has grown to 300 employees. Today, the human resources area is currently revising many of the company's employment policies and writing a new employee manual while the designing, marketing, and production areas are busy on their first custom toy in six years, called Beeg Bird. The MIS and financial departments are busy implementing new General Ledger, Accounts Receivable, and Accounts Payable systems. The employees have been actively chipping in to cut costs and improve revenues.

When John Leetle took over the company, sales were still small, at only $500,000. But by 1989, sales had reached $11 million; this year, they are expected to top $30 million. Not bad at all for a company whose biggest product is a small fluorescent orange bug.

To celebrate the company growth and employee dedication, the vice presidents would like to select at least three employees to honor at an awards banquet about six months from now. The current human resources vice president, Sam Parker, who has been with the company for 15 years, is leading the call for the banquet. You have been assigned to manage the awards project.

Because of this large increase in production, the company is finding that the time delays involved in the existing purchasing system are shutting down production. To compensate, the shop has had to increase inventory on hand, which is affecting cash flow. It is likely that the senior management will be initiating an investigation into a replacement purchasing package in the near future.

CONFERENCE CENTER RENOVATION

The Leetle Toy Company executives are big supporters of the local historic preservation group. The preservation group has recently incorporated a subsidiary nonprofit, which has purchased a run-down building. Sam Parker, the Senior Vice President of Human Resources, has volunteered you to help the group to manage the building restoration.

The building is an old meetinghouse that has been vacant for the past two years; prior to that, it was a soup kitchen for nearly 30 years. It's a three-story commercial Queen-Anne-style building built in 1884 and a contributing building in a National Historic District. It's brick on the first floor, frame on the second and third, with a full basement with a Medina sandstone foundation. The original wood siding on the top two floors has been covered or replaced by asbestos siding. The roof appears to have been last done in the 1960s and has major leaks in several places. Several windows are broken and covered with plywood, but most are the original 16 × 16. The heat and electrical systems will all need to be replaced and the foundation supports must be repaired.

The nonprofit group intends to restore the building, with a caretaker's third-floor apartment, using the library as an office and using the auditorium and dining rooms as training and banquet facilities, both for internal use and to rent.

FYI Additional information on each project will be presented as needed in future lessons.

HOUR 2
Initiating a Project

- Listing project needs.
- Determining project feasibility.
- Evaluating project risk.
- Writing a project recommendation.
- Identifying a sponsor.
- Obtaining authorization to proceed.

A project always starts with someone uncovering a need he or she thinks a project can satisfy. Often, though, this need is ill defined or is too small to justify the project required to meet that need. Yet, the common approach is to plunge in anyway. In the following sections of this hour, you'll learn the steps to take before taking the plunge.

LIST PROJECT NEEDS

Projects often start out as fuzzy images of a need to do something. You may see a problem that needs fixing, opportunities to exploit a new market niche, or a way to cut costs. But without developing a list of needs up front, two problems could occur. You could create a project that doesn't meet the true need, or you could create a project that will end up costing more than it will save. For these reasons, it's best to start any project with a simple list of the business or personal needs driving the project.

You need to consider several categories of business when creating your list. They include the following:

- Capital improvements
- Legal requirements
- New product development
- Process improvement
- Problem removal

While it isn't necessary to categorize your needs when you are listing them, the categories are helpful in getting you started on what your individual project needs may be. Let's look at each of these categories in a little more detail.

JUST A MINUTE

Make sure that the business needs you list in this section correspond with your company's strategic goals.

Consider Capital Improvements

Many corporate projects can be classified as capital improvements. Some of the more common needs in this category include the need for more office, warehouse, or training space; the need to upgrade the HVAC (Heating, Ventilation, and Air Conditioning) infrastructure; or the need to upgrade manufacturing or other equipment.

Consider Legal Requirements

The needs that fall under legal requirements include the need to improve employee or consumer safety, the need to improve employee or consumer health, the need to comply with current building or other codes, and the need to comply with changing federal banking or other regulations.

JUST A MINUTE

Writing down the business needs for a project not only clarifies them in your mind but also helps you to verify them with other project participants.

Consider Product Development

Product development needs include the need to design new products, to refine existing products, or to change marketing programs to increase market share.

Consider Process Improvement

Process improvement needs include new computer software systems, revised employment policies, new project management processes, and *ISO certification.*

> Receiving **ISO certification** means that your organization has proven it meets certain standards of your specific industry.

Consider Problem Removal

The largest problem removal need is generally some type of cost reduction, but this category would also include computer software and hardware bug fixes and redesigning products with known defects. The need for training might also fall under the problem-removal category.

Note that some of the needs can overlap. For instance, the need to improve the HVAC systems may be driven by a code compliance need. In cases where this occurs, you may want to list the legal requirement as the primary need and the improvements as a secondary need.

Now that we've looked at some types of business needs, let's look at the project needs for the case studies.

List Awards Banquet Needs

Take a few minutes to reread the awards banquet case study in Hour 1, "Understanding Project Management."

It appears that two primary needs are driving this project. One is the need to recognize the corporate achievements of the past few years and the other is to recognize the specific contributions of a select number of individuals.

List Conference Center Needs

Take a few minutes to reread the conference center restoration project case study from Hour 1, and then list two to five project needs. The conference center needs are listed in Appendix A, "Sample Documents."

Determine Project Feasibility

Once you've listed your project needs, you're ready to review the feasibility of the project. You can take several approaches to assessing feasibility, but perhaps the most inclusive is to do the assessment by *constraint* category.

> A **constraint** is something that limits a project.

Common constraint categories include the following:

- Technical
- Financial
- Operational
- Geographic

- Time
- Resource
- Legal
- Political

Let's see how considering these constraint categories can also help us assess feasibility.

CONSIDER TECHNICAL FEASIBILITY

When reviewing the technical feasibility, you compare the technical requirements of a project with your current technical capabilities and/or your ability to acquire the necessary technical skills. For instance, if the project is to develop a new computer system, technical feasibility issues may include whether or not the type of data arrangement required could be handled by your existing database and whether or not the existing hardware could run the new software.

If the project is some type of event, such as a conference, training seminar, or wedding, technical feasibility would include such questions as "Is there a facility available that will accommodate the event?" and "Are there suitable speakers for the event topic?"

For construction projects, technical feasibility would include questions like "Can this lightweight structure actually support the weight of the roof?" or "Can our equipment lathe the number of balusters needed?"

CONSIDER FINANCIAL FEASIBILITY

The major financial feasibility issue is whether or not you have enough money to properly execute the project. This particular aspect of financial feasibility is defined in some projects as part of the cost/benefit analysis.

Some other financial considerations include whether or not a new product will be ready before a similar product by the competition (time to market), whether a project would have a negative impact on a company's image (hence revenue), and what the ongoing support requirements might be. Many times, organizations and individuals can afford the costs of a project but cannot afford the time, people, or cash to support the product of the project.

FYI Cost/benefit analysis will be discussed in more detail later in the "Perform High-Level Cost/Benefit Analysis" section, later in this lesson.

In the case of a new computer software system, evaluating financial feasibility includes considering any escalating hardware requirements, programmer and operations support, and any annual software maintenance fees.

If the project is some type of event, such as a conference, training seminar, or wedding, most of the financial feasibility issues are covered in the cost/benefit analysis. There are limited ongoing costs for these types of projects.

For construction projects, financial feasibility would include ongoing operating costs such as heating and electricity, as well as regular maintenance costs such as painting.

CONSIDER OPERATIONAL FEASIBILITY

Operational feasibility refers to how the project fits in with the way things are done in your company. If it takes three weeks for purchase orders to run through your purchasing system, this makes a project to purchase something next week infeasible. If half of the workforce works second or third shift, it might make a weeknight evening event infeasible.

When working on personal projects, operational feasibility may refer to how the companies you are doing business with work. For example, airlines requiring a three-week advance purchase and Saturday night stay may make something operationally infeasible.

In addition to processes, other operational issues include the number of departments, divisions, or companies involved in a project. The larger these numbers are, the more difficult it is to complete a project successfully.

PROCEED WITH CAUTION

Listing operational deficiencies in your feasibility study may bring criticism by other project participants. You will need to justify the negative impacts you see.

A third operational issue to consider is whether or not the project conflicts with other projects currently in work. A project to reduce costs by 15 percent may be in conflict with a project to train everyone on the new release of the corporate standard word-processing system.

With a new computer system, replacing a single accounting system may be operationally infeasible because of its tight integration with the other accounting systems.

If the project is some type of event, such as a conference, training seminar, or wedding, operational feasibility would include the availability of an appropriately sized and equipped facility.

For construction projects, operational feasibility issues might include the way proposals for bids are created.

CONSIDER GEOGRAPHIC FEASIBILITY

When project *stakeholders* and/or team members are geographically dispersed, it makes a project harder to coordinate and may make certain solutions infeasible.

STRICTLY DEFINED

A **stakeholder** is anyone who will be affected by a project.

When developing a new computer network in multiple countries, the geographic isolation of some locations may make certain types of networks infeasible.

With event projects, geographic feasibility would include flights into the proposed conference airport or coordinating across multiple time zones.

For construction projects, geographic feasibility would include getting materials to remote sites or coordinating across multiple time zones.

CONSIDER TIME FEASIBILITY

The time feasibility of a project is one of the most critical considerations yet one of the hardest to quantify. If you need to complete a six-month project by May and it's already April, then the project isn't time feasible. The problem, however, is in determining that the project is a six-month project. One way to estimate possible project duration at this early point is to compare the project with similar ones completed in the past. Even though each project is unique, a past project with similar scope should give you a ballpark time.

For example, if a new computer system is needed in three months and the last new system project took a year, then the project is not time feasible. The new system may still be needed in three months, however, so rather than developing a system in-house, the project may need to be changed to purchasing a new system.

PROCEED WITH CAUTION

In many cases, you may still need to perform a project with an unrealistic deadline. In those cases, changing project strategies, scope, and resources may make a project time feasible.

In event projects, facility and speaker availability on certain dates may make the event not feasible. You can handle this by changing the event date.

For construction projects, building a house in two months when the owners haven't purchased a lot yet would not be time feasible.

CONSIDER RESOURCE FEASIBILITY

Resource feasibility is not just whether you have enough resources for the job, but also if you have the right resources for the job and whether they will be available when needed.

This means that you should consider not just the number of resources needed for your project, but categorize that number by skill type and skill level. Once you've determined resources by skill, you then need to look at the availability of those resources during the timeframe of your project. If you won't have the appropriate number of resources available when needed, your cost/benefit analysis will need to include the cost of external resources.

JUST A MINUTE

Remember that people are not the only project resources. Equipment, training rooms, and building materials might also be resources to your project. Instead of skill level for these types of resources, consider capacity, quality, and so on.

When developing a new computer system, you may need two systems analysts, one database administrator (DBA), five C++ programmers, and two system testers. Your project might allow the programmers to range in skill level from novice to expert but would require an expert DBA. When you look at the availability of the DBA, you see she is already committed to five projects. If this is the case, you may want to reconsider the timing of your project or include hiring an external DBA for your project in the cost/ benefit analysis.

In an event project, you might need an administrative assistant to answer phone questions, do mailings, and take reservations, and a marketing person and/or graphic artist to design the event brochure, speakers, meals, and rooms that would accommodate the appropriate number of participants.

For construction projects, you may need six carpenters, one plumber, one electrician, and three roofers. Because of the odd contours of the roofline, the roofers would all need to be experts.

CONSIDER LEGAL FEASIBILITY

To evaluate the legal feasibility of a project, consider whether or not the project meets existing legal obligations, both contractual and governmental.

PROCEED WITH CAUTION

 To adequately evaluate the legal aspect of feasibility, you may need to consult with your legal and/or contracts expert.

Legal feasibility is not generally a concern with computer system projects but might be if you would be contracting for a system and the terms of the new system contract ran counter to terms in other preexisting contracts.

With an event project, you may need to consider ADA compliance and health and safety issues as well as speaker contracts, copyright of handout materials, and the like.

For construction projects, legal feasibility would include whether or not the proposed project would be ADA compliant and satisfy zoning codes, safety codes, and so on.

CONSIDER POLITICAL FEASIBILITY

Political feasibility considerations include whether or not a project would conflict with either corporate or governmental politics. A project to implement a new project management process would not be politically feasible if the president of the company doesn't believe in project management.

Some organizations evaluate feasibility through a form of Risk Management or Portfolio Management. Find out if your organization has a formal process for evaluating project feasibility at the initiation phase.

PRACTICE WITH AWARDS BANQUET FEASIBILITY

Take a few moments to reread the awards banquet case presented in Hour 1. Let's look at how feasible this project is.

Awards banquets are held frequently, so the project is technically feasible. The main financial issue is cost/benefit, which we will evaluate in the next section. There are no ongoing costs to consider, so at this point the project is financially feasible. There are no internal operational issues that would make the project infeasible, so the project is operationally feasible. All the employees of the Leetle Toy Company are local, so the project is geographically feasible. Six months is a reasonable amount of time to plan the event, so the project is time feasible. The project would require the time of an administrative assistant, the project manager, a team of employees to evaluate and select the award winners, and a hall in which to hold the banquet. The Leetle Toy Company has the appropriate internal human resources for the job but will need to consider the renting of the hall in the cost/benefit analysis. Still, at this point, the project is resource feasible. There are no legal restrictions on the project, nor does anyone in senior management oppose the project, so it's both legally and politically feasible.

DETERMINE CONFERENCE CENTER RESTORATION FEASIBILITY

Review the restoration case study and evaluate the project feasibility. An answer is included in Appendix A.

PERFORM HIGH-LEVEL COST/BENEFIT ANALYSIS

At the beginning of a project, not a lot is known about the exact costs likely to be encountered or the benefits to be accrued. Still, a project manager and the project sponsor must have some idea of the order of magnitude of the costs to evaluate whether or not the potential benefits would outweigh those costs. If project approval will be based on the availability of external funding, you should list the potential amounts from each funding source.

For large-dollar value projects, it may be practical to enlist the aid of a financial expert to help you with more in-depth cost analyses such as Net Present Value.

DETERMINE HIGH-LEVEL COST

To determine a high-level cost estimate, the first thing to do is to list the general categories of expenses. Some categories to consider are wages, materials, postage, travel, equipment, training, and fees/penalties. Next, break these categories down to the lowest possible level of detail and estimate the costs. Wages would be estimated for each resource, materials listed by type, travel by numbers and destination, training per person, and the like.

DETERMINE HIGH-LEVEL BENEFITS

Common project benefits include reducing cost, increasing revenues, and removing problems. Benefits are similar to the needs discussed earlier but differ in format and content. Benefit statements can include both tangible and intangible benefits. Tangible benefits should be quantified. That is, if a project benefit is to reduce costs, the benefit statement should include an estimate of the actual dollar value.

Benefits may sometimes be negative statements, explaining what would happen if the project isn't completed. An example of this might be, "We will not incur the daily $250 noncompliance fee for building counter to the zoning code."

QUANTIFY POTENTIAL FUNDING SOURCES

Once you have an idea of the costs and benefits of a project, you should consider how you would meet those project costs. For most internal projects, costs come from some budget center, but external projects may need to generate cash before the project is approved. For public and not-for-profit projects, don't forget to consider federal, state, or community grant programs; private foundations and membership fees; and other donations as potential funding sources.

EVALUATE BANQUET COST AND BENEFITS

For the awards banquet project, list the project benefits, and then list the cost categories and potential funding sources.

Benefits:

- Sustain or improve employee morale by demonstrating that positive performance is rewarded.
- Improve employee performance by demonstrating that positive performance is rewarded.
- Encourage employee cost containment by demonstrating that cost containment is rewarded.

Costs:

Banquet Hall Rental	$0
Dinners for 200 at $30	$6,000
Award Plaques	$300
Employee Time 225h at $30	$6,750
Invitation materials	$300
Postage	$80
Total	$13,430

Project Funding:

The cost of the awards banquet will come from the administrative account in the Human Resources department.

Note that specific costs were not given in the case study but are presented here to show one possible way to format the data. Your answer should have come up with the same cost categories, however. If you had intended to hire speakers or entertainment at the banquet, an additional cost may have been speaker or entertainment fees and travel expenses.

EVALUATE RESTORATION COST AND BENEFITS

Develop a cost/benefit analysis for the restoration project. An answer is provided in Appendix A.

PROCEED WITH CAUTION

 In their zeal to get projects approved, many unconsciously exaggerate potential benefits or funding sources. While this may increase project approval rates, it nearly always has negative long-term effects when the project doesn't deliver what was promised. Be careful that successful implementation of your project can guarantee all your benefits, and you can raise the promised funding.

WRITE A PROJECT RECOMMENDATION STATEMENT

Once the preliminary cost/benefit analysis has been completed, you're ready to develop a project recommendation. This recommendation can be a simple statement, either written or presented to senior management, or it may be a lengthy document or presentation. Organizations that use a formal document approach may have a *template* for the components that go into the document. Typical sections of this template mirror the sections discussed previously, such as including a statement of the business needs for a project, the project feasibility, and cost/benefit analysis. They may also include a formal risk assessment and some type of recommendation statement.

STRICTLY DEFINED

A **template** is a specially formatted document with a standard layout for the required sections. It may also contain instructions for use. Project management templates are usually word-processing documents for forms and reports, spreadsheet documents for risk and cost/benefit analysis, or scheduling software files for work breakdown structures.

When you use the recommendation statement, it needs to do two things.

First, it needs to convince the decision-makers that the project can be successfully completed. It does this by reviewing all the information discussed earlier, including a summary of the project, but doing so in an upbeat, salesy way. It also helps to list the tasks for the next phase and give a tentative phase schedule. This tells people that you not only have looked at the high-level project but also have an idea on immediate next steps if the project is approved.

The second purpose of the recommendation statement is to tie the project's needs to the overall organization's strategic plans. When the project is directly supported by a strategic initiative, state which one.

PRACTICE WITH AWARDS RECOMMENDATION STATEMENT

From the needs listed, feasibility issues explored, and the cost/benefit analysis performed, it appears that the awards banquet would be a good project for the Leetle Toy Company. Even though this project ostensibly already has management support, it's good practice to write a formal recommendation.

Recommendation to Proceed:

Annual office expense is $125,000 per year, which equates to $500 per employee. If 10 percent of the employees decrease their spending by 10 percent, the company would save $1,250.

Annual sales revenue is $2 million, which equates to $200,000 per sales person. If only one sales person increases his/her revenue by 10 percent, the company would earn an additional $20,000.

Because it is likely that both of these scenarios are not only feasible but also probable, the expense of the awards banquet is justified and we recommend proceeding with the project.

DEVELOP RESTORATION RECOMMENDATION STATEMENT

Summarize the initiation results in a recommendation statement for the restoration project. An answer is provided in Appendix A.

IDENTIFY THE PROJECT SPONSOR

The project sponsor is the most important person to the project, as it's the sponsor who approves the project funding. On internal corporate projects, sponsors are usually senior managers in the organization. On external projects, the sponsor is usually a senior manager in the client organization. On personal projects, you are most likely the sponsor and the project manager, except perhaps on weddings and graduations, where a parent might be the sponsor.

PRACTICE IDENTIFYING AWARDS BANQUET SPONSOR

This project has several potential sponsors, but the most likely candidate is the senior vice president of Human Resources, Sam Parker. It's his role to encourage employee development, which is akin to the needs of this project. Another candidate would be the vice president of sales and marketing, since an increase in sales would specifically benefit his work objectives. However, because the case study reads, "Sam Parker … is leading the call for the banquet," this makes him the more likely choice.

IDENTIFY RESTORATION PROJECT SPONSOR

Based on the facts of the case study presented in Hour 1, identify the project sponsor for the restoration project. The answer is provided in Appendix A.

OBTAIN AUTHORIZATION TO PROCEED

In this step, you get the authority to proceed with the planing portion of a project. This authority is granted in a variety of ways, depending on the type of project. For corporate projects, the authority to proceed generally comes from the internal project sponsor. With an external project, the authority to proceed usually comes from the client sponsor. The paperwork for this authority may just be an internal document signed by the sponsor and project manager or it may be a formal contract with an external client. Some organizations refer to this formal authority to proceed as a *project charter*.

STRICTLY DEFINED

A **project charter** is a document signed by the sponsor and/or client agreeing to the definition of the project and authorizing the continuation of the project.

Some organizations—either as part of granting the authority to proceed or shortly thereafter—also prioritize the project. These priorities may be assigned by the project sponsor or by a corporate *steering committee*.

STRICTLY DEFINED

A **steering committee** is a small group of senior executives who approve, prioritize, and monitor projects.

Unlike some of the other initiating activities noted previously, this process is often repeated throughout the project. That is, in a system using four phases in a project management life cycle, the project manager gets the authority to proceed with the planning phase of a project, gets the authority to proceed with the executing phase, and then gets the authority to close the project.

Hour 3
Starting a Project Plan

LESSON PLAN:

In this hour you will learn about ...

- Defining the project goal.
- Creating project objectives.
- Determining project scope and exclusions.
- Defining project deliverables.
- Evaluating project constraints.

Once a project has been authorized to move into the planning phase, it's time to flesh out some of the components started in the initiation phase and to add additional components. In the following sections of this hour, you'll learn how to create some of the components of a project plan.

Define the Project Goal

Once you've received authorization to start planning a project, you need to start developing the project plan. For short-duration, uncomplicated projects, the project plan can be a three- to five-page document. For larger, more complicated projects, it may be 30 to 40 pages long. The purpose of the project plan is to document the proposed project in as much detail as possible before any work on the project's products begins. This helps solidify the project in the minds of all the stakeholders, and it gives everyone a chance to adjust the plan before any work is started.

While the sections in the project plan are presented sequentially in the next three lessons, keep in mind that developing the project plan is really an iterative process. You will most likely start with the project goal and objectives, but once these two are completed, they will prompt you to think of items that belong in other project plan sections. This is fine. The only thing to make sure of is that you've considered each section in the plan.

JUST A MINUTE

Although most organizations call the project initiation document the project charter, some organizations call the project plan the project charter.

Also keep in mind that developing your first few project plans will seem very time-consuming. This is also normal. It will most likely take you three to five project plans before you feel comfortable creating them. After that, you will be able to create them much more easily and much more quickly.

The first component of a project plan is the project goal. The project goal or mission is a very high-level statement of *why* you are performing the project. Developing and writing a solid goal statement helps the project in two ways. First, when you're still planning the project, the goal statement helps you and the team to define the rest of the project plan and to communicate that to the project stakeholders. Once a project moves into the execution processes, the goal statement, combined with the scope statement discussed later in this lesson (see the section "Determine Project Scope and Exclusions"), will help you evaluate proposed changes to the project.

JUST A MINUTE

Goal or mission statements may also include a time component if that time component is critical to project success.

Goals are expressed in verb statements; that is, they start with action verbs such as "provide," "prepare," "develop," "build," and the like. While a goal statement is high level, the phrasing should adequately limit potential solutions right from the start.

For instance, if you're developing a registration process for a one-time-only banquet, a goal statement might be …

To facilitate the timely registration for this year's awards banquet.

If, however, your task was to develop a registration system to be used on an ongoing basis, a goal statement might be …

To facilitate the timely registration for this and future awards banquets.

While the two statements are very similar, if what you're developing will be used regularly, this should be included in the goal. Why? Because it's likely that the process developed for a one-time event would not be adequate to be used regularly. With everyone on the project knowing about the future requirement, the team will be able to think in those terms when designing the process.

The goal for a new computer system might be ...

> To provide a new purchasing system for the company that will reduce purchase-order turnaround to three days and will cut the purchase of excess inventory by 10 percent.

Potential new purchasing systems can be evaluated and then added to the short list or eliminated, based on whether or not they can meet the criteria in the goal. If it is found that no systems can meet these criteria, then the company must write its own system, recast the project goal, or abandon the project before wasting further resources on it.

For construction projects, a goal might be ...

> To select an appropriate lot on the Michigan peninsula and build a 4,000-square-foot log cabin home by June 1.

In this case, this project has four criteria limiting potential solutions. The lot must be on the Michigan peninsula, the house must be a log cabin, it must be 4,000 square feet, and the entire project must be completed by June 1. If the owners have already purchased a lot, the goal could be recast to read ...

> To build a 4,000-square-foot log cabin home on the Michigan peninsula by June 1.

If the project is some type of event, such as a conference, training seminar, or wedding, the goal statement might be ...

> To hold a barn restoration conference for up to 100 people on August 25.

This goal has three limiting criteria. The conference theme must be related to barn restoration, the facility must hold up to 100 people, and the date will be August 25. If the location was already set, this, too, should be added to the goal. If, however, the location, date, and conference size were flexible, the goal might be ...

> To hold a barn restoration conference within the next six months.

PRACTICE WITH AWARDS BANQUET GOAL

Take a few moments to consider what the goal statement for the awards project might be.

One possible answer is …

> To recognize the achievement of Leetle Toy Company employees.

Note that this goal statement leaves a variety of options open. If the intent is that only an awards banquet will do, then the following, more specific goal should be used:

> To hold an awards banquet for all employees, honoring the achievements of at least three selected employees.

JUST A MINUTE

You may find creating a project notebook to be very helpful. Put in the notebook any project standards, all versions of your project plan, schedules, and revisions, as well as change documents, status reports, timesheets, authorities to proceed, contracts, and any product-specific documents, such as building plans. That way everything is in one convenient, portable place.

CREATE THE RESTORATION PROJECT GOAL

Reread the Conference Center case study in Hour 1, "Understanding Project Management," and create the restoration project goal. A possible answer is given in Appendix A, "Sample Documents."

CREATE PROJECT OBJECTIVES

Project objectives are also high-level statements, but rather than explain the *why*, they explain the *what*. Just what will this project do?

Each organization that has a methodology has its own definition of objectives, but, in general, objectives should be specific, measurable, realistic, and—where necessary—time-framed.

Objectives are also expressed as verb statements. Four or five objectives will usually cover the entire project. If you find yourself developing more than that, it probably means you're getting into more detail than necessary at this point.

Using the goal for the new computer system in the previous section, some objectives might be …

1. Research and select replacement purchasing system within two months of receiving project go-ahead.

2. Install, train users, and implement new system within three months of selection.

For the log cabin construction project, some objectives would include the following:

1. With owner, research and select appropriate lots for cabin within two months.

2. With owner, research and select cabin plans and specifications within one month of selecting lot.

3. Construct appropriate cabin within three months of closing on lot purchase.

Note that this represents a six-month time frame. If it's past December, this set of objectives would not meet the stated goal of completion by June 1. It may be that the June 1 date in the goal was not necessary and should be removed. However, if it's necessary to meet the June 1 date, the objectives may need to be adjusted. These types of considerations will be obvious in your own projects. Considerations such as these are another reason for planning the project in more detail before starting work.

PROCEED WITH CAUTION

While it's tempting to include bringing the project in on time and within budget as objectives, these really aren't objectives; they're success criteria. The meeting of objectives enables us to measure when a project is done and a project can be done without meeting either of those two success measurements.

Objectives for the barn conference could be ...

1. Locate and rent a facility that would hold general sessions of up to 100 and breakout sessions of up to 40 by May 10.

2. Develop and implement a preregistration and registration system by June 10.

3. Hold a conference with at least six one-hour sessions on August 25.

AWARDS BANQUET PROJECT OBJECTIVES

Compare the sample objectives we've just listed with their goals, and then review the awards banquet goal and create the objectives.

Two objectives are associated with the goal of the awards banquet:

1. Select up to three outstanding employees to honor within four months.

2. Hold an awards banquet for all employees honoring the award winners within six months.

CONFERENCE CENTER RESTORATION PROJECT OBJECTIVES

Write the objectives for the conference center restoration project. The answer is given in Appendix A.

DETERMINE PROJECT SCOPE AND EXCLUSIONS

Project scope refers to the total amount of work involved in a project. Traditionally, project scope is represented in the project plan as a statement of the work components included in the project. This scope statement consists of one or two simple sentences summarizing the significant work.

PROCEED WITH CAUTION

 The term scope means widely different things to different people and organizations. Make sure that you understand how your organization uses the term.

In some organizations, there's no such thing as a separate scope statement. These organizations use project objectives and deliverables to determine when something is within scope. The concern with this approach is that it's more difficult for all the project stakeholders to understand the project boundaries. Taking the time, up front, to develop a succinct statement of the scope will help everyone in the long run, especially when evaluating whether later changes are within scope.

Equally important to the project scope is a statement of project scope exclusions, that is, what is *not* included. Why state scope exclusions? Because one of the most common causes of scope creep is that the project team believed components were not part of the scope and the client believed they were. Stating the exclusions up front enables you to discuss them and add them to the project, if necessary, before any estimates are given.

The scope exclusions may be written in a separate section of the project plan or in a portion of the scope section.

JUST A MINUTE

 To make sure that everyone sees and understands the scope exclusions, it's generally better to list them in their own section of the project plan.

The scope statement and exclusions for the new purchasing system project might be …

Scope:

Research, select, and install a replacement purchasing system, and train the end users.

Exclusions:

- Development of the training program
- Ongoing system support

For the log cabin construction project, the scope statement and exclusions could be …

Scope:

With owner, research and select appropriate lot for cabin; research and select cabin plans and specifications, and construct the cabin.

Exclusions:

- Septic system
- Landscaping
- Interior papering and painting

The scope statement and exclusions for the barn conference would be …

Scope:

Locate and rent an appropriate facility, develop and implement a preregistration and registration system, recruit at least six speakers, and hold the conference.

Exclusions:

- Lodging, travel, and expenses for speakers
- Computer projection equipment

GO TO ▶
Refer to Hours 4, "Adding to Your Plan," and 5, "Developing Project Control Plans," for additional ways to control scope creep.

DETERMINE AWARDS BANQUET SCOPE/EXCLUSIONS

The scope of this project is simple:

Select and honor up to three employees at a banquet for all employees.

The scope exclusions were not stated in this case description. You'll find that is almost always true on your real projects as well. You'll need to list what you think are exclusions, remembering that the client may want those components included, which then will change your scope. Two logical exclusions for this project are the following:

- Dinners for spouses and families
- Travel and transportation to and from the banquet facilities

DETERMINE RESTORATION PROJECT SCOPE/EXCLUSIONS

Write the scope statement for the restoration project. Then list the scope exclusions. The answer to this exercise is in Appendix A.

DEFINE PROJECT DELIVERABLES

The project deliverables are the tangible results—the products or services of the project. There are two categories of deliverables:

- Intermediary deliverables are those that are produced to be used in subsequent portions of the project.
- End or final deliverables are those that are turned over to the client at the end of the project.

JUST A MINUTE

 If a project has many intermediary deliverables, it's better to list just the major deliverables in the main body of the plan. This enables the other people using the plan to concentrate on these major deliverables.

If the concept of a deliverable is new to you, listing deliverables may be difficult for you at first. It may help you to try one or both of the following techniques to develop your list.

The first way to develop the list is to look at each objective and decide what is being produced by that objective. The combined lists from each objective give you the list for the entire project.

Another way to list deliverables is to think of the categories of deliverables. The two main categories are products and services, but each has subcategories.

For instance, products may include computer software, computer hardware, user manuals, training, buildings, designs, program schedules, and reports. Deliverables from the training category might include training manuals, training classes, and the trained participants. Deliverables from the report category may include status reports or selection of a building lot, house design, and so on.

Typical service deliverables include product warranty, computer support, expert opinion, and the like. Let's look at some more specific examples.

Objective 1 for the purchasing system gives us four intermediary deliverables, which are the following:

- Survey of potential systems
- Short list of systems to investigate further
- Investigation results of each system
- Selected system

Final deliverables from objective 2 are as follows:

- The installed purchasing system
- Trained end users
- New purchasing process

For the log cabin construction project, the intermediary deliverables from objective 1 include the following:

- Survey of potential lots
- Short list of lots to investigate further
- Results of lot investigations
- Selected lot

The intermediary deliverables from objective 2 include the following:

- Survey of potential plans
- Short list of plans to investigate further
- Results of plans investigations
- Selected plan

The final deliverable from objective 3 would be the completed cabin on the selected lot. Major intermediary deliverables would be as follows:

- Plumbing pipes and fixtures
- Electrical wiring and fixtures
- Heat ducts, furnace, and so on
- Walls, roof, ceilings, and so on

As shown in this lesson, deliverables are generally nouns and are listed in bullet format in the project plan.

The intermediary deliverables for the barn conference from objective 1 include the following:

- Survey of potential facilities
- Short list of facilities to investigate further
- Results of facilities investigations
- Selected facility

The intermediary deliverables from objective 2 would be the following:

- Conference brochure
- Preregistration process
- Registration process

The final deliverables from objective 3 would be as follows:

- Six speakers
- Six sessions
- Lunch for 100
- Morning and afternoon breaks for 100
- Handout packages

PRACTICE WITH BANQUET PROJECT DELIVERABLES

Take a few moments to consider the project deliverables for the awards banquet project.

The deliverables from objective 1 would include the following:

- A process for selecting winners
- Winner nomination forms
- Completed winner nominations
- Selected winners

The deliverables from objective 2 would include the following:

- Plaques for each winner
- Selected banquet hall

- Dinner for 200 employees
- Invitations

PROCEED WITH CAUTION

Many stakeholders may not understand the concept of deliverables, which means you may have to explain to them why you're using them in the plan.

LIST RESTORATION PROJECT DELIVERABLES

List the final deliverables and major intermediary deliverables of the restoration project. The answer is in Appendix A.

EVALUATE PROJECT CONSTRAINTS

As you learned in Hour 2, "Initiating a Project," a constraint is something that limits a project. In the constraints section of the project plan, you list the constraints of this particular project. You list these for your own purposes, to help clarify the parameters of the project, but also so that project stakeholders can understand project-limiting factors, too. This way, you help to manage the stakeholders' expectations, especially as the project moves into the execution processes.

To help uncover these constraints, you can use the categories noted in Hour 2. These included Technical, Financial, Operational, Geographic, Time, Resource, Legal, and Political categories. Constraints are usually given in sentence format.

For the software project, a technical constraint would be that the new package must run on the existing infrastructure. An operational constraint may be that the purchasing system can never be off line, so the current system must run in parallel to the new system until the team is ready to cut over to the new system. A resource constraint would be the availability of the DBA.

For the log cabin project, there is the geographic constraint of the lot being on the Michigan Peninsula. Depending on the exact circumstances of the general contractor hired, there may also be an operational constraint of coordinating and scheduling the subcontractors.

With the barn conference, there is a geographic constraint, with the location limiting the conference attendance primarily to residents in the immediate area. There is also the time constraint of August 25 for the conference date.

In the actual project plan, these constraints would be phrased and listed as follows:

Constraints:

- The new package must run on the existing computer infrastructure.
- Because the purchasing system can never be offline, the current system must run in parallel to the new system until cut over to the new system.
- The DBA may not be available to work on the project when needed.
- The lot must be on the Michigan peninsula, which will limit potential sites.
- The coordinating and scheduling of the subcontractors may delay some of the project tasks.
- The location of the conference may limit conference attendance primarily to residents in the immediate area.
- The August 25 date may limit the availability of conference facilities and may limit conference attendance.

LIST AWARDS PROJECT CONSTRAINTS

Take a few moments to consider the awards banquet constraints. They would include the following:

- The banquet facility must hold at least 200 employees.
- A banquet facility must be available when the selected award winners are available.

LIST RESTORATION PROJECT CONSTRAINTS

Now consider the restoration project constraints. List them as shown in the examples. An answer appears in Appendix A.

PROCEED WITH CAUTION

When listing constraints, don't list just the constraint category. Every project has resource constraints. Specify each of them for the readers.

HOUR 4

Adding to Your Plan

CHAPTER SUMMARY

LESSON PLAN:

In this hour you will learn about ...

- Defining the project approach.
- Determining required resources.
- Listing and evaluating project stakeholders.
- Listing project assumptions.
- Developing critical success factors.

The project goal, objectives, scope, exclusions, deliverables, and constraints are important components of your project plan, but they aren't sufficient to fully describe the project. This lesson introduces five additional project plan sections to help you further define the project for both your team and your clients.

DEFINE PROJECT APPROACH

Each project manager approaches a project in a slightly different way. This section specifies how the project manager and team intend to approach a project so that everyone understands the approach and may suggest better alternatives. Depending on the methodology in place, this section may also be called strategies.

To help you think about potential approaches to a project, go back and review your objectives. Just as each objective helped trigger ideas for deliverables, these same objectives can help you determine approaches. In the first draft of a project plan, you may want to list multiple suggested approaches and let the team and other project stakeholders decide on the approach. This will encourage buy-in for the project.

The objectives we discussed in Hour 3, "Starting a Project Plan," for the software system project included researching, selecting, and installing the new purchasing system and training the users. The objectives gave a time frame of approximately five months. To be able to do this within five months, some approaches might be to ...

- Gather requirements through a *Joint Requirements Planning* (JRP) session.
- Purchase an existing package rather than develop a system in house.
- Implement the system in stages, starting with corporate headquarters and then distributed to the various divisions.

STRICTLY DEFINED

A **Joint Requirements Planning** session is a technique for gathering and agreeing to system requirements more quickly.

The objectives for the log cabin construction project included researching and selecting lots, researching and selecting log cabin plans, and constructing the cabin. The objectives gave an approximate six-month time frame for the project.

To help meet a six-month time frame, potential approaches for building the log cabin might be to …

- Limit plan selections to a single vendor.
- Purchase a kit to minimize construction time.
- Install all off-the-shelf products rather than customized ones.

For the barn conference project, the objectives were to locate and rent a facility, develop and implement a preregistration and registration process, and hold a conference with at least six one-hour sessions. Approaches for this might be to …

- Hire an event planner to organize the conference.
- Use the department secretary as the single point of contact for all conference inquiries.
- Choose speakers from a list of previous speakers.

PRACTICE WITH AWARDS BANQUET APPROACH

We know that the management of the Leetle Toy Company wants this awards ceremony both to honor past achievements and to encourage future success. One way to help increase the chances that this will happen is to use an employee-inclusive approach to the project:

- Solicit nominations for awards.
- Appoint a team of three employees to review the nominations and select the winners.
- Schedule the banquet based on winner and facility availability.

DETERMINE RESTORATION PROJECT APPROACH

What types of approaches might you use as project manager of the conference center restoration project? Write them down in the bulleted sentence format shown in the examples. Answers are in Appendix A, "Sample Documents."

DETERMINE REQUIRED RESOURCES

During project initiation, you evaluated project feasibility based on the resources and skill levels needed to successfully perform the project. In this section of the project plan, you detail those resource requirements. If known, you assign specific resources to specific project *roles* at this point. Otherwise, the resources listed here are still generic. If you have some idea of the time commitment necessary for each resource, include it in this section.

STRICTLY DEFINED

A **role** in project management refers to the type of work the resource will be performing on the project. In smaller organizations, a single person may perform multiple project roles.

For the new purchasing system project, this section might look like the following:

Team Resources:

- Betty Lo, senior systems analyst, for five hours per day for three weeks
- Phyllis Johnson, systems analyst, for six hours per day for six weeks
- Jackie Lee, senior DBA
- One junior C++ programmer, for three months
- Three C++ programmers, for three months
- One senior C++ programmer, for three months
- Phil Johnson, system tester, for six hours per day for two weeks
- Bob Samuels, system tester, for three hours per day for two weeks

For the log cabin project, resources might be ...

Team Resources:

- Six carpenters full time for the project duration
- Jack Mason, plumber, as needed
- Ben Yanks, electrician, as needed
- Three expert roofers from Roofing Specialists, Inc., as needed

The resources for the barn conference could be the following:

Team Resources:

- Flora Adams, administrative assistant, to answer phone questions, do mailings, and take reservations, for two hours per week
- Jenna Rich, marketing, to design the event brochure, for 20 hours over first two weeks
- Project manager to locate and select speakers, meals, and venue, for approximately five hours per week until the conference

Equipment, and so on:

- Large room to seat 100
- Breakout rooms for 50 each
- Two slide projectors and screens, and two overhead projectors

DETERMINE AWARDS BANQUET REQUIRED RESOURCES

Team Resources:

- One project manager, for approximately five hours per week for the next six months
- One administrative assistant to coordinate mailings, RSVPs, and so on, for approximately two hours per day for the last two months of the project
- Three employees to select the award winners, for approximately two hours per week for four months

Equipment, and so on:

- Slide projector and screen available at banquet facility

DETERMINE RESTORATION REQUIRED RESOURCES

Review the details of the restoration case study and list the resources and skill levels required for this project. Remember that, in this case, you work in a toy company and you're not expected to be a restoration specialist. How will this affect your resources? The answer is listed in Appendix A.

LIST AND EVALUATE PROJECT STAKEHOLDERS

Project stakeholders are people affected by the project. They include the project sponsor, the team members, and the clients. In government-related projects, stakeholders would also include the people authorizing spending, such as congress, mayors, city councils, and so on.

Why is it important to understand the project stakeholders? Because these people will have a vested interest in the outcome of the project. They will need to be informed about the possibility of the project, may have a say in the project planning and approval, and will want to receive updates on project status.

In this book, we use a separate section for listing stakeholders, although some organizations do not do this. Instead, they list stakeholders in the resource section. When using a separate stakeholders' section, list only nonteam stakeholders, as team members were already listed in the resource section. Also, if you know specific names for people, use their names, titles, and roles. Otherwise, list the roles, remembering to add specific names and titles as you learn them.

Stakeholders of the new purchasing system project would include the following:

- Project sponsor (likely the manager in the purchasing area or his or her boss)
- Purchasing department staff
- All employees involved in the purchasing process
- Sales people and others at the companies on the vendor short list

For the log cabin project, some of the stakeholders include the following:

- Project sponsors (the homeowners)
- General contractor
- Subcontractors (electrical and plumbing)
- Suppliers
- Lot owners

EVALUATE AWARDS BANQUET PROJECT STAKEHOLDERS

Let's look at the potential stakeholders for the awards banquet. The only named participant noted so far in the case is Sam Parker, the Vice President of Human Resources. Remember that in Hour 2, "Initiating a Project," we listed Parker as the project sponsor in the initiation document. We would do that again here in the project plan. The remaining stakeholders would be listed by role.

- Sam Parker, Vice President of Human Resources, sponsor
- All employees
- Management
- Banquet facility staff
- Selected award winners

Notice that the selected award winners and all employees are listed as separate items, as are Parker as sponsor and other members of management. Because the primary reason for listing stakeholders is to not forget anyone when planning our project communications, it's good practice to separately list individuals or subset groups with different communication needs. Then, when you create your communication plan, it's less likely that you'll overlook a critical communication channel.

EVALUATE RESTORATION PROJECT STAKEHOLDERS

GO TO ▶
The communication plan and communication channels are explained in detail in Hour 5, "Developing Project Control Plans."

List the project stakeholders for the conference center restoration project. An answer is located in Appendix A.

LIST PROJECT ASSUMPTIONS

We all make estimates of costs and times based on our own set of assumptions. In the project plan, we specify these assumptions so that everyone involved in the project can review them and decide whether or not the assumptions are valid. Listing assumptions is often one of the most difficult sections of the plan to complete. Sure, we always make assumptions, but we don't usually realize it. This means it may take you a while to recognize when you and your team members are making assumptions.

Be careful not to go overboard with assumptions. List the major assumptions that can have severely negative impacts on the project's success if they turn out not to be true. Don't create a laundry list of minor assumptions. As with objectives, each project should have four to five assumptions. If you list more than that, people are likely to stop reading them and/or not take them seriously.

The only possible exception to this general guideline is when assumptions are included in a contract. In that case, you may want to list major assumptions in the assumptions section, add a line that says "and all other standard assumptions as listed in the appendix," and then create an appendix with those standard minor assumptions.

For the new purchasing system project, based on the objectives and approaches listed previously, assumptions could include the following:

- The DBA will be available when needed.
- There will be a package that will meet the project requirements.
- The existing computer infrastructure will support the new package.

As noted in the initial feasibility and in the resource section, the DBA has multiple commitments, and if she's unavailable, the project could be significantly delayed. If a package could not be found, the project approach would need to be changed, which would certainly increase project time. If the existing computers can't support the new system, there would be an additional cost.

Assumptions for the construction project might be the following:

- The owners will be able to find a suitable lot.
- The owners will be able to find a suitable plan.
- The general contractor will be able to find qualified subs available at the appropriate times.

The first two assumptions, if proven false, would cancel the project. If the third assumption is false, the quality of the completed home could decrease, the cost could increase, and the duration could increase.

The barn conference project's assumptions would include the following:

- A suitable facility is available on August 25.
- Six speakers will be available on August 25.
- All six speakers will actually arrive at the conference.

If no facility is available, the project would be canceled or rescheduled. If six speakers are not available, it may be necessary to use a smaller number, which could then limit the number of people attending. If all six speakers don't show, it may cost more to find alternates or attendees may ask for refunds.

GO TO ▶
Everything listed in the assumptions section may prove to be false. Coping with this possibility is covered in Hour 12, "Facing Project Risk."

Notice from these examples that assumptions, constraints, and exclusions are very similar. It's not uncommon for a single aspect of a project to be listed in two or more sections of the project plan. As long as a factor should truly be considered in multiple sections, go ahead and include them. This helps ensure that people reading your plan will get the complete project picture.

List Awards Banquet Project Assumptions

Based on the approaches and objectives listed earlier, some assumptions for the awards banquet include the following:

- Employees will submit award nominations.
- At least three employee nominations will be different and will be for deserving employees.
- Appropriate local banquet facilities will be available.
- Two hundred of the two hundred fifty employees will be able to attend the banquet.

If employees do not submit nominations for awards or if they do not submit at least three unique nominations, another method of selection will need to be developed. If the facilities are not available, an alternate date will need to be chosen. If fewer than 200 or more than 200 attend, it may change the pricing on dinners as well as room availability.

List Restoration Project Assumptions

List the assumptions for the conference center restoration project. The answers are included in Appendix A.

JUST A MINUTE

To practice listing project assumptions, start with listing simple daily assumptions. For instance, planning on a 20-minute drive to work assumes that you can quickly find your keys, your car will start, the traffic lights will be functioning as usual, and so on. Once you get used to looking for your daily assumptions, they will be easier to find in project situations.

Determine Critical Success Factors

In Hour 1 we noted that there are five common measurements of success: on time, within budget, happy customer, met objectives, and no casualties. The critical success factors section of a project plan lists the conditions that must be met to help ensure successful project completion. You may also include performance goals in this section or in the deliverables and objectives noted previously.

In the new computer system project, one critical success factor related both to meeting objectives and to happy clients would be that the purchasing manager and staff be actively involved in selecting the replacement system. Another factor relating to keeping on time would be that key resources be available when necessary.

For the log cabin construction project, a critical success factor also related both to meeting objectives and to happy clients would be that the owner be actively involved in selecting the lot and the house plans and major fixtures in the new home. Another factor relating to keeping on time would be that electrician, plumber, and other subcontractors be available when necessary. Also relating to time would be that selecting and closing on the lot proceed quickly. Delay at this early point could significantly affect the schedule later.

With the barn conference, critical success factors for a happy customer would include that the facility accommodate enough people, both for the lecture sessions and for lunches and breaks. A factor for time would be that the selected speakers submit their session descriptions and handouts when needed, so that conference brochures can be mailed and handout packets can be reproduced. A cost factor may be that at least 75 registrants are required in order to break even.

These success factors are generally listed by criteria. The combined factors discussed might be listed as follows:

Critical Success Factors

Time Factors:

- Key resources, especially the DBA, must be available when necessary.
- The electrician, plumber, and other subcontractors must be available when necessary.
- Selecting and closing on the lot must proceed quickly.
- Selected speakers must submit their session descriptions and handouts when needed so that conference brochures can be mailed and handout packets can be reproduced.

Meeting Objectives Factors:

- The purchasing manager and staff need to be actively involved in selecting the replacement system.

- The purchasing manager and staff need to be actively involved in testing the replacement system.
- The purchasing manager and staff need to be actively involved in training on the replacement system.
- The (log cabin) owners need to be actively involved in selecting the lot and the house plans and major fixtures in the new home.

Happy Customer Factors:

- The facility must accommodate enough people, both for the lecture sessions and for lunches and breaks …

    … plus all the factors listed under meeting requirements would be listed under happy customers, too.

Cost Factors:

- At least 75 registrants are required to break even.

JUST A MINUTE

Some organizations do not share the success factors with anyone other than the core project team and the sponsor. If phrased correctly, however, sharing these factors with all the project stakeholders can encourage their buy-in and enable the project to run more smoothly.

DETERMINE BANQUET CRITICAL SUCCESS FACTORS

Review the analysis and listing of success factors stated previously and consider the success factors for the awards banquet project. Two primary success factors appear.

Meets Requirements Factors:

- The three award winners must all be available on the same night.
- A suitable hall must be available on that same night.

DETERMINE RESTORATION CRITICAL SUCCESS FACTORS

Review the project plan for the restoration projected created so far, and determine the critical success factors for that project. An answer appears in Appendix A.

HOUR 5

Developing Project Control Plans

CHAPTER SUMMARY

LESSON PLAN:

In this hour you will learn about ...

- Defining a communication plan.
- Writing a change control plan.
- Creating a quality management plan.
- Developing a procurement plan.
- Outlining a completion plan.

Hours 3, "Starting a Project Plan," and 4, "Adding to Your Plan," introduced 11 important project plan components that are used to describe various aspects of the project. This lesson introduces the five project control plans that you'll use to execute and control the project. We will look at controlling project communications, project changes, project quality, project procurement, and project completion.

UNDERSTAND PROJECT CONTROL PLANS

Five project control subplans are commonly added to a project plan. These subplans are used not only to execute and control the project, but also, in the planning process, to gain commitment to the control processes from the major project stakeholders.

The project communications plan explains the major types of communication that will take place during the project. The change control plan explains how project changes will be handled. The quality management plan lists how quality will be evaluated and controlled. The last two plans, the project procurement and project completion plans, are not used in all organizations, but are useful when projects will have to deal with contracts and when project managers may have difficulty closing out a project.

TIME SAVER

Although subplans can be very detailed and lengthy, once a good subplan has been developed, it can be used from project to project because, at least within a given organization, the way these project aspects are handled does not vary greatly.

DEVELOP A COMMUNICATION PLAN

Perhaps the most important component of a project plan is the communication plan because managing expectations is key to a successful project, and the best way to do that is through effective communications. The communication plan describes who will speak to whom, when, why, and in what format. Let's take a closer look at each of these pieces of information.

DETERMINE CHANNELS OF COMMUNICATION

A *communication channel* is the line of communication between two parties. In a project, there are lines of communication within the team and from the team to external stakeholders.

STRICTLY DEFINED

A **communication channel** represents the communication line between two people or two groups of people. To calculate the channels of communication in a project, use the formula: $C = n(n - 1) \div 2$, where n represents the number of people on the project team.

The primary lines of communication in any project include the following:

- Project manager and team
- Project manager and sponsor
- Project manager and stakeholders
- Team and team

Each communication line is bidirectional although the information passed in each direction will vary greatly.

When you consider the type of communication that should take place on each line, make sure you also consider the "level of abstraction" of that data. That is, you'll need to consider how much detail to present. Communications with team members generally use more detailed data than do those with stakeholders or senior managers.

While the communication plan is not intended to cover every single line of communication in the project, it does need to address the most significant lines. In addition to the lines noted previously, the plan might need to specify communications with other senior managers who are not the sponsor, with different categories of stakeholders, or with specific people from within the team.

DECIDE ON MEDIA

Once you've considered the various communication channels in your project, you need to decide how you want to communicate the information. The two main communication types are verbal and nonverbal, with verbal consisting of either written or oral communications.

The oral communication can be delivered one on one, in small groups (meetings), or in large groups (presentations). It can be delivered face to face, via telephone, or via videoconference. The written media used in projects include letters, memos, e-mail, forms, reports, newsletters, project plans, and contracts.

As you can see, you can use various types of media. While it's tempting to try to use one medium for all your communications, you should take some time to choose a medium most appropriate for the message and the recipients. It will make those communications much more effective. The benefits and drawbacks of a few of the media are given here.

Face-to-face—whether one on one, in meetings, or in presentations—is still the preferred project management communication method. You're speaking with one or more individuals. They can see you, and you can see them. Most people prefer to communicate this way because they can read the nonverbal elements of the conversation. This makes it easier to receive feedback and adjust your message. The drawback to face-to-face is scheduling the communication, especially when many people are involved or the parties are in geographically dispersed areas. This can lead to delaying any decisions that need to be made.

Telephones are also indispensable in project communications. They can be used one on one, in meetings, or in audio-conferences. Phone conversations are good for quick communications when immediate decisions are necessary and when the individuals are geographically dispersed. With more than two people involved, though, scheduling can still be a problem. They're also not useful for people who are frequently away from their desks.

To spread news about the project within your department or your company or to a larger group of stakeholders, you may want to use a newsletter. Designed to be informative and fun, newsletters are a great way to pass on needed information while gaining visibility. Newsletters may be written and published in traditional hardcopy, but many organizations are also starting to use intranet-based newsletters.

E-mail has also become very popular, especially with large organizations with geographically dispersed divisions or organizations with a large base of external vendors and/or clients. The advantage to e-mail is that you can send a message when you want and the recipients can answer when it's convenient for them. E-mail has several drawbacks, however. Many people still don't read their e-mail on a regular basis. And, as with other written media, there are no nonverbal cues, which may lead to misunderstandings.

JUST A MINUTE

Another problem with e-mail is that the sender tends to think of it as a form of talking, which means the sender communicates less formally. To the recipient, however, e-mail often comes across as a formal written communication. Keep this in mind when you're sending project-related e-mails.

DESIGN THE FORMATS

After you've evaluated the strengths and weaknesses of the various media for your communications, you're ready to design the format for these communications. The major formats to consider at this point are project time sheets and project status reports. You can decide on formats for other communications, such as newsletter articles and presentations, once the project is under way.

The timesheet format must allow a space for the team member's name, the tasks on which he or she is working, the dates for the seven days in the current time period, a daily total row, and a task total column (see the following figure).

Organizations use two types of status reports. One type of status report summarizes the entire project to date. If used, these are generally issued monthly by the project manager. The most common status report, though, is the weekly status report, which briefly describes project progress since the last report. These reports are usually written by the team members and sent to the project manager, who then summarizes them and distributes the summary document back to the team and on to other interested parties.

EMPLOYEE:

TASK	/ /	/ /	/ /	/ /	/ /	/ /	/ /	TOTAL
WEEKLY TOTAL								

A sample time sheet showing the minimum fields to include.

The team member status reports should include the team member's name and the project name and allow space to write what was accomplished during the week. They generally include space for next week's plans and any potential problems on the horizon.

TIME SAVER

 Once you've agreed on a format for a status report, resist the temptation to tweak it. People get into the habit of looking for information in specific places and will be able to write them and read them more quickly if the information stays put.

Evaluate Response Times

Another component of the communication plan might be the response times required for certain types of communications. For instance, you might note that when people are called they should return the call within 24 hours, when they are e-mailed they should reply within 4 hours, and when they are paged they should answer within 2 hours. These response times can be added to a traditional communication plan or they may be a separate section of the plan.

Although this section is not needed in all project plans, it's especially useful if you'll be contracting with external resources. It's also helpful when working with team members or clients who have not communicated in a timely manner in past projects.

Write the Communication Plan

After thinking about each of the communication plan components, you're ready to write the actual plan. The specific details in communication plans vary greatly among organizations, but they all show the project's communication channels, type, and frequency of communication.

These plans tend to come in three main formats:

- **Matrix** format plans list the communication lines in columns or rows and give the corresponding type and frequency data.
- **Paragraph** format plans list the line of communication as a header and then explain the type and frequency in sentences.
- **Graphic** format plans show the communication lines, type, and frequency in a visual format.

PROCEED WITH CAUTION

Don't try to cram too much information into a graphic format communication plan. The graphic format for the communication plan can be the easiest to read, but a poorly designed graphic format may actually be harder to read.

WRITE THE AWARDS COMMUNICATION PLAN

To start the communication plan, we need to review the people and roles defined so far. The team members listed in Hour 3 included a project manager, an administrative assistant, and three employees to select the award winners. The stakeholders listed in Hour 4 included Sam Parker (as sponsor), all employees, corporate management, banquet facility staff, and the selected award winners.

Now we create a matrix shown as follows:

From	To	Frequency	Format	Media
PM	Sam Parker	Monthly	Status	Meeting
PM	Employees	Two months prior	Invitations	Printed
PM	Employees	Bimonthly	Article	Corp. newsletter
PM	Team	Weekly	Status	E-mail
Team	PM	Weekly	Timesheets	Hardcopy
Team	Team	As needed	As needed	As needed
Admin.	Facility	As needed	As needed	As needed
Employees	Team	As needed during first three months	Nominations	Written via e-mail or hardcopy

From	To	Frequency	Format	Media
PM	Nominators	As needed	Questions and follow-up	As needed
Sponsor	Employees	End of month four	Announcement of winners	Memo

Notice that another subgroup of employees—nominators—was added in the plan. These are the employees who decide to submit award nominations. Once identified as a group with separate communication needs, this group should also be added to the stakeholder list.

The following figures display examples of two matrix communication plans as well as a paragraph and a graphic communication plan.

Communication Plan-Matrix Style One

From	To	Frequency	Form	Type
PM	Team	Weekly	Status	E-mail
Team	PM	Weekly	Time	Hardcopy

A sample matrix-format communication plan.

Communication Plan-Matrix Style Two

	PM	Team	Sponsor	
PM	X	Weekly revised schedule	Monthly written status	
Team	Weekly written timesheets	As needed	X	
Sponsor	As needed	X	X	

Another sample matrix-format communication plan.

A sample paragraph-format communication plan.

> *Communication Plan-Paragraph*
>
> **PM to Team**
> Once a week, on Tuesdays, the PM will summarize the status from the previous week and distribute via e-mail.

A sample graphic-format communication plan.

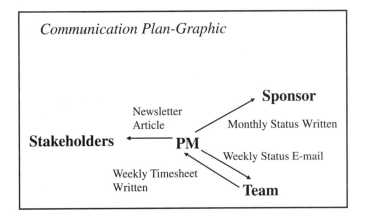

Communication Plan-Graphic

WRITE THE RESTORATION COMMUNICATIONS PLAN

Review the project objectives, resources, and stakeholders for the restoration project and write the communication plan. Choose a matrix, paragraph, or graphic format. An answer is in Appendix A, "Sample Documents."

DEVELOP A CHANGE CONTROL PLAN

The primary purpose of the change control plan is to minimize project scope creep. It does this by giving you and your team a way to evaluate proposed changes to a project once project execution has started. It specifies how you'll evaluate those changes, how you'll report the effects of the change to the stakeholders, and who needs to approve the change.

DETERMINE WHAT CONSTITUTES A CHANGE

Before you can outline the change process, you and your team need to decide on what will constitute a project change. In some organizations, any potential variation in the project deliverables or tasks constitutes a change. In other organizations, only task variations are project changes.

For our purposes in this book, we'll consider anything that will change our time and/or cost estimates to be a project change.

OUTLINE CHANGE NOTIFICATION PROCESS

Team members, the project manager, the sponsor, or any stakeholder can request changes. These requests can be formal written requests or informal oral requests, but it's generally better to use formal written requests. This enables the project manager to keep accurate records of all changes, both for tracking the current project and for better planning for the next project.

PROCEED WITH CAUTION

If you decide to accept oral change requests, it's best to fill out the paperwork yourself and circulate it as you would a written request. That way, the team and other major stakeholders are not surprised by changes.

DESIGN A CHANGE FORM

If your organization does not have a standard change control form, you will need to design one for your project (see the figure that follows as an example). The form should include blanks for at least the following pieces of information:

- Project name
- Project number
- Project manager name
- Requestor name
- Request date
- Resolution requested by date
- Description of change
- Reason for change
- Impact on scope and/or deliverables
- Impact on time and cost

- Impact on resources and quality
- Change accepted or rejected
- Spaces for signatures for the project manager and/or project sponsor and dates signed

A sample change form showing the minimum fields to include.

CHANGE REQUEST FORM

Project Name:	Project Number:	Project Manager Name:
Requestor Name:	Request Date:	Resolution Requested By:

Description of Change:
Reason for Change:
Impact on Scope and/or Deliverables:
Impact on Resources and Quality:
Impact on Time and Cost:

Change Resolution:		Accepted ☐		Rejected ☐
Project Manager:			Date:	
Project Sponsor:			Date:	

DEVELOP EVALUATION CRITERIA

Changes are generally evaluated against the normal success measures:

- How much work (scope) does this add/subtract?
- How much cost and time will this change add/subtract?
- How will it affect the team resources and project quality?

Project scope changes are generally noted by the addition or removal of tasks, cost is noted in dollars, time is noted in *duration* and/or *effort*, resources are noted in percentages of full-time workers, and quality is usually noted in number of defects.

STRICTLY DEFINED

Duration is the number of days, weeks, and so on that a project task will take. **Effort,** on the other hand, is the actual amount of work, usually expressed in resource hours. This will be explained in more detail in Hour 8, "Developing Project Estimates."

CONSIDER LEVELS OF AUTHORITY

Because project changes often negatively impact the project cost and schedule, the change control plan must establish who can approve what types of changes. Common levels of authority include the following:

- The project manager can approve any changes that don't increase time or cost. The project sponsor must approve any changes increasing time or cost.

- The project manager can approve any individual change within a +/–10 percent impact on the time or cost. The project sponsor can approve changes between 10 percent and 20 percent. Any change higher than that must be approved by the steering committee.

A common concern with the latter authority level description is what happens when cumulative changes run higher than the 10 percent or 20 percent approval levels. If this is a concern in your organization, too, you may want to put another condition on the approvals:

- The project manager can approve any individual change within a +/–10 percent impact on the time or cost as long as that change does not bring the cumulative changes higher than 15 percent. The project sponsor can approve individual changes between 10 percent and 20 percent as long as that change does not bring the cumulative changes higher than 25 percent. Any change(s) higher than that must be approved by the steering committee.

PROCEED WITH CAUTION

Don't confuse project change control with the production change control process used in Information Systems and other industries. Production change control processes deal with maintenance or operational changes to systems or products. In the new purchasing system example, one of the project tasks would be to turn the system over to production, which would then start the production change control processes.

DETERMINE FEEDBACK PROCESS

The feedback process outlines how the requestor and other stakeholders will be notified of the disposition of the change request. Generally, a copy of the updated change request form is circulated to the original requestor, sponsor, and team members; the original is filed in the project notebook. Then the appropriate changes are made to the project plan and schedule.

WRITE THE CHANGE CONTROL PLAN

Once you've considered all the preceding factors, you can write the project change control plan.

WRITE AWARDS CHANGE CONTROL PLAN

Review the project criteria for the awards project specified to date and formulate the project change control plan.

Given the parameters discussed so far, a possible change control plan is …

- Changes must be requested on form CC-1, Change Control Request Form.
- The project manager can change the date of the banquet until the contract with the facility is signed.
- No changes to the budget can be made without sponsor approval.

WRITE RESTORATION CHANGE CONTROL PLAN

Review the communication plan and other plan components, and develop the change control plan. If your company has a standard change form, refer to this in your plan. If not, use the sample form. An answer is provided in Appendix A.

DEVELOP A QUALITY MANAGEMENT PLAN

Measuring and maintaining quality is a complicated process, and it varies greatly from industry to industry and organization to organization. Just looking at the five types of projects we've been considering in this book should show you why. The quality measures for a software system would vary significantly from those in a construction project, and both would be different from those of a conference.

FYI A good quality control resource is PMI's *Guide to the PMBOK*. It explains the basic concepts of quality management and briefly discusses quality management in a variety of industries.

For these reasons, this section will only briefly discuss the concepts of quality and quality management plans. It will cover enough to get you started, but if you work in an industry with complex quality issues, you may want to find customized materials.

The quality management plan in a project explains how quality issues will be addressed. The plan looks at both the quality of the project and the quality of the products/deliverables. It's important to consider quality during the planning process because the desired levels of quality may require scope, cost, or schedule changes. It's best to learn that as soon as possible.

Three processes are involved in monitoring quality: quality planning, quality assurance, and quality control. The next three sections look briefly at these processes.

CONSIDER QUALITY MEASURES

When you start the quality planning process, you first need to decide what measures of *project quality* you'll use. If your organization has standard quality measures, your plan will simply say that your project will follow those standards for quality. If your organization does not have quality standards, however, you'll need to develop them.

STRICTLY DEFINED

Project quality is defined as the ability to meet the project's requirements. It does not mean meeting a client's expectations, but properly managed, a project can still do both.

In information systems, some quality standards are no bugs (defects) in the code, screen layouts that are consistent throughout the system, mathematical calculations that are appropriate, and so on. In construction, meeting codes is a major quality issue, as are such things as fixtures being installed and functioning correctly, roof and windows that are watertight, and so on.

DEVELOP QUALITY ASSURANCE PLAN

The quality assurance plan explains what you will do to assure quality in your project and/or in your project's product. The most common technique for quality assurance is a quality audit, which examines products and processes at random to see if quality standards are being met. If problems are discovered during the audits, corrective action will be necessary. Any of these actions must be approved through the change control process noted in the previous section.

In information systems, assuring consistent screen layouts would include developing a screen layout guide for all designers to follow. In construction, quality assurance might be using materials from only one well-known vendor.

DEVELOP QUALITY CONTROL PLAN

In the quality control plan, you explain want you'll do to inspect the quality of completed products and processes and how you'll correct problems. In our barn conference project, proofreading the brochure prior to printing might be a control. Fixing the errors and proofreading again might be the corrective action. In information systems, controlling consistent screen layouts would include reviewing all screens to make sure they match the standards. If they don't, they would need to be corrected. In construction, quality control would mean simulating a heavy rainstorm to make sure the roof didn't leak.

WRITE THE QUALITY MANAGEMENT PLAN

Once you've decided what to evaluate and how to assure and control quality, you are ready to write the quality control subplan of your project plan. You simply explain the measures you've agreed upon with your team and stakeholders. The section can be divided into the three sections noted previously, but for simple projects, it's often just a series of bulleted statements.

JUST A MINUTE

Quality assurance is generally concerned with preventing quality problems, while quality control is concerned with correcting them if they occur.

WRITE AWARDS QUALITY MANAGEMENT PLAN

Review the project criteria for the awards project and write the project quality management plan.

Given the parameters discussed so far, a possible quality plan is …

- Selection team will meet with managers of at least three potential banquet facilities to verify quality/quantity of dinners and service.

- Dates and times will be verified with award recipients and facilities.

- All memos, articles, and invitations will be proofread by at least one person other than the writer.

WRITE RESTORATION QUALITY MANAGEMENT PLAN

Review the communication plan and other plan components, and develop the quality management plan. If your company has standard quality assurance and control processes, then refer to them in your plan. If not, develop this section as noted previously. An answer is provided in Appendix A.

TIME SAVER

 While you want your team to share in the development of the project plan to encourage team buy-in, it's generally faster if you develop a draft of the plan first and then distribute it for comments. Most people can comment on existing material more quickly than they can develop it from scratch.

DEVELOP A PROCUREMENT PLAN

The procurement plan (or contract plan) subsection of the project plan is optional, but very beneficial when you'll be contracting for products or services from external sources. The plan specifies how you will solicit bids, how you will select the winners, and what standards and procedures the winning bidders will be expected to follow.

DETERMINE ANNOUNCEMENT METHOD

You can announce the opportunity for project contracts in several ways. The most common way is to issue a *Request for Proposal* (*RFP*), asking for organizations to bid on your project. An RFP is a document that lists the products and/or services that you want to procure and what your requirements and selection criteria are. RFPs are usually sent to a short list of contractors with whom you've dealt in the past, as well as advertised in the local newspapers or online.

A **Request for Proposal (RFP)** is a document in which you list the products and/or ser-vices that you want to procure and your requirements and selection criteria.

On smaller projects, or on nongovernment projects, you may just call a few organizations and tell them about the opportunity.

Determine Selection Method

This section covers how you will process the various bids. When you issue a formal RFP, the usual selection method is to review the formal, written responses to that RFP. In other cases, resumes may be reviewed, and then con-tractors called in for personal interviews or perhaps for telephone interviews.

Determine Selection Criteria

For this section, you need to consider how you'll choose the vendor. Some organizations require selecting strictly on the lowest bid; others evaluate each vendor's quality, reliability, and so on, as well as price. Some selection processes require complicated point systems for selection, and others go with gut feel.

Whatever selection criteria you decide to use are included in this section and in the formal RFP so that all bidders understand the selection criteria.

Outline Contract Standards and Procedures

To make sure that contractors follow your established standards and proce-dures, you need to specify which ones they'll be accountable for meeting. You list these in this section and again in any formal RFP that you issue.

Write the Procurement Plan

Once you've considered the announcement and selection process and the standards the contractors must follow, you're ready to write the procurement plan.

If you work in a large, departmentalized organization, you may want a procurement plan section even if you're not using external contractors. In this case, the section will explain how you intend to get and use corporate resources such as training rooms, computer equipment, and the like.

WRITE AWARDS PROCUREMENT PLAN

Review the project criteria for the awards project and write the project procurement plan.

Given the parameters discussed so far, a possible procurement plan is …

- Selection team will identify at least three potential facilities and will get menus and price lists from each.
- Selection will be made based on price as well as on quality measures noted.
- Invitations will be printed internally.
- Plaques will be purchased from the same vendor as for last year's awards.
- All vendors will submit invoices after rendering services to be paid within 30 days.

WRITE RESTORATION PROCUREMENT PLAN

Review the communication plan and other plan components and develop the procurement plan. If your company has a standard for issuing RFPs and selecting vendors, refer to this in your plan. If not, develop this section as noted previously. An answer is provided in Appendix A.

DEVELOP A COMPLETION PLAN

The last control subplan is also an optional component. It's most useful in organizations that have traditionally had difficulty closing projects and in contract situations where payments are issued "on completion."

The plan usually addresses two main questions:

- How do you know when you're done?
- What do you do when you're done?

Both of these questions are discussed in the next sections.

DETERMINE COMPLETION CRITERIA

The first thing to determine in a completion plan is how to decide when the project is over. Generally, a project is over when all the deliverables have been finished to the quality specified in the quality plan and have been turned over to the client. This section lists the critical deliverables that must be completed.

DEVELOP COMPLETION PROCEDURES

The completion activities generally include the following:

- Verifying that all the deliverables are complete
- Turning the deliverables over to the client
- Closing out project charges
- Providing any warranty or support for the deliverables
- Conducting the lesson-learned session

The completion plan explains how each of these activities will be performed.

WRITE THE COMPLETION PLAN

Once you've determined the completion criteria and have considered how to perform each of the completion activities, you're ready to write the completion plan.

WRITE AWARDS COMPLETION PLAN

Review the project criteria for the awards project and write the project completion plan.

Given the parameters discussed so far, a possible completion plan is …

The project will be considered complete when all outstanding invoices have been received and paid, and the sponsor has written one last article on the banquet for the employee newsletter.

Because the vendors in this case (plaque sellers/engravers, banquet facility) generally require advanced payment, the process for final invoicing is not complicated. In projects with several contracts and different contract terms, the completion plan would need to cover each one of these.

HOUR 6

Creating a Work Breakdown Structure

During project initiation we did a high-level cost/benefit analysis. Before we can estimate in more detail how long a project will take and how much it will cost, we need to get a more complete picture of the work involved. We do this with a Work Breakdown Structure (WBS), which is used to divide the total work of a project into manageable units. This lesson shows you how to create a Work Breakdown Structure.

UNDERSTAND THE WORK BREAKDOWN STRUCTURE

To get a more complete picture of the work involved in a project, we divide the total work of a project into manageable units. Different companies have different terms for the various units, but the hierarchy, regardless of the names at each level, is always called your Work Breakdown Structure (WBS).

The purpose of the WBS is to organize your project into various summary-reporting levels. Some of the more traditional reporting levels in information systems, training development, and engineering projects include the following:

- Stages
- Steps
- Tasks

Or:

- Phases
- Activities
- Tasks

CHAPTER SUMMARY

LESSON PLAN:

In this hour you will learn about …

- Understanding the need for a WBS.
- Determining WBS approach.
- Determining tracking levels.
- Creating WBS detail.

JUST A MINUTE

Whether you have standard reporting levels or not, remember that the sole purpose of these higher levels is to group your detail tasks so that you can create summary information for your detail tasks.

GO TO ▶

For more information on some of the popular project management software packages available today, see Hour 24, "Choosing a Project Management Package."

In either of these level-naming schemes, the top name is considered level one, the middle is level two, and the third is level three. In either of these schemes, you could only get three levels of detail. Because of the computer scheduling packages available today, many organizations now use WBSs with more than three levels and have stopped naming the various levels. In these organizations, the lowest levels are called *detail tasks*, and everything else is called a *summary task*.

DETERMINE WBS APPROACH

As noted, the WBS organizes your project work into a hierarchical reporting structure. The traditional way of viewing the WBS was graphical, like in an organization chart, but today very few project managers use this graphic view because most software products don't support it. Instead, the new products display the WBS in what is called an *indented list format*.

Despite how the WBS is displayed, you can organize the WBS in three ways:

- By phase
- By deliverable
- By skill or role

Each of these is described in more detail in the following sections.

CONSIDER ORGANIZING BY PHASE

The most common WBS organization scheme is by phase. With this organization scheme, the highest level in the WBS is a project or product phase. Some examples of WBS phases are Initiation, Design, Construction, and Post-Construction in building construction, or Initiation, Analysis, Design, Coding, Testing, Implementation, and Post-Implementation in Information Systems. The second level breaks the phases down further. If necessary, that second level is divided again.

A partial WBS example of the phase approach with three levels for the new purchasing system project might be the following:

1 Initiation

 …

2 Analysis

 2.1 Research Potential Replacement Systems

 2.2 Develop Short List of Contenders

 2.3 Contender Evaluation

  2.3.1 Evaluate System XYZ

  2.3.2 Evaluate System PQR

  2.3.3 Evaluate System JKL

 2.4 Make Selection Recommendation

3 Design

 …

4 Coding

 …

5 Testing

 …

6 Implementation

 …

7 Post-Implementation

 …

The numeric scheme in front of each summary and detail task is called the WBS Code. The traditional scheme is shown in the previous example and in the accompanying figure, although some organizations use four- to eight-digit numbers (with 1 equaling 1000, 2.3.1 equaling 2310, and so on) or alphanumeric schemes (A.1 for Analysis.1, and so on).

A graphical representation of a WBS.

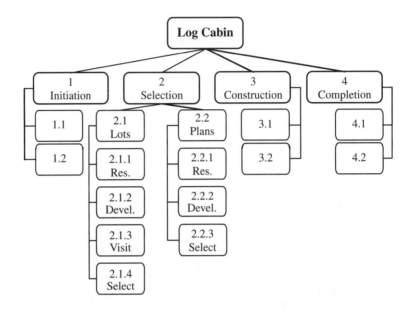

Using the log cabin project, a portion of the WBS with three levels might be as follows:

1 Initiation

    ...

2 Selection

    2.1 Lots

        2.1.1 Research Potential Lots

        2.1.2 Develop Short List of Lots

        2.1.3 Visit Each Lot

        2.1.4 Make Selection

    2.2 Plans

        2.2.1 Research Potential Plans

        2.2.2 Develop Short List of Plans

        2.2.3 Make Selection

3 Construction

    ...

4 Completion

...

A partial three-level WBS for the barn conference project might be as follows:

1 Initiation

...

2 Development

2.1 Facilities

2.1.1 Research Potential Conference Centers

2.1.2 Develop Short List of Facilities

2.1.3 Visit Each Facility

2.1.4 Make Selection

2.2 Program

2.2.1 Determine Topics

2.2.2 Identify Potential Speaker

2.2.3 Hire Speakers

2.2.4 Develop Conference Brochure

2.2.5 Mail Brochure

2.2.6 Arrange Meals and Breaks

2.2.7 Pre-Register Participants

2.2.8 Register Participants

2.2.9 Sign in Participants at Site

2.2.10 Introduce Speakers

2.2.11 Reproduce Handout Packages

3 Implementation

...

4 Post-Implementation

...

CONSIDER ORGANIZING BY DELIVERABLE

When you organize by product or deliverable, the first level in the WBS represents your major project deliverables. Under each deliverable, at lower and lower levels, are the tasks needed to complete that deliverable.

JUST A MINUTE

In some cases, you will have multiple, large, and final deliverables with very complicated or detailed separate work flows. You may want to consider each of these as subprojects of the larger project and then create WBSs for each subproject.

A partial WBS example of the deliverable approach with two levels for the new purchasing system project might be as follows:

1 Installed Purchasing System

    1.1 Survey potential systems

    1.2 Create short list of systems to investigate further

    1.3 Perform investigation

    1.4 Develop investigation report

    1.5 Select system

2 Trained end users

    2.1 Develop training

    2.2 Hold classes

For the log cabin project, a portion of the WBS with two levels might be like the following:

1 Lot

    1.1 Research Potential Lots

    1.2 Develop Short List of Lots

    1.3 Visit Each Lot

    1.4 Make Selection

2 Plans

    2.1 Research Potential Plans

    2.2 Develop Short List of Plans

    2.3 Make Selection

FYI The Project Management Institute standards group is working on tentative guidelines for creating WBSs. More information on this is available on the PMI Web site, www.pmi.org.

A partial two-level WBS for the barn conference project might be as follows:

1 Facilities

    1.1 Research Potential Conference Centers

    1.2 Develop Short List of Facilities

    1.3 Visit Each Facility

    1.4 Make Selection

2 Program

    2.1 Determine Topics

    2.2 Identify Potential Speaker

    2.3 Hire Speakers

    2.4 Develop Conference Brochure

    2.5 Mail Brochure

    2.6 Arrange Meals and Breaks

    2.7 Pre-Register Participants

    2.8 Register Participants

    2.9 Sign in Participants at Site

    2.10 Introduce Speakers

    2.11 Reproduce Handout Packages

TIME SAVER

 It's often hard to tell detail tasks from summary tasks in an indented list format. If you have difficulty with this, try naming each summary task with nouns and the detail tasks with verbs. This way, just by glancing at the name, you can tell whether or not it's a detail task.

CONSIDER ORGANIZING BY SKILL OR ROLE

When you organize by skill or role, the first level in the WBS represents your major skills/roles. Under each role, at lower and lower levels, are the tasks that will be completed by the resources assigned to those roles.

Using the new purchasing system project, a portion of the WBS organized by skill or role would be as follows:

1 Analysts

    1.1 Research Potential Replacement Systems

    1.2 Develop Short List of Contenders

    1.3 Contender Evaluation

        1.3.1 Evaluate System XYZ

        1.3.2 Evaluate System PQR

        1.3.3 Evaluate System JKL

    1.4 Make Selection Recommendation

2 Programmers

    ...

3 DBAs

    ...

4 Testers

    ...

5 Purchasing End Users

    ...

PROCEED WITH CAUTION

If you are working in an organization with a project management office and/or project management WBS templates, it's likely that you will need to follow the organization method used in the templates. Be sure to check on this before creating the WBS for your first project.

Using the log cabin example, a potential skill/role WBS would be the following:

1 Owner

    1.1 Research Potential Lots

    1.2 Develop Short List of Lots

    1.3 Visit Each Lot

    1.4 Make Selection

    1.5 Research Potential Plans

    1.6 Develop Short List of Plans

    1.7 Make Selection

2 General Contractor

    …

3 Electrician

    …

4 Plumber

    …

5 Carpenter

    …

For the barn conference project, an example would be the following:

1 Project Manager

    1.1 Research Potential Conference Centers

    1.2 Develop Short List of Facilities

    1.3 Visit Each Facility

    1.4 Make Selection

2 Caterer

    …

3 Speakers

    …

4 Administrative Assistant

    …

DECIDE ON APPROACH

Once you have reviewed the plusses and minuses of each organization method, choose the one that best meets your project scheduling and tracking needs. Then you are ready to proceed to the next step of deciding on WBS detail.

DETERMINE TRACKING LEVELS

In this step, you decide how much detail you'll use in your WBS and what you'll require your team members to track. You have two considerations here: what your organization will use for historic metrics and how much detail is too much.

CONSIDER TRACKING METRICS

Many organizations today still track projects only at the project level. That means that any project resource who works on the project only needs to track time spent on that project, not on what task in the project. The problem with this approach is that, although we know the total project actuals, we do not gather the historic task metrics that make estimating individual tasks easier on subsequent projects.

PROCEED WITH CAUTION

 If you plan on changing the way people track time on your projects, make sure that they understand the rationale. Time tracking is a very sensitive issue for some people.

Another approach to time tracking is to track the phase or deliverable level. For phased approaches, as used in computer systems, this means that resources note *whether* they are working on design, coding, or testing, but not *what* they are designing, coding, and testing. For the deliverables approach, as applied to construction, this means that they track if they are working on the roof, the basement, or the garage, but not what they are doing with that component.

Again, the difficulty with these approaches is the lack of detail on individual tasks. While we would know how long it took to do the garage, we would not know that it took 8 hours to design it, 6 hours to purchase the material, 47 hours to construct it, and 13 hours to do the interior work.

If you are interested in collecting metrics to be used later in estimating, the best approach is to track time down to the task level. But this approach also has problems. First, you have to make sure your resources understand *why* you are tracking to this level of detail. Second, you need to make those tasks's metrics meaningful without making too many tasks. Some guidelines to help you in this are explained in the next section.

UNDERSTAND DECOMPOSITION GUIDELINES

Because the WBS is used to estimate the project schedule and to track progress, you should consider several things when determining if you have decomposed a summary level into appropriate detail. The first is that you must be able to tell when the task starts and ends and how many hours of effort it took to complete. If a person cannot tell you when he or she started the task or cannot track the effort while working on the task, the task may still be too large or it may have been divided too far.

Detail tasks should also be assignable to one person or to one role. For instance, in software or construction projects, it's okay to leave, as a task, work that will be assigned to multiple programmers or multiple carpenters as long as each can tell you when the task started, ended, and how long it took. What you don't want to do, however, is to create a task that requires programmers and DBAs or carpenters and plumbers to perform different work on the same task. Tasks that would lead to this should be further divided into the carpenters' work and the plumbers' work so that they each can track it.

Because we don't want thousands of tasks in each project, detail tasks should have a reasonable amount of effort associated with them. Some project managers say that tasks should have at least eight hours of work, but the more important guide should be whether it is trackable by start date/time, end date/time, and effort.

On the other hand, you don't want to overwhelm your team members with very large tasks. It's daunting to think of tasks that will take hundreds of hours of effort. It's generally better to divide these larger tasks into detail tasks, providing that doing so does not violate the other considerations noted previously.

JUST A MINUTE

Don't expect to get a complete WBS on the first pass. Just as with the other sections, developing the WBS is iterative. You and your team may discover missing tasks during estimating and scheduling. While it's better to have an accurate WBS prior to executing, it's not uncommon to find missing tasks during project execution.

Here are two other things you should keep in mind when decomposing summary level tasks. A summary level task cannot have only one detail task, so you need to either find a way to make two detail tasks or remove the summary task. Also, the detail tasks, when completed, must fully complete the summary task. If they do not, then you need additional detail tasks.

CONSIDER WORK PACKAGES

Another way to help you think about how to create your WBS is the concept of a *work package*. Because you have to delegate the majority of the tasks in a project to other resources, you have to be able to explain the task to them. You have to be able to tell them the intended deliverable as well as any standards they must follow in completing that deliverable, how long they have to complete that deliverable, and what the tentative schedule is.

STRICTLY DEFINED

A **work package** is the collective name given to a project task and all its relevant work information. Generally included in this package are the task name, scheduled start and end date, duration, effort estimate, deliverable, completion measurements, quality measurements, and standards.

If you cannot pass on this information, then it's likely that the task is too detailed. On the other hand, if a task would have multiple deliverables or a variety of different standards to follow, it may need to be further divided.

CREATE WBS DETAIL

After you have decided on the WBS organization method and have considered tracking levels and work packages, you're ready to develop the WBS. Work packages will not be created, however, until after a project schedule has been developed.

CREATE AWARDS WBS

Let's look at what a complete WBS for the awards banquet might be. Take a few minutes and think about how you might organize this WBS and what tracking levels you might use, and then sketch out the WBS. When you're done, compare it to the answer that follows.

Since this project had two major objectives, which gave us two major deliverables (the award winners and the banquet), we'll look at this project WBS by deliverable. A potential WBS is …

Awards Banquet Project

1 Winners

    1.1 Create Team

    1.2 Create Process for Selecting Winners

    1.3 Develop Nomination Forms

    1.4 Gather Nominations

    1.5 Evaluate Nominations

    1.6 Select Winners

    1.7 Announce Winners

    1.8 Create Plaques

2 Banquet

    2.1 Determine Potential Dates

    2.2 Determine Potential Halls

    2.3 Review Hall Menus

    2.4 Create Short List of Halls

    2.5 Dine at Each Potential Hall

    2.6 Select Hall

    2.7 Announce Banquet

    2.8 Send Invitations

    2.9 Gather RSVPs

    2.10 Finalize Dining Arrangements

    2.11 Choose Entertainment

    2.12 Choose Speakers

    2.13 Choose Photographer

    2.14 Hold Dinner

Note that the three "choose" tasks could be divided into detail tasks much like the facility task itself. That is, each might have the four detail tasks as follows:

Determine Potential ___, Create Short List of ___, Gather Detailed Data on Each ___, and Select ___.

GO TO ▶
Although we discussed work packages in this section, they will not be created until we start executing the project. This will be covered in Hour 13, "Doing the Work."

If it's important for tracking purposes to track at this level, or if you intend to give the detailed tasks to separate people, then it's fine to create the additional 12 tasks. If neither of these is the case, however, as the effort in the "choose" tasks is relatively small, then it's probably best to not decompose these tasks.

CREATE RESTORATION WBS

Based on the data provided in the case study in Hour 1, "Understanding Project Management," and this additional information, create the restoration WBS. Additional project data is as follows:

There is a large diagonal crack in the brick in the western elevation. The original double entrance doors are in place but are badly damaged, as is the intricately carved woodwork over the door, and the transom has been covered with plywood. The rear door has been replaced with a smaller steel door, and its transom is also covered with plywood.

On the interior, the first floor contains a front entrance hall, a theater with balcony and stage, a rear entrance hall, and dressing rooms currently used as storage. Wainscoting runs around the theater and the entrance halls. The original wood floor is intact in the theater, as is the pine tongue-and-groove ceiling, but all the ceiling fixtures have been removed, as have the wall sconces. Traces of an old frieze run around the top of the walls to about 18 inches below the ceiling. The flooring in the front and rear entrance halls is 1950s linoleum; the floor in the dressing rooms is unknown.

TIME SAVER

If you have difficulty arranging your WBS in the indented list format and your software does not have a graphical WBS, then use sticky notes instead. Put each detail task or summary level task on its own sheet and then arrange the tasks as you would an organization chart. Then when you're happy with the arrangement, enter them into the software.

The second floor, reached by the front stairs through the balcony or by the rear stairs, has a large dining room, a kitchen, a bathroom with only one toilet and sink, and two small rooms, one currently used for storage and one as an office. The kitchen has oak wainscoting, with a double pocket door to the dining room and a single pocket door to the hall, both nonfunctioning at this time. There's a fireplace on the east wall of the dining area, but the mantel and decorative tiles have been stolen. The flooring is all 1950s linoleum. The ceiling is a 1970s drop ceiling, but the original plaster ceiling, complete with mahogany boxed beams, is still underneath, though highly damaged from the roof leaks.

On the third floor, accessed from the second floor hall, is an apartment. It has a kitchen, bath, living room, three bedrooms, and a large room on the south that was once a library. The built-in oak shelves, which housed beveled leaded glass doors and ran on three sides of the room, have been stolen. Most of the walls along the hall are missing, presumably demolished to aid in the theft of the shelves. The walls and ceilings have also been extensively damaged by the roof leaks. The floor in the library is the original wood; the hall, kitchen, and bath floors are linoleum; and the rest of the floors are currently carpeted.

The basement holds two furnaces, neither of which works, but which were used with hot-water heat through the existing radiator system. The electric is fuses, not circuit breakers, and two of the three lateral brick support walls are crumbling in spots. The basement floor is concrete. The flooring under the dressing rooms shows signs of fire, probably in the 1930s or 1940s, based on the repairs performed.

An answer appears in Appendix A, "Sample Documents."

PART II

Developing Project
Plan Details

Hour 7

Creating Your Project Team

CHAPTER SUMMARY

LESSON PLAN:

In this hour you will learn about ...

- Reviewing required resources.
- Considering resource availability.
- Considering work styles.
- Developing organizational plans.
- Planning to acquire appropriate resources.

In some organizations, the project team is assembled during project planning; in others, it's organized after the planning is complete. In this lesson you'll learn to review your resource needs, evaluate your resource pool, develop an organizational plan, and plan to acquire the appropriate resources for your project.

REVIEW REQUIRED RESOURCES

In the project initiation hour (refer to Hour 2, "Initiating a Project") we looked at the resources we would need at a high level and in Hour 4, "Adding to Your Plan," we discussed the resources again in the resource section of the project plan. In this hour, we'll expand on our resource discussion by reviewing the project requirements and developing a team and organization plan.

One of the most important aspects of the resource effectiveness of the team is the members' skill level on various types of work. This is important for two reasons. First, it may affect the resource's availability. Second, it may affect the effort estimates as developed in Hour 8, "Developing Project Estimates." When you are reviewing the required resources, verify the skill levels noted earlier in the project plan. Compare this skill level with those of the resources you have to draw from and select the resources that have the appropriate skill levels.

In some organizations project managers have no input into the resource selection process, so you should check to see how resources are allocated in your own organization.

CONSIDER RESOURCE AVAILABILITY

There are several aspects of availability to consider when looking at resources. Those that affect project work the most are the number of other projects a resource is assigned to, how many hours per day that resource can work on projects, and what external commitments such as vacation and training may limit availability. Let's look at each of these in more detail.

Although we would all like to think that our projects are top priority and should be able to use the highest skill-level resources, this is rarely the case. When determining which skill levels you need for tasks, you may want to establish a minimum as well as a preferred. This gives you a broader potential resource pool and may minimize resource bottlenecks.

REVIEW SIMULTANEOUS PROJECTS

Many resources are assigned to multiple simultaneous projects. This impacts projects in three ways. First, a critical resource may be working on another project when he or she is most needed on your project. Second, splitting time between multiple projects decreases the productivity on each project. Third, resources may be swapped across project tasks, which also decreases their productivity.

While we account for some of this in the estimates we create in Hour 8, if at all possible, it's preferable to work with resources that are not assigned to multiple projects. At the least, don't assign workers to more than four simultaneous projects.

EVALUATE HOURS PER DAY

Another aspect to consider when assigning resources to tasks is the number of hours per day that a resource can dedicate to project work. While the standard number of hours per day, at least in the United States, is eight hours, very few people work a full eight-hour day, especially on project work.

Team members who mix project work with operational work may have only an hour per day available to the project. Similarly, people who work part time will have less time available to project work.

You will need to understand these aspects of your resource assignments prior to moving into the estimating step.

REVIEW NONWORK TIME

Other nonwork time to be considered when evaluating potential resource assignments includes vacation, sick time, leaves of absence, and training sessions. Sick time is not generally scheduled in advance, but potential resources who have already scheduled vacations, leaves of absence, and/or training sessions may not be available during critical project timeframes. So, if other equivalent resources are available, you should consider assigning them instead.

After you've selected and assigned your resources, your project management software package can handle the mathematical effect on the schedule, but you will need to evaluate the qualitative effect on the project.

GO TO ▶
For more information on factors affecting dedicated project time, see Hour 8.

REVIEW AWARDS PROJECT RESOURCE AVAILABILITY

The noted human resources needed for the awards project included you as project manager, an administrative assistant for answering questions and taking reservations, and a three-employee selection committee. The nonhuman resources were the banquet facility, a slide projector, and a screen. These latter three will be considered during project execution.

We know this about our potential resource pool. You are working on this project and the restoration project. Three potential administrative assistants are available to the project. All are above-average performers at their jobs. Connie Shoup has been with the company for six years and works mornings Monday through Wednesday and afternoons Thursday and Friday. She is not currently assigned to any special projects but does have her normal operational tasks to perform. Sally Kirk has been with the company for three years, works full time, and has one other project to work on a few hours per week in addition to her operational tasks. Phyllis Jacobs has been with the company for 10 years, works full time, and has one other project to work on two hours per day in addition to her operational tasks. She also has a two-week cruise scheduled for the last two weeks before the banquet.

From the data given, which administrative assistant might be best for this project?

All three have similar skills, but Connie doesn't work full-time. While she'd have the physical amount of time to work on the project, it would be better to have someone who could answer questions at any time during the normal workday. That leaves Phyllis and Sally. But Phyllis will be gone during a critical time period, so the best choice at this point is Sally.

REVIEW RESTORATION PROJECT RESOURCE AVAILABILITY

Using the answers in Appendix A and other information provided on the restoration project, review the resource availability for potential resources. An answer is in Appendix A, "Sample Documents."

CONSIDER RESOURCE STYLES

The most effective teams are those with skills and styles that complement one another. Perhaps as important to you as a project manager, then, is how a resource works. As we noted in the skill section, you may not be able to select your team based on work styles, but understanding a little about their styles will help you work with them.

In this section we'll take a look at some of the more popular personality and communication style typing methods. We'll examine the different categories proposed in each method and look briefly at the characteristics associated with those categories.

First, some background. During the twentieth century, many individuals and organizations performed research on people's work preferences. Some of this research was done on what are called "personality styles," some on the dominant quadrant of the brain, and some on communication patterns. All these studies provided interesting data about working with people, but the most common and most relevant to project management include the following:

- Carl Jung
- Myers-Briggs
- Johari Window
- Whole Brain

Let's look at each of these in the following sections.

UNDERSTAND CARL JUNG'S METHOD

One of the first forays into personality typing was started in the 1920s by Carl Jung, a compatriot of Sigmund Freud. Jung's primary work divided people into the four categories of Intuitor, Thinker, Feeler, and Sensor. Let's look at some characteristics of each of these:

- *Intuitors* are generally imaginative and idealistic. They tend to think about the future and global issues, often to the detriment of the present.

- *Thinkers* are generally realistic and structured. They like detail work and decisions that require logic and good organization of facts.

- *Feelers* are generally emotional and spontaneous. They are nostalgic about the past and are generally very loyal to friends, family, and work.

- *Sensors* are generally aggressive and competitive. They are driven to succeed and tend to forget everything not directly related to success.

To determine which of these types most closely resembles your dominant style, you can take a type test. Jungian-based tests are usually designed around 20 to 30 quadrilles of adjectives; you rank each adjective on how closely it describes you.

JUST A MINUTE

Personality typing actually goes back well before Jung, especially if you count astrology as a typing method. But most authorities recognize Jung as the father of modern personality typing.

UNDERSTAND MYERS-BRIGGS TYPING METHOD

A few years after Jung created his typing scheme, Isabel Briggs Myers and Katherine Cook Briggs, daughter and mother who were amazed by the very different personalities of their in-laws, enhanced his work. The work of Myers and Briggs expands Jung's four types into a 16-type matrix, based on your preferences for performing certain tasks. The traditional Myers-Briggs test, called an *MBTI*, is similar to the Jungian-based test.

STRICTLY DEFINED

MBTI stands for Myers-Briggs Type Indicator. It's currently the registered trademark of Consulting Psychologists Press, Inc.

The Myers-Briggs preferences and their components are shown in the following table:

Preference	Definition	Options	Characteristics
Energizing	What types of activities energize you	Introverted	Gain energy from self and own thoughts
		Extraverted	Gain energy from other people and things
Attending	What types of things you pay attention to	Sensor	Gather information by using the five senses
		Intuitor	Gather information by perceiving and interpreting
Deciding	What kind of information you base your decisions on	Thinker	Make objective, logical decisions
		Feeler	Make subjective, value-driven decisions
Living	What kind of life you live	Judgment	Live a planned, regimented life
		Perception	Live an unstructured, spontaneous life

FYI Instead of going through the MBTI testing process, you may want to use a book called *LIFETypes,* by Sandra Hirsh and Jean Kummerow (Warner Books, Inc., 1989). The book enables you to get your type by picking one option from each of the four preferences, or you can read descriptions of each of the 16 possibilities and determine your type that way.

While many people have difficulty agreeing that they display some of the characteristics in the Jungian typing method, you'll find you fit almost exactly into one of the 16 MBTI types.

Some organizations even use the MBTI to determine what jobs people are best suited to. The concern with this, however, is that most "thinking outside of the box" solutions to problems come from people with different viewpoints. When everyone in the same job description has the same personality type, where is the innovation going to come from?

UNDERSTAND THE JOHARI WINDOW METHOD

In 1955, Joseph Luft and Harrington Ingram put forth a new theory of communication styles they called the Johari Window. They described four types known as Open, Hidden, Unknown, and Blind. In the original Johari Window, the panes (types) were not really personality types but dealt with data that you knew about yourself and showed, knew about yourself and didn't show, didn't know about yourself but didn't show, and didn't know about yourself but showed.

Since that time, a variety of researchers have built upon the Johari Window concepts, and the extension most applicable to project management is the one that discusses "disclosure patterns." According to this research, these patterns describe how people gather and disclose information. They noted four patterns and changed the naming slightly from the original, calling the patterns Open, Closed, Hidden, and Blind. Let's look briefly at each type.

As the name implies, Open communicators disclose information about themselves and their work. They also actively seek new information from others. On the opposite side of the window are the Closed communicators. They naturally neither disclose any information nor seek any new information.

Halfway between open and unknown, Hidden communicators rarely disclose information, but constantly seek it. They are good at keeping secrets. Also halfway between open and unknown, Blind communicators disclose a lot, but they rarely seek new information. They think they know it all already.

TIME SAVER

In a project situation, the most difficult of these disclosure patterns to deal with tends to be Blind communicators. You may want to focus your attention on these people to make sure the information they spread is accurate.

As with the other typing methods, we all have some components of each disclosure pattern. What's perhaps most important about this typing method is that the disclosure patterns can be applied to team members, whole teams, and entire organizations.

When using this method to think about team members, you need to understand that each type will have different communication needs. Open and Hidden communicators will want to have as much information, in as much detail, as possible. They tend to like the detail to make their own decisions.

Closed and Blind communicators, on the other hand, may have to be spoon-fed information they need to know since they tend not to gather it naturally.

In terms of disclosing, Open and Blind communicators will share their knowledge. Both types, in fact, tend to enjoy sharing knowledge and may actually share things they shouldn't. Closed and Hidden communicators, though, don't naturally share. If they are the experts on your team or if they are your clients, you may need to work harder to gather the information that you need from them.

When working in departments, these disclosure patterns also apply. Open and Blind departments will willingly share information with you, while Hidden and Closed will not. In these latter cases, you will need to look for an Open or Blind individual in that department or you will have to use special questioning techniques. Classes on interviewing techniques may help you with this.

Whole organizations also have set communication patterns. Some organizations openly communicate with employees and external contacts while others remain hidden or closed. If you are an Open communicator working in or working with a Closed organization, you are likely to have more project-related stress.

UNDERSTAND THE WHOLE BRAIN METHOD

Ned Herrmann and his Whole Brain Institute (now known as Herrmann International) categorize people by their dominant brain quadrant. The quadrants/thinking modes were originally called Facts, Feelings, Form, and Future, but now are simply lettered A through D.

- The left cerebral quadrant (Facts/A) is factual and logical.
- The right cerebral (Future/B) is visual and conceptual.
- The left limbic (Form/C) is organized and procedural.
- The right limbic (Feelings/D) is emotional and relationship-oriented.

Some Whole Brain theorists believe that you can learn to use all the quadrants of your brain. In this way you can adjust your thinking style to the type of problem at hand.

 FYI For more information on Whole Brain and Myers-Brigggs, check out the following sites: Whole Brain, www.hbdi.com; Myers-Briggs, dir.yahoo.com/Social_Science/ Psychology/Branches/Personality/Myers_Briggs/. For additional information on Jung and the Johari Window, your best bet is to locate their original works in your local library.

UNDERSTAND WHY TYPING MATTERS

What all these methods, and the dozens of others not covered, provide us with are ways to consider our interactions with others. If you believe the typing methods that use four types, then the assumption is that about 25 percent of the population fit in each type. This means that you have a 75 percent chance of working with someone with a different style. These people with different styles will handle information differently, make decisions differently, handle time differently, and relate to one another differently. Understanding this will help you to have more patience with your team and to increase the chance of project success.

CONSIDER AWARDS PROJECT STYLES

Now let's review the style information on our awards project resources. Sally Kirk, who is the primary candidate as administrative assistant at this point, is an Open communicator. This is consistent with the role she'll need to play, both to answer questions and to take registrations.

CONSIDER RESTORATION PROJECT STYLES

Using the answers in Appendix A and other information provided on the restoration project, review the resource work style of the potential project resources. An answer is in Appendix A.

DEVELOP AN ORGANIZATIONAL PLAN

Once you've considered your resources, you can start thinking about the team functions and organization. The organizational plan explains three things: how the team will be organized in terms of reporting relationships, when the individuals will be needed, and what their individual roles and responsibilities will be.

JUST A MINUTE

 Unless your organization routinely tests employees on work and/or personality styles, you will generally not know the styles of all your potential resources. You may have to infer the styles from previous work with them.

DETERMINE THE ORGANIZATIONAL STRUCTURE

The organization of a project team often depends on the underlying structure of the company performing the project. There are three primary organizational structures in use in companies today:

- **Hierarchical structure.** This is where employees are organized by the type of function they perform within the organization. For instance, in a manufacturing company, major departments may include finance, manufacturing, and engineering, with the heads of those departments reporting directly to the company president or CEO.

- **Projectized structure.** A relatively new structure in which project managers report directly to the CEO or company president. They are full-time project managers and they have full-time project staffs.

- **Matrix structure.** A cross between projectized and hierarchical. While there are project managers with authority over project resources, these resources still report to the functional managers in terms of performance appraisals, development, and the like.

When you work in a matrix or functional (hierarchical) organization, you will need a plan to acquire resources for your projects. This is discussed in the "Plan to Acquire Appropriate Resources" section later in this hour.

When you work in a matrix or functional (hierarchical) organization, it is unlikely that your resources will report directly to you, so in this step, you create the organization chart for your project.

The reporting relationships are generally given graphically in a typical organization chart. An example of one is shown in the following figure. This organization chart should be consistent with the communication lines in the communication plan.

DEVELOP THE STAFFING PLAN

The staffing plan is similar to a project budget, except that instead of giving dollar amounts per time period, it gives resource hours per time period. They can be summarized for all resources per time period, by resource type per time period, or by individual resource per time period. You can display this plan in a traditional table format or in a more visual histogram format (see the following figures).

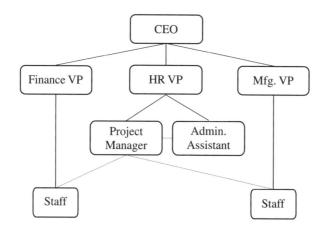

A sample project organization chart.

ID	Name		August 2002					September 2002				October 2002		
		29	05	12	19	26	02	09	16	23	30	07	14	21
Res1	Resource 1	16.00	40.00	40.00	0.00	0.00	0.00	0.00	0.00	0.00	0.00	0.00	0.00	0.00
Res2	Resource 2	16.00	24.00	0.00	8.00	0.00	0.00	0.00	0.00	0.00	0.00	0.00	0.00	0.00
Res 3	Resource 3	0.00	0.00	0.00	0.00	0.00	0.00	40.00	0.00	0.00	0.00	0.00	0.00	0.00
Res 4	Resource 4	16.00	24.00	0.00	0.00	0.00	0.00	0.00	16.00	40.00	24.00	0.00	0.00	0.00

A sample staffing-plan table.

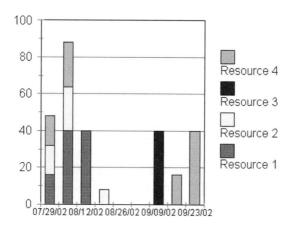

A sample staffing-plan chart.

DETERMINE THE ROLES AND RESPONSIBILITIES

Another important resource-planning component is who will do what on the project. A convenient way to display the various stakeholders and their contributions to the project is with a roles-and-responsibilities matrix.

A typical roles-and-responsibilities matrix lists the WBS in indented list format in the left column of the matrix and lists one resource per column across the rest of the matrix. In a simple roles-and-responsibilities matrix, an X is placed in each cell where a resource has any involvement on the task. In a more comprehensive roles-and-responsibilities matrix, the person's role in the task is coded with letters, numbers, or colors. Both are displayed respectively in the following figures.

A simple roles-and-responsibilities matrix.

Resource	Res1	Res2	Res3
Task			
2 Analysis			
2.1 Research Potential Replacement Systems	X	X	X
2.2 Develop Short List of Contenders	X		
2.3 Contender Evaluation			
2.3.1 Evaluate System XYZ		X	
2.3.2 Evaluate System PQR			X
2.3.3 Evaluate System JKL			X
2.4 Make Selection Recommendation		X	

A roles-and-responsibilities matrix showing individual roles.

Resource	Res1	Res2	Res3
Task			
2 Analysis			
2.1 Research Potential Replacement Systems	A	W	W
2.2 Develop Short List of Contenders	W/A		
2.3 Contender Evaluation			
2.3.1 Evaluate System XYZ		W	
2.3.2 Evaluate System PQR			W
2.3.3 Evaluate System JKL			W
2.4 Make Selection Recommendation		W/A	

A = Approver   C = Contributor   R = Reviewer   W = Worker

In these more complicated roles-and-responsibilities matrixes, the coding scheme may include the following responsibilities: worker, approver, contributor, reviewer, and so on. Each responsibility would then be given a code. Using the named responsibilities in the preceding scheme, the code could be the first letter of the responsibility, so a worker would be coded "W," an approver, "A," and so on. You could also use numbers and colors to display the coding scheme.

REVIEW AWARDS PROJECT RESOURCE ORGANIZATION

Review the work on the awards project to date and develop an organization chart and a roles-and-responsibilities matrix.

The organization chart for this project is straightforward. The Leetle Toy Company is a functional hierarchical organization, so the project resources will all have indirect reporting relationships through the project manager for the duration of the project and will still have direct relationships to their managers.

The roles-and-responsibilities matrix might look like this:

Awards Banquet Project Roles and Responsibilities

	PM	Admin	Committee	Winners
Winners				
Create Team	X			
Create Process	X	X	X	
Develop Forms			X	
Gather Nominations		X		
Evaluate Nominations			X	
Select Winners			X	
Announce Winners	X			
Create Plaques		X		
Banquet				
Determine Dates	X	X		
Determine Halls		X		
Review Hall Menus		X		
Create Short List	X	X	X	
Dine at Each	X	X	X	
Select Hall	X	X	X	
Announce Banquet	X			
Send Invitations		X		
Gather RSVPs		X		
Finalize Dining		X		
Choose Entertainment		X		
Choose Speakers		X		
Choose Photographer		X		
Hold Dinner	X	X		

REVIEW RESTORATION PROJECT RESOURCE ORGANIZATION

Review the work on the restoration project to date and develop an organization chart and a roles-and-responsibilities matrix. An answer is in Appendix A.

PLAN TO ACQUIRE APPROPRIATE RESOURCES

In most organizations, the project resources are not actually acquired until the execution phases, so this section describes how you plan to acquire the resources.

You acquire resources in three main ways:

- By preassignment
- By negotiation
- By procurement

Resources tend to be preassigned to project managers in projectized organizations because they are direct employees, but in hierarchical (functional) organizations and in matrix organizations they may also be preassigned. In these cases, the resources could be preassigned by a steering committee at project initiation.

When resources are not preassigned, you need to negotiate with functional managers to use their resources or go outside the organization to procure them. Negotiation success will depend on the other commitments the resources already have and to relative project priorities. To procure external resources, you will need to budget for them and get the cost approved by the sponsor.

REVIEW AWARDS RESOURCE ACQUISITION PLAN

Review the resources we've discussed so far and develop an acquisition plan for this awards project.

Based on the project data so far, you, the project manager, were preassigned to the project, but you can negotiate with Sally's manager for her administrative time. The three employees on the award-winner selection team are probably best acquired by asking for volunteers and then negotiating with their managers.

REVIEW RESTORATION RESOURCE ACQUISITION PLAN

Develop an acquisition plan for the restoration project. An answer is provided in Appendix A.

TIME SAVER

 Like the project control plans in Hour 5, "Developing Project Control Plans," the roles-and-responsibilities matrix can generally be reused with minor modification from project to project.

HOUR 8
Developing Project Estimates

Once you've created a project work breakdown structure and have reviewed your resource requirements, you're ready to estimate how long each of the project tasks will take. This lesson introduces a variety of bottom-up estimation methods to help you create these estimates. Bottom-up means that you estimate per task and then total the individual estimates to get a total project time and cost estimate.

PREPARE FOR ESTIMATING

This section discusses some of the activities you need to perform prior to developing your estimates. It discusses the nature of estimates, the types of estimates, and the other portions of a project plan to review prior to estimating.

UNDERSTAND ESTIMATES

The first thing you need to do when estimating tasks is to realize that estimates are just that. They are guesses at how long we think a task will take. This hour discusses some methods for refining estimates to make them more accurate, but it's part of the nature of projects that we cannot predict exactly how long something will take.

Part of the problem with estimating is that accurately predicting what will happen in the near future is difficult, but predicting the distant future is virtually impossible.

LESSON PLAN:

In this hour you will learn about …

- Understanding estimates.
- Developing standard estimates.
- Adding estimate adjustments.
- Using special situation estimating techniques.
- Creating cost estimates.

Many organizations account for this difficulty by recognizing a variety of estimation levels. Most commonly, there are three levels.

The first level of estimates is given at *project initiation*. Because there is little actual detail on the project at this point, these estimates tend to be 50 percent to 75 percent under the actual time and cost of the completed project. The second level of estimates is given at *project planning*. These estimates are more accurate because we know more about the project at this point. They are usually still low, however, by 30 percent to 50 percent of the actuals at completion. At the beginning of *project execution*, these estimates are reviewed and revised and will be, on average, 10 percent to 30 percent off the actuals at completion.

Task estimates within plus or minus 10 percent of actuals are very good. In fact, even if task estimates vary more than that, cumulative estimates keeping the project within plus or minus 10 percent is considered by many organizations to be "on time."

JUST A MINUTE

Because both success criteria of on time and within budget depend on the accuracy of your estimates, you need to make sure that your management and clients understand the average accuracy of estimates at the various levels. You may want to include notes to this effect in your project initiation documents and your project plans.

UNDERSTAND TASK TYPES

When you create estimates, they will be either resource-constrained estimates or time-constrained estimates. The most common tasks are resource-constrained tasks. This means that the duration of the task is based on how many resources are assigned to it and how many hours per day they work on it. When you estimate resource-constrained tasks, you estimate the total amount of work effort involved in the task. Effort is generally expressed in hours, although it can also be expressed in days, weeks, months, or even years.

In the new software, log cabin, and barn conference projects we've been working with, the majority of the project tasks would be resource-constrained. For example, researching potential software vendors, researching potential lots and potential cabin plans, and researching potential conference facilities could all be performed by multiple people to shorten the task duration.

The duration of time-constrained tasks, on the other hand, is fixed by the nature of the task. Adding more resources to time-constrained tasks does not decrease the duration. Typical time-constrained tasks include training classes, meetings, certain types of machine operations, and order times. Most time-constrained tasks are estimated in days, although they, too, can be estimated in any time unit.

In the new software project, ordering the software and holding training classes would be time-constrained tasks. In the log cabin project, meetings with the owners would be time-constrained. In the barn conference project, signing in participants at site and introducing speakers would be time-constrained tasks. These latter two might be considered resource-constrained, too, but assuming that on-site sign-in is open only for the first hour and that each speaker gets a two-minute introduction just prior to his or her presentation makes these tasks time-constrained.

FYI   Some organizations call resource-constrained tasks resource-driven or effort-driven tasks.

It's important to remember that, even though the durations of some tasks are time-constrained, they still have effort associated with them. Some time-constrained tasks, such as training classes, will have effort equal to the duration multiplied by the number of participants. Other time-constrained tasks, such as ordering products, will have some up-front effort associated with them but no additional effort. Still other tasks, such as monitoring equipment that produces something, will have periodic effort throughout the duration of the task.

If you will not be estimating and tracking costs, it's not necessary to estimate these effort amounts because they generally don't affect the schedule, but they will affect the cost.

Now that we've reviewed the types of tasks and estimates, let's look at the estimating steps.

REVIEW WBS

Estimates are created from your tasks, so your first step should be to review the WBS and make sure that it's organized the way you'd like it to be. Also make sure that you haven't missed any tasks.

REVIEW RESOURCES

Next, review the resource assignment to each task. If any assignments have changed since you originally assigned resources, then modify them.

CREATE TASK ESTIMATES

After you've reviewed the WBS for completeness and you've reviewed and verified your resource assignments, you're ready to start estimating. This section describes an estimating method that helps you to account for various resource skill levels, multiple project assignments, and the normal nonwork time during a standard day. Other nonwork time, such as vacations, are accounted for in scheduling (discussed in Hour 10, "Determining the Project Schedule").

DEVELOP STANDARD ESTIMATES

The first step in this estimating method is to develop a standard estimate for each task. This estimate represents the amount of effort a task would take given no interruptions, optimal work conditions, average skill level, and assignment to just this project.

This standard estimate can come from various sources. It may be based on a historical database of effort actuals from previous projects, from expert opinion, or some other technique. If a historical database is available, this is generally the best source for the standard estimate.

JUST A MINUTE

Top-down (analogous) estimating is where you estimate total current projects based on actuals from similar past projects. If a project took 20 percent of its hours in the planning phase, then this project should also. While some organizations use this method as the primary estimation method, it's generally better used as a reality check for a bottom-up method.

ADD WORK INTERRUPTION FACTORS

Even when someone is diligently working on a project task, he or she will encounter project-related and nonproject-related interruptions throughout the day. These are not scheduled tasks, but they take time away from the tasks and need to be accounted for in our estimates.

The three most common work interruption factors are meetings, communications, and idle time. In most organizations, meetings, phone calls (nonproject), and other breaks account for a 10 percent loss factor. "Communications" here refer to project communications, including project phone calls, walk-ins, and the like. In most organizations, this is also a 10 percent loss factor. Although it sounds similar, "idle time" as used here is not the same as breaks. It represents the time lost to staring off into space, listening in on nearby phone conversations, singing along with the radio, and the like. Idle time is also generally estimated as a 10 percent loss factor.

This means that work-interruption factors alone cause workers to lose 30 percent of their days. This is why some organizations schedule work for less than eight hours per day. If your organization has been collecting data on internal work-interruption factors, you may have different values for this factor, but 30 percent is typical.

PROCEED WITH CAUTION

Another common value used for the communications work-interruption factor is 1 percent per team member, with a minimum of 10 percent. This would mean that a team of 30 would lose 30 percent to communications and an overall 50 percent to work-interruption factors.

ADD PART-TIME EFFECT

When team members are working on multiple tasks simultaneously, we need to add time to the standard estimates for them to switch gears between tasks. This is generally referred to as the part-time effect. When people are working on only one project, there's no additional loss. When they're working three-fourths' time on your project, there's a 10 percent loss, half time means a 15 percent loss, and one-fourth time a 20 percent loss.

ADD SKILL FACTORS

When people have varying proficiencies on a certain type of work, there's a wide swing in effort hours. This, too, needs to be accounted for in the estimates. The standard estimate presumed an average skill level, so you will need to adjust the estimate as follows for different skill levels:

Expert: .50
Highly Skilled: .75

Average: 1.00

Junior: 1.25

Novice: 1.50

As with work interruption factors, if your organization has its own skill factors, you would use them instead.

JUST A MINUTE

If the novice is very new to the type of task involved, you may actually want to use 2.0 as the skill factor.

Do the Math

Once you've determined the effects of each of the factors noted, you need to calculate the real expected effort on a task. To do this, you use the following formula:

Adjusted Effort = Standard × 100 ÷ (100 − WIF) × 100 ÷ (100 − PTE) × Skill Factor

Let's look at an example.

On the new purchasing software project, some of the tasks in the WBS were as follows:

Analysis

2.1 Research Potential Replacement Systems

2.2 Develop Short List of Contenders

2.3 Contender Evaluation

       2.3.1 Evaluate System XYZ

       2.3.2 Evaluate System PQR

       2.3.3 Evaluate System JKL

2.4 Make Selection Recommendation

On task 2.1, let's presume that expert opinion says that it takes an average analyst 15 minutes to scan write-ups on potential systems to see if they meet your criteria, and there are 24 potential systems. The standard estimate would then be 6 hours.

Now let's say your analyst is working on three other projects, and she has never done a systems survey. This would give a 20 percent loss for part-time effect and a skill factor of 1.5.

The adjusted effort would be $6 \times 100 \div 70 \times 100 \div 80 \times 1.5$.

This gives us an adjusted effort of 16 hours.

PROCEED WITH CAUTION

 When adding skill factors to an estimate, you need to be careful of where the standard estimate comes from. If you ask experts how long it will take them to perform a task, they are already factoring in their expertise. You don't want to then multiply their number by .5 or the task will be severely underestimated.

CALCULATE AWARDS ESTIMATES

According to the historical database of project information at the Leetle Toy Company, on similar special event projects the actuals have averaged as follows:

Create Teams, 1 hour per team member

Create Processes for Selecting Winners, 4 hours per team member

Develop Forms, 12 hours

Create Plaques, 2 weeks from vendor

Surveying Potentials, 15 minutes per potential

Reviewing Potentials, 10 minutes per potential

Printing Invitations, 2 weeks from print shop

The team size is 5. You are an averaged-skilled project manager, and Sally (the administrative assistant) is also average, but the members of the selection committee are novices. You're all working on 2 projects, but Sally also has operational duties. There are 4 potential dates, 32 potential halls, 4 potential photographers, 8 potential acts, and 20 potential speakers. The short list of halls will have 3 selections. Calculate the expected amount of effort for each of the awards banquet tasks.

For task 1.1, Create Teams, we have 5 team members, so this would be 5 hours. This task would most likely not be affected by other factors, so we'll leave the estimate at 5.

On task 1.2, Create Process for Selecting Winners, the standard estimate (s) would be 20 hours. Presuming an average part-time effect of 15 percent and using the lowest skill level of novice, this would yield an adjusted estimate (ae) of 50 hours. The rest of the tasks would look like this:

1.3 Develop Nomination Forms = 12 s; 30 ae

2.1 Determine Potential Dates = 1 s; 2 ae

2.2 Determine Potential Halls = 8 s; 20 ae

2.3 Review Hall Menus = 5 s; 13 ae

2.4 Create Short List of Halls = 5 s; 13 ae

2.6 Select Hall = 1 s; 2 ae

2.11 Choose Entertainment = 4 s; 10 ae

2.12 Choose Speakers = 5 s; 13 ae

2.13 Choose Photographer = 2 s; 5 ae

No historical data was provided for the following tasks, so you would need to use expert opinion or comparisons to similar tasks.

Task 1.5.1, Evaluate Nominations, is likely to be similar to the surveying tasks. With an assumption of 10 nomination forms, this yields 2.5 hours standard, 6 ae.

Using the same logic would give a 6-hour ae on the following tasks, also:

1.6 Select Winners

1.7 Announce Winners

2.7 Announce Banquet

The rest of the tasks are time-constrained.

1.4 Gather Nominations: Allow 3 weeks

1.8 Create Plaques: 2 weeks

2.5 Dine at Each Potential Hall: 3 days (1 day per each facility)

2.8 Send Invitations: 2 weeks

2.9 Gather RSVPs: Allow 3 weeks

2.10 Finalize Dining Arrangements: Required 1 week prior

2.14 Hold Dinner: 4 hours

Even though these tasks are time-constrained, each one has effort associated with it. Because these tasks tend to be worked on over time, the effort estimates on time-constrained tasks are not normally adjusted for the factors noted earlier. The possible exceptions to this might be repetitive tasks, such as mailing the invitations, where you might be slower because of interruptions or skill. For our purposes, we will not calculate any adjustments to these effort estimates.

For task 1.4, it should take about 15 minutes per nomination to open, copy, and file each. With 10 forms, that would be 2.5 hours. Task 1.8 should take 1 hour to place the order for the plaques, task 2.5, 6 hours to dine, task 2.8, 1 minute each to stuff and stamp invitation for 2 hours, task 2.9, 4 hours, and task 2.10, 1 hour.

With task 2.14, we're going to leave the effort at zero because the Leetle Toy Company is not paying the employees for their time at the dinner. If they were being paid, the effort would be 800 hours, which is the 4-hour dinner times all 200 employees who are estimated to attend.

JUST A MINUTE

Even when you have a historical metrics database, not every task will be present. When possible, select similar tasks for your standard estimate or use expert opinion.

Calculate Restoration Project Estimates

The Leetle Toy Company has never managed a restoration project, but the nonprofit organization has managed two other projects. The actuals from those projects for some of the tasks are as follows:

Engineering reports: 2 weeks from vendor

Architectural plans: 3 weeks from vendor

Getting detailed estimates: 2 weeks from vendor

Roof replacement/repair: 4 weeks from vendor

Foundation repair: 2 weeks from vendor

Window/door replacement/repair: 4 weeks from vendor

Wall repair: 4 weeks from vendor

Floor refinishing: 2 weeks from vendor

Siding and brick replacement/repair: 4 weeks from vendor

Painting: 2 weeks from vendor

Project Manager Administrative Tasks: 16 hours per week

Given the skill factors, team sizes, and project assignments discussed in earlier examples, calculate the expected amount of effort for each of the restoration project tasks. An answer is given in Appendix A, "Sample Documents."

Use Special Situation Estimating Techniques

When you don't have good metrics on which to base estimates, you still need a way to try to develop relatively reasonable estimates. These next three estimating techniques may be helpful in those situations.

Understand Weighted Average

Originally a component of developing estimates in the Program Evaluation and Review Technique (PERT) method of scheduling, *weighted average* is still used by project managers to estimate projects that are highly volatile and/or highly visible. In this method, three sets of estimates are developed: most likely, optimistic, and pessimistic.

STRICTLY DEFINED

WAVE, which stands for **Weighted AVErage,** is often used as another name for the weighted average technique.

The most likely estimate, as the name implies, is how long, preferably in terms of effort, you think a task will most likely take. The optimistic estimate, also referred to as best case, is how long you think a task will take if everything goes perfectly. The pessimistic estimate, also referred to as worst case, is how long you think a task will take if everything that can go wrong does.

You create these estimates for each detail task in your project. These three estimates are then averaged, with a weight of four on most likely. The formula is as follows:

WAVE = [Optimistic + 4 × (Most Likely) + Pessimistic] ÷ 6

In most cases, the resulting estimate ends up being slightly higher than the most likely estimate. While this helps allocate contingency time in the schedule, perhaps an even greater advantage to this method is that four separate schedules can be produced, giving a range of potential time and cost estimates.

The optimistic schedule is generally the most enlightening schedule. Remember that this schedule is the one that represents every task running perfectly. The odds of every task running perfectly are slim to none, so if your optimistic schedule says you will not finish the project in time for your deadline, then you need to renegotiate the scope or the deadline.

The disadvantage of using weighted average estimates, of course, is that it's tedious to create four sets of estimates. Even if you have a software package to calculate the weighted average, creating the original three estimates is very time-consuming, especially in projects that have hundreds of tasks.

USE EXPERT OPINION

Another common estimating method is expert opinion. In this method, you ask an expert in the task how long it should take to perform that task. The disadvantages to this technique are in locating that expert and in making sure his or her assumptions are valid for your project and environment.

UNDERSTAND THE DELPHI TECHNIQUE

The Delphi Technique is similar to expert opinion, but rather than get the opinion of one expert, you use a group. The method is often used to get group consensus on estimates or as a way to include a variety of possible estimates. The Delphi Technique starts with a team of estimators, usually five or seven. Each person in the team estimates a task and gives his or her assumptions. Each person then reads the other estimates and assumptions and reestimates the task. The revised estimates are then averaged to come up with a final estimate. In some versions of this technique, the high and low are discarded and the remaining estimates averaged. Other versions of the technique use three rounds of estimating.

The advantage to this method is similar to that of weighted average. By getting a variety of estimates, the estimates tend to be higher and more accurate. The disadvantage is that, as with weighted average, it's a long process to get estimates on a large number of tasks. Another disadvantage is that if the team has little experience with the tasks they are estimating, they will all really be guessing.

CREATE COST ESTIMATES

Once you have effort estimates for your tasks, you can consider cost. We looked at high-level cost estimates in the project initiation phase, and in this phase we can get more detailed estimates. This section looks at the two major types of costs in a project—fixed costs and variable costs.

JUST A MINUTE

Each organization has its own way of classifying fixed and variable costs. Make sure you check with your accounting department on how to classify costs if you will be feeding accounting systems from your project data.

ESTIMATE FIXED COSTS AND VARIABLE COSTS

Fixed costs for a project generally include materials, designs, fixed-bid services, and the like. They are generally associated per task and totaled for the whole project.

In most organizations, variable costs are those associated with resource cost. The primary variable cost is wages. In some cases, the overhead associated with those wages is also considered a variable cost. Costs are calculated by multiplying the resource rate by the number of units of the resource used per task. With human resources, this means multiplying a person's hourly rate times the number of hours assigned to the task.

TIME SAVER

Most of the major project management software packages on the market today can do the cost estimate math for you. There are some, though, that do not provide in-depth costing features. If this aspect is important to you, make sure that you carefully evaluate each package.

Let's look at two examples.

In the new purchasing software project, the major fixed cost would be the cost of the software package. These can run from $2,000 to $2,000,000 depending on the individual package. Because at this stage you won't know the exact package, so you don't know the exact cost, you should use the cost used in the cost/benefit analysis. You should also add an assumption related to the cost in your assumptions section of the plan.

In the building the log cabin project, each piece in the log cabin will have its own material cost as well as the time-related costs for installing the materials. If, as project manager of this project, you are the owner, it's unlikely you would know the variable costs on the project. You will be working with the bid prices you've received. On the other hand, if you work for the contractor building the cabin, you will want to estimate and track your actual cost to be able to bid more accurately on future projects.

CALCULATE AWARDS COST ESTIMATES

Let's practice estimating costs with the awards banquet project.

To calculate cost, assume each resource has a rate of $32 per hour. When you know which specific resources will be assigned to the project, you can adjust the rate per resource, but this will give a good second-level estimate of cost.

Fixed costs are estimated at $300 for the plaques, $50 for the hall, $200 for the photographer, $400 for entertainment, and $1,000 for speakers. The invitations will cost about $250 to print plus 68 cents each to mail out and receive RSVPs. The dinners will cost approximately $30 per attendee with tip, tax, and service charges.

Awards Banquet Cost Estimates	Hours	Variable	Fixed	Total
1 *Winners*				
1.1 Create Team	5	160	160	
1.2 Create Process	50	1,600	1,600	
1.3 Develop Nomination Forms	30	960	960	
1.4 Gather Nominations	2.5	80	80	
1.5 Evaluate Nominations	6	192	192	
1.6 Select Winners	6	192	192	
1.7 Announce Winners	6	192	192	
1.8 Create Plaques	1	32	300	332
2 *Banquet*				
2.1 Determine Potential Dates	2	64		64
2.2 Determine Potential Halls	20	640		640

continues

Awards Banquet Cost Estimates	Hours	Variable	Fixed	Total
2.3 Review Hall Menus	13	416		416
2.4 Create Short List of Halls	13	416		416
2.5 Dine at Each Potential Hall	6	192	270	462
2.6 Select Hall	2	64	50	114
2.7 Announce Banquet	6	192		192
2.8 Send Invitations	2	64	420	484
2.9 Gather RSVPs	4	128		128
2.10 Finalize Dining Arrangements	1	32		32
2.11 Choose Entertainment	10	320	400	720
2.12 Choose Speakers	13	416	1,000	1,416
2.13 Choose Photographer	5	160	200	360
2.14 Hold Dinner	0	0	6,000	6,000
TOTAL	203.5	$6,512	$8,640	$15,152

CREATE RESTORATION COST ESTIMATES

Calculate the estimated cost of the restoration project based on the following information: Although you're not charging the preservation group for your time, your hourly rate needs to be included in the cost calculations. With overhead, your billable rate is $72 per hour.

In terms of materials, you will not be buying any of the products directly, but instead will be contracting with a variety of providers for both their time and the materials. At this point, you're hoping to go with fixed-price bids from each vendor, so you will presume that the bids are fixed and that you will not track any hours on the project except your own.

An answer is given in Appendix A.

HOUR 9

Creating a Network Diagram

CHAPTER SUMMARY

LESSON PLAN:

In this hour you will learn about ...

- Understanding task relationships.
- Determining inter-task relationships.
- Creating a PERT chart.
- Creating a CPM diagram.

Now that we've created a Work Breakdown Structure, assigned project resources, and estimated our task times and costs, we're ready to look at creating a project schedule. The first step in creating a schedule is to create a network diagram. In the following sections of this hour, you'll learn about the various network diagramming techniques and how to apply them to your projects.

UNDERSTAND TASK RELATIONSHIPS

In Hour 1, "Understanding Project Management," we noted that, by definition, a project is a series of connected activities. In Hour 6, "Creating a Work Breakdown Structure," we created a work breakdown structure that defined the activities. Now we'll take a look at those connections and see how they affect our project schedules.

All we've done so far is to break down the projects into a series of tasks. If the project were to be scheduled now, the tasks would be scheduled to run simultaneously. But many of the tasks are really dependent on one another, meaning that the start or completion of one task is somehow related to the start or completion of another task. These relationships are referred to as inter-task dependencies.

There are four types of inter-task dependencies:

- Finish-start
- Start-start
- Finish-finish
- Start-finish

The tasks that come first are called the *predecessor tasks*, and those that follow are *successor tasks*.

STRICTLY DEFINED

A **predecessor task** is a task on which another task depends. That dependent task is called the **successor task.**

Let's take a look at each of these four dependency types.

CONSIDER FINISH-START RELATIONSHIPS

The most common dependency is the finish-start (FS) relationship. In the FS relationship, the predecessor task must finish before the successor task can start. Some examples of this type of relationship are as follows:

Construction example—Cement must be mixed before it can be poured.

Small Business example—Invoices must be received before checks can be cut.

Information Systems example—Systems design must be done before coding can start.

In most cases, the successor in the finish-start related tasks could start as soon as the predecessor finishes. This is called an *As Soon As Possible* or ASAP relationship. Sometimes, however, tasks have an *As Late As Possible* or ALAP relationship.

GO TO ▶
Refer to Hour 10, "Determine the Project Schedule," to see how dependencies and ASAP and ALAP relationships can affect a schedule.

An example of ALAP might be blowing up balloons for a party. The task of blowing up the balloons must be completed before the party starts, but it can be done anytime before then. However, if we blow these balloons up two weeks before the party, they'll be deflated again before we start the celebration. So these two tasks have an ALAP relationship.

When you're defining your dependencies, you need to consider not just the dependency type, but these ASAP and ALAP relationships, too.

STRICTLY DEFINED

As Soon As Possible (ASAP) relationships mean that the start of the successor task will be scheduled as close to the finish of the predecessor task as possible. **As Late As Possible (ALAP)** relationships mean that the finish of the predecessor will be scheduled as late in the schedule as possible.

Another aspect of dependency relationships to consider is delay. Sometimes a time delay must occur between the finish of one task and the start of another. This is called lag time.

An example of two tasks with lag time between them would be ordering a book and reading the book when shipping the book takes two weeks. The lag would then be the two weeks.

Lag time can be expressed in time units or in percentages of the duration of the predecessor task. Most often, lag is expressed in time units.

TIME SAVER

Many clients and managers don't understand the concept of lag time, especially as it displays on schedules. Although it lengthens your WBS, you may want to consider creating tasks to represent the lag. It saves on the questions later. So, in the example of ordering the book, you could add a task called "waiting for shipment" between the ordering and reading tasks.

The converse of lag time is lead-time. Lead-time allows tasks to overlap.

Say, for instance, that although there's a finish-start relationship between designing a computer system and coding a computer system, the design for the complete system need not be done in order to start coding some of the components already designed. You could say that coding could start when design is 70 percent complete—that 70 percent is the lead-time.

Lead-time can be expressed either in time units or in percentages of the duration of the predecessor task, but it's usually expressed in percentages. That way, if something elongates the predecessor task, the lead-time will also elongate.

PROCEED WITH CAUTION

The major project management software packages do not use the term "lead-time." To allow a 70 percent lead-time on a finish-start relationship in these packages, you would have to code a negative 30 percent lag time.

Consider Start-Start Relationships

The start-start (SS) relationship is a less common dependency relationship. In the SS relationship, the predecessor task must start before the successor task can start. This relationship is often erroneously interpreted as meaning that both tasks start at the same time. While it sometimes happens that these tasks start at the same time, that's not always the case.

Some examples of this type of relationship are ...

Construction example—The pouring of cement must have started before the cement curing can start.

Small Business example—The printing of checks must have started before the signing of checks can start.

Information Systems example—The setting up of interviews must have started before the interviews can start.

Start-start relationships can also have delay. Another way to model the relationship between designing a computer system and coding a computer system might be with a start-start. You could still say that coding could start when design was 70 percent complete.

PROCEED WITH CAUTION

Be careful when setting any dependencies other than traditional finish-start that you're modeling how the real project will work. Misunderstanding your task-dependency relationships can have a serious impact on the schedule.

Consider the Finish-Finish Relationship

The finish-finish (FF) relationship is also a less common dependency relationship. In the FF relationship, the predecessor task must finish before the successor task can finish. This relationship is often erroneously interpreted as meaning that both tasks finish at the same time, but, as noted in the start-start section, this is not always the case.

Some examples of this type of relationship are ...

Construction example—The painting cannot finish until priming has finished.

Small Business example—The printing of checks must have finished before the signing of checks can finish.

Information Systems example—Testing cannot finish until programming has finished.

Delay can also be used with finish-finish relationships. With our example of the relationship between designing a computer system and coding a computer system, the coding of the complete computer system cannot be completed until design for the complete system is completed. Without delay, this relationship would schedule the tasks to be done nearly simultaneously, but this is not realistic. A certain amount of work on coding still needs to happen after design is done. You could say that coding couldn't finish until three weeks after design was complete.

CONSIDER THE START-FINISH RELATIONSHIP

A very uncommon relationship is the start-finish relationship. This means that the predecessor task must start before the successor task can finish. Although it's possible to use the start-finish relationship without delay, this relationship really makes sense only when used with delay. With a start-finish relationship, you tie the start of the predecessor task to the finish of the successor task.

Say that a task must finish 10 days after its predecessor task starts. You could use one of the other relationships to try to figure out how to create the correct time lag, but it's much simpler to use the start-finish relationship with a 10-day lag.

JUST A MINUTE

Some project management software packages do not enable you to use the start-finish dependency relationship. This is such an uncommon relationship, however, that this is not a major deficiency in the tool.

CONSIDER EXTERNAL PROJECT RELATIONSHIPS

There will be times when project tasks depend not only on internal tasks, but on external tasks as well. Say that your project is to install a new software package; however, before doing that, your organization needs to install a new computer system. This is not part of your project, but you can't proceed with some of the tasks in your project until the other project is finished. So, the install task of your project would be the successor in a finish-start relationship with the install hardware task.

DETERMINE INTER-TASK RELATIONSHIPS

One of the keys to running on-time projects is in the modeling of the task interdependencies. Now that we've reviewed the types of dependency relationships, we're ready to look at the dependency relationships in our projects.

PROCEED WITH CAUTION

 Don't code resource conflict as dependencies. Project management software packages handle resource conflict in a different way. If you physically code dependencies, you will most likely forget to remove them if the resource conflict goes away.

DETERMINE RELATIONSHIPS IN EXAMPLES

One of the WBSs we created for the purchasing system was as follows:

1 *Installed Purchasing System*

   1.1 Survey potential systems

   1.2 Create short list of systems to investigate further

   1.3 Perform investigation

   1.4 Develop investigation report

   1.5 Select system

2 *Trained end users*

   2.1 Develop training

   2.2 Hold classes

Let's look at the dependency relationships in this project. Task 1.1 would be the first task in this project, so it would have no dependencies. Task 1.2 would have a finish-start dependency on task 1.1. Task 1.3 would have a finish-start dependency on task 1.2. Task 1.4 would have a finish-start dependency on task 1.3. Task 1.5 would have a finish-start dependency on task 1.4.

Next, however, we see a problem. We can't start developing training on the system until we've installed the system, so we see that several tasks under the Installed Purchasing System deliverable are missing. You may often notice missing tasks when you consider the relationships. We need to add four more tasks, as shown:

1.6 Purchase system

1.7 Install system

1.8 Test system

1.9 Turn over to production

Now the remaining dependencies are as follows:

Task 1.6 would have a finish-start dependency on task 1.5. Task 1.7 would have a finish-start dependency on task 1.6. Tasks 2.1 and 1.8 would have a finish-start dependency on task 1.7. Task 2.2 would have a finish-start dependency on task 2.1. Task 1.9 would have a finish-start dependency on tasks 1.8 and 2.2.

In the paragraph format, these relationships are hard to see, so you may find it more useful to use one of the two table formats shown here.

Relationship Table for the New Purchasing System

Task	Depends On
1 *Installed Purchasing System*	
1.1 Survey potential systems	—
1.2 Create short list	1.1
1.3 Perform investigation	1.2
1.4 Develop investigation report	1.3
1.5 Select system	1.4
1.6 Purchase system	1.5
1.7 Install system	1.6
1.8 Test system	1.7
1.9 Turn over to production	1.8, 2.2
2 *Trained end users*	
2.1 Develop training	1.7
2.2 Hold classes	2.1

TIME SAVER

 Because finish-start dependencies are the most common, when creating your dependency tables there's no need to note finish-start relationships unless there is lead or lag.

Relationship Table for the New Purchasing System

Predecessor	Successor
1 *Installed Purchasing System*	
1.1 Survey potential systems	1.2
1.2 Create short list	1.3
1.3 Perform investigation	1.4
1.4 Develop investigation report	1.5
1.5 Select system	1.6
1.6 Purchase system	1.7
1.7 Install system	1.8, 2.1
1.8 Test system	1.9
1.9 Turn over to production	—
2 *Trained end users*	
2.1 Develop training	2.2
2.2 Hold classes	1.9

DETERMINE RELATIONSHIPS IN AWARDS PROJECT

Now that we've looked at some sample dependency relationships, let's look at those in the Awards Banquet Project. Take a few minutes to review the WBS and consider the relationships.

JUST A MINUTE

Although you can time-phase some PERT charts and CPM diagrams to get a better visual image of the schedule, the visual format most widely used for the schedule is the Gantt chart, discussed in Hour 11, "Creating a Gantt Chart."

The way this WBS is defined, the first task is to create the team. The rest of the tasks have traditional finish-start relationships with one another until we get to the banquet tasks. The first banquet task depends on the selection of the winners, and most of the following banquet tasks also have traditional finish-start relationships with one another.

We do have three tasks—choosing photographer, entertainment, and speakers—that depend on the selection of the hall but on nothing else. And the last task, holding the banquet, depends on several earlier tasks, but still in a traditional finish-start relationship.

The dependency table looks like the following:

Awards Banquet Project

Task	Depends On
1 *Winners*	
1.1 Create Team	—
1.2 Create Selection Process	1.1
1.3 Develop Nomination Forms	1.2
1.4 Gather Nominations	1.3
1.5 Evaluate Nominations	1.4
1.6 Select Winners	1.5
1.7 Announce Winners	1.6
1.8 Create Plaques	1.6
2 *Banquet*	
2.1 Determine Potential Dates	1.6
2.2 Determine Potential Halls	2.1
2.3 Review Hall Menus	2.2
2.4 Create Short List of Halls	2.3
2.5 Dine at Each Potential Hall	2.4
2.6 Select Hall	2.5
2.7 Announce Banquet	1.7, 2.6
2.8 Send Invitations	2.6
2.9 Gather RSVPs	2.8
2.10 Finalize Dining Arrangements	2.9
2.11 Choose Entertainment	2.2
2.12 Choose Speakers	2.2
2.13 Choose Photographer	2.2
2.14 Hold Dinner	1.8, 2.7, 2.10–2.13

FYI A classic text on these systems is *Network-Based Management Systems (PERT/CPM)* by Russell D. Archibald and Richard L. Villoria, published by Wiley in 1966.

DETERMINE RELATIONSHIPS IN RESTORATION PROJECT

Review the information on the restoration project presented so far, and create a dependency-relationship table for each task in the restoration WBS.

CREATE A PERT CHART

Once you've determined the dependency relationships in a project, you're ready to create a network diagram that will then be used to create a project schedule. In this section, we'll talk about the PERT chart network diagram.

UNDERSTAND PERT CHARTS

Program Evaluation and Review Technique (PERT) charts were developed in the 1950s by the United States Navy as a way to more accurately schedule the development of the Polaris submarine. As noted in Hour 8, "Developing Project Estimates," this scheduling technique also used the WAVE estimating technique, but in this hour, we'll look at the type of network diagrams created with this technique.

Traditional PERT charts always started with a node called the start node. From the start node, arrows were drawn representing any tasks that had no dependencies. At the end of the arrows, additional nodes were drawn. Then, from these nodes, the dependent tasks were drawn until all tasks were connected. The last task(s) was/were then connected to a finish node. This type of graphical arrangement is called "activity on arrow" because the activities take place on the arrows connecting the nodes.

A major drawback to PERT charts is that when tasks depend on the completion of more than one other task, the additional relationships have to be shown with what's called a "dummy activity." Dummy activities are differentiated from real activities by a dashed arrow rather than a solid one (see the following figure).

A sample PERT chart.

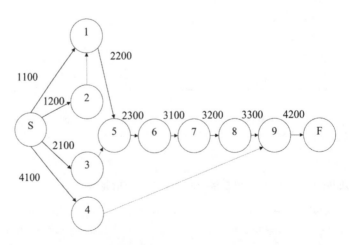

CREATE PERT CHART IN EXAMPLES

Let's look at how to create a PERT chart from the dependencies in the new purchasing system project. The first thing we do is to draw a start node. From that start node, we draw lines representing the independent tasks in the project. In this project, though, we have only one independent task, task 1.1, so we draw only one line and create another node, which we label node one. From node one, we draw arrows representing all the tasks that depend on task 1.1. Because there's only one of these, we draw only one line and then draw node two. We continue drawing arrows and nodes until we've drawn each task, with the last task going to the finish node.

PROCEED WITH CAUTION

Although many of today's project management software packages enable you to do so, it is generally best *not* to assign dependency relationships at the summary level. Rarely does one task depend on every task in a summary level; scheduling to meet those relationships can artificially extend the project completion date.

But what happens with task 1.9? It depends on both 1.8 and 2.2. We need to draw a dummy activity from node 10 to node 9 to represent this relationship.

The following figure shows the resulting PERT chart.

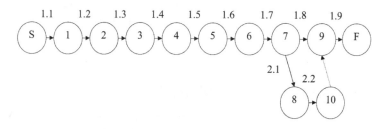

The PERT chart for the new purchasing system.

CREATE AWARDS PROJECT PERT CHART

Based on the dependencies given earlier in this hour, create the PERT chart for the awards banquet project. Take about 10 minutes to think about how you would organize this chart and then sketch it out. The PERT chart in the following figure shows an answer.

Note that in this project, many of the tasks are sequential. The only real parallel tasks are the choosing of the entertainment, speakers, and photographer (2.11, 2.12, and 2.13).

The PERT chart for the awards banquet.

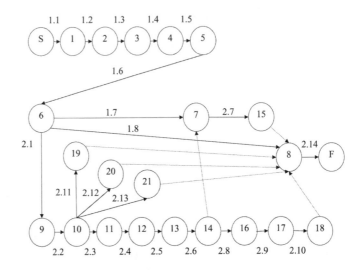

CREATE RESTORATION PROJECT PERT CHART

Based on the dependency relationships we looked at in the restoration project, create the PERT chart for the restoration project. An answer is shown in Appendix A, "Sample Documents."

TIME SAVER

Use a project management software package to create your network diagram. It frees you from redrawing the network if you created it incorrectly or if it changes as the project develops.

CREATE A CRITICAL PATH METHOD DIAGRAM

Another networking technique is the Critical Path Method (CPM) diagram. This section discusses the background of the CPM diagram, its advantages over a PERT chart, and how to create this from your dependency tables.

UNDERSTAND CPM DIAGRAMS

The CPM diagram was created in the 1950s at DuPont to schedule renovations to its chemical plants. The major difference between PERT charts and CPM diagrams is the graphic representation of tasks. Where the PERT chart uses activity on arrow and round nodes, CPM uses activity on node and rectangular nodes.

This means that each node is a task, which eliminates the problem with dummy tasks. To show the relationships on the CPM diagram, you simply draw arrows from predecessor to successor.

This method of representation also enables us to model dependency relationships other than finish-start, which the PERT chart does not.

CREATE A CPM DIAGRAM IN EXAMPLES

Now that we've discussed the concept of a CPM diagram, let's see how to create one. We'll use the purchasing system project to be able to compare the PERT and CPM diagrams.

We start the CPM diagram by drawing a rectangular node for each independent task, which in this case is only task 1.1. Then we draw an arrow to its successor task, 1.2, and on through the project (see the following figure).

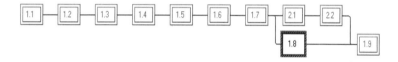

A CPM *diagram for the new purchasing system project.*

CREATE AWARDS PROJECT CPM DIAGRAM

Based on the dependency relationships we looked at in the awards banquet project, let's look at the CPM diagram. As with the purchasing project, we start by drawing rectangles for the independent tasks. In the awards project, 1.1 is the only independent task. We then connect the remaining tasks as we did earlier.

The answer is shown in the following figure.

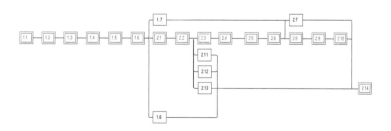

The CPM diagram for the Awards Banquet project.

CREATE RESTORATION PROJECT CPM DIAGRAM

Based on the dependency relationships you determined earlier, draw the CPM diagram for the restoration project. An answer is shown in Appendix A.

JUST A MINUTE

Despite the fact that most of the major project management software packages call the network diagrams they draw "PERT charts," the diagrams are actually CPM diagrams.

HOUR 10

Determining the Project Schedule

For most people interested in your project, the bottom line is when can we get this done. But before you can create a realistic schedule, you should consider some additional pieces of data. After you have created the Work Breakdown Structure (WBS), estimated your tasks, and determined the task interrelationships, you are ready to create a project schedule. In this hour you'll learn how to use your estimates and CPM diagram to calculate a project schedule.

UNDERSTAND THE PROJECT SCHEDULE

Because being "on time" in a project is one of the project success factors, creating an accurate schedule is critical to this success measurement. Still, as we noted in Hour 8, "Developing Project Estimates," on estimating, estimates are predictions, and because the schedule is based on these predictions, it, too, is not infallible. You may need to remind your clients and sponsor of this after you have created a project schedule.

CHAPTER SUMMARY

LESSON PLAN:

In this hour you will learn about …

- Calculating task duration.
- Applying the project calendar.
- Performing a forward pass.
- Performing a backward pass.
- Determining the critical path.

JUST A MINUTE

Although the mathematical examples in this hour show you how to schedule from the project start date, you can use similar math to schedule from the finish date.

This hour discusses the CPM scheduling process in detail. The good news is that the project management packages will do the heavy mathematics in this hour for you. The bad news is you still need to go through this hour or you won't understand how your package creates the schedule, which is vital to understanding how to make appropriate schedule changes.

REVIEW RESOURCE ASSIGNMENTS

Before creating the project schedule you'll need to review your resource assignments. You need to make sure that you have resources assigned to each task, then look at how many resources are assigned to each task, and verify the skill levels of those resources.

REVIEW ESTIMATES

After you have reviewed the resource assignments, review the estimates for each task. If the skill level of the assigned resource has changed, or the work-interruption factors or part-time effect of any of the assignments have changed, update the estimates.

REVIEW CPM DIAGRAM

Once you have verified your estimates and made any necessary adjustments to the estimates, review the dependency relationships as noted in your CPM diagram. What you'll especially need to note during this review are the tasks that need to be scheduled As Late As Possible (ALAP).

CALCULATE TASK DURATION

After you have reviewed the resource assignments, estimates, and CPM diagram, you're ready to calculate the task durations. These calculations will vary depending on whether or not the task is resource or time-constrained. The next two sections explain the calculations.

PROCEED WITH CAUTION

Many beginning project managers skip the majority of the work in the estimation step by creating elapsed time estimates for tasks that are really resource-constrained. While this is easier to estimate, it makes accurate scheduling and tracking nearly impossible. Take the time up front to create the appropriate type of estimates for each type of task.

DETERMINE DURATION ON RESOURCE-CONSTRAINED TASKS

The majority of the tasks in your project will be resource-constrained tasks. To calculate the duration of resource constrained tasks, you use the following formula:

D = effort ÷ hours per day ÷ number of resources

So, a resource-constrained task with an estimate of 40 hours, assigned to one person working an 8-hour day, would have a duration of 5 days. If that person worked only 4 hours per day, the duration would be 10 days. And if two people worked on the task 8 hours per day, they could complete it in 2.5 days.

In the new purchasing system project, we had the following adjusted effort estimates:

1 Installed Purchasing System	Adjusted Effort
1.1 Survey Potential Systems	16
1.2 Create Short List	4
1.3 Perform Investigation	48
1.4 Develop Investigation Report	24
1.7 Install System	8
1.8 Test System	80
1.9 Turn Over to Production	8
2.1 Develop Training	100

Tasks 1.1, 1.2, 1.3, and 1.4 are assigned to an analyst working 8 hours per day. Tasks 1.3 and 1.4 are also assigned to two additional analysts working 8 hours per day. The systems programmer installing the system and turning it over to production will only be available to the project 2 hours per day, but the two system testers and the instructional designer work 8-hour days.

In calculating the duration of tasks 1.3 and 1.4 in the purchasing system project, we used three resources. If you are not positive you will have more than one resource on each task, however, then the calculation needs to be based on only one resource.

This gives us the following durations:

1 Installed Purchasing System	Duration
1.1 Survey Potential Systems	2
1.2 Create Short List	.5
1.3 Perform Investigation	2
1.4 Develop Investigation Report	1
1.7 Install System	4
1.8 Test System	5
1.9 Turn Over to Production	4
2.1 Develop Training	12.5

DETERMINE DURATION ON TIME-CONSTRAINED TASKS

Calculating the duration on time-constrained tasks is easy. You simply use the time constraint as the duration. So, the duration of a time-constrained two-day conference is two days.

Three time-constrained tasks were in the purchasing system project, and they had the durations shown here:

1.5 Select System	2-hour meeting
1.6 Purchase System	30 days
2.2 Hold Classes	2 days

CALCULATE AWARDS BANQUET DURATIONS

Let's take another look at how this would work with the awards banquet project.

The project manager is working 5 hours per day on this project, the administrative assistant 2 hours per day, and the three volunteers as needed.

PROCEED WITH CAUTION

Remember to include your lag times in the calculations of your schedule, or you'll end up with a schedule that is not long enough. When calculating your early start dates, you'll need to add the duration of the lag to the early finish date of the predecessor task.

Task 1.1, Create Team, assigned to the project manager, had an effort estimate of 5 hours, which yields a 1-day duration. On task 1.2, Create Process for Selecting Winners, the adjusted effort was 50 hours. If the project manager and the three volunteers worked on the process 5 hours per day, which was the project manager's allocated time to the project, the duration would be 2.5 days.

The remaining tasks would have the following durations:

Task	Effort	Duration
1.3 Develop Nomination Forms	30	1.5
1.5 Evaluate Nominations	6	.3
1.6 Select Winners	6	.3
1.7 Announce Winners	6	.3
2.1 Determine Potential Dates	2	.1
2.2 Determine Potential Halls	20	1
2.3 Review Hall Menus	13	.7
2.4 Create Short List of Halls	13	.7
2.6 Select Hall	2	.1
2.7 Announce Banquet	6	.3
2.11 Choose Entertainment	10	.5
2.12 Choose Speakers	13	.7
2.13 Choose Photographer	5	.25

The durations on the time-constrained tasks are as follows:

Task	Effort	Duration
1.4 Gather Nominations	2.5	3 weeks
1.8 Create Plaques	1	2 weeks
2.5 Dine at Each Potential Hall	6	3 days
2.8 Send Invitations	2	2 weeks
2.9 Gather RSVPs	4	3 weeks
2.10 Finalize Dining Arrangements	1	1 week prior to
2.14 Hold Dinner	0	.5 days

Calculate Restoration Project Durations

Based on the exercise answers given to date, calculate the restoration project durations. An answer is given in Appendix A, "Sample Documents."

Determine Schedule from Date

Before calculating the schedule, we need to consider our schedule from date. We can schedule from the project start date, or we can schedule from the proposed deadline.

JUST A MINUTE

After you've done these examples manually, try them in your project management software package.

The most common method of scheduling is to schedule from the start. The advantage to scheduling in this direction is that you may find that the schedule created actually shows that the project can be completed prior to its proposed deadline. Unfortunately, though, what usually happens is that the scheduled completion date is past the deadline. Then it is time to renegotiate the project scope, resources, and the like.

Scheduling from the proposed deadline has the advantage of telling you when the project should start. The disadvantage is that the scheduled start date may be well before the current date. Obviously you can't go back in time to start the project, so as noted earlier, it is time to renegotiate.

Apply Schedule Adjustments

Now that we have calculated durations for each of our tasks, we need to consider and apply project adjustments. Some of the considerations include project nonwork days, project time constraints, assigning effort to time-constrained tasks, and resource overallocation. Each of these is discussed in more detail in the following sections.

Consider Project Nonwork Days

The next aspects to consider in the schedule are project nonwork days. There are three types of nonwork days:

- Corporate
- Project
- Resource

In most organizations, weekends are nonwork days. Government holidays, planned facility shutdowns, and other corporate-wide events would also be corporate nonwork days.

At the project level there may be other nonwork days. Team training sessions and trips to various sites are examples of project nonwork days.

TIME SAVER

Project level nonwork days can also be scheduled at the individual level, but it is less work if your software package enables you to schedule them at the project level.

Scheduled individual nonwork days include vacations, training days, leaves of absence, and other scheduled time away from work. These need to be considered for each resource in the project so that the work they are assigned to can be rescheduled around these individual nonwork days.

EVALUATE PROJECT DATE CONSTRAINTS

There may be date constraints on our project that will affect the schedule. The most common are that tasks must be started or completed on a specific date. These are normally stated as follows:

- Must Finish On
- Finish No Earlier Than
- Finish No Later Than
- Must Start On
- Start No Earlier Than
- Start No Later Than

JUST A MINUTE

Project-level nonwork days can also be scheduled as tasks in the WBS. For instance, a team training class can be listed as a task and then each team resource can be assigned to that task. If you want everyone to be able to visually see why no additional project work can be done during that time frame, this is the better approach.

As their names imply, the two "Must" constraints mean that the tasks must be scheduled on those dates. Whenever possible, try not to use these two constraints. They generally yield less-than-optimal schedules. However, if these date constraints are a true model of reality, you need to use them to model the schedule correctly.

The No Earlier Than and No Later Than date constraints are preferable because they give us more scheduling options, which generally give us a faster schedule.

CONSIDER PROJECT MILESTONES

Other date-related considerations in a project schedule are *milestones*. Milestones occur at a specific point in time and are tied to significant project accomplishments. Milestones generally have "Must" time constraints as described previously. An example of a dated milestone would be the expected arrival date of a materials shipment, the completion date of a major project deliverable, and the like.

STRICTLY DEFINED

A **milestone** is a specific point in time tied to a significant project accomplishment.

Milestones may also be "floating." This means that they are still tied to an event, but that event does not have a specific schedule date. Examples of this type of milestone are go/no-go decisions on the project. They have to occur between phases, but not on any required date.

Because milestones are just a point in time, they do not have any duration that changes the schedule. But if they have "Must" dates and successors, those Must dates may affect the successor's schedule.

CONSIDER EFFORT ON TIME-CONSTRAINED TASKS

We noted in Hour 8 that even though a task is time-constrained, it still has effort associated with it. Effort can be allocated to the task in three main ways. The first is at the beginning of the task, the second is at the end of the task, and the third is evenly throughout the task.

For example, in the new purchasing system project, task 1.5, Select System, is a two-hour meeting, and the effort would also be two hours per attendee, scheduled evenly. The effort on the two-day task 2.2, Hold Classes, would be 16 hours per participant, scheduled evenly. The effort of two hours on the

30-day task 1.6, Purchase System, however, should be scheduled in the beginning because this task was deigned to represent ordering the software and waiting for it to be shipped. The only effort involved on the team's part is in placing the order.

CONSIDER RESOURCE OVERALLOCATION

From looking at the resources assigned to the tasks as arranged in the CPM diagram, we can see whether or not any resources will be overallocated to tasks. Simply put, this means that the resource would be scheduled to work more than his or her normal hours per day on any given day. While we may end up needing to ask resources to work some overtime, we don't want to start the schedule that way.

You can eliminate this overallocation in two ways. The first way is to assign a different resource to the task. Because our resources are limited, though, this is generally not possible. This leaves us with the other choice of moving one or more of the tasks to eliminate the resource conflict. Although we can move the tasks either forward or back, we usually need to move the tasks forward, extending the schedule.

This moving of tasks is automatically done for us in our project management software packages. The term they use for this is called *resource leveling*.

STRICTLY DEFINED

Resource leveling is the adjusting of task schedules to eliminate resource overallocation.

PERFORM FORWARD PASS

After you have calculated durations, considered nonwork days, date constraints and milestones, and reviewed resource assignments, you are ready to develop a schedule. Creating a schedule in the traditional CPM method involves performing two sets of calculations. The first set of calculations is called the forward pass.

UNDERSTAND EARLY START AND EARLY FINISH

Early start is the earliest that a task can start based on dependencies, task priorities, and constraints. By definition, the early start of the first task in the network is day 1. In finish-start relationships, the early start of subsequent tasks is the early finish of the predecessor task plus one. (The assumption is that the task is finishing at the end of the early finish date, so the earliest the next task can start is the following day.) On tasks with lead-time, it is the early start of the predecessor task plus the lead-time.

Early finish is the earliest a task can finish if everything goes according to plan. Early finish equals early start plus the task duration minus one.

STRICTLY DEFINED

Early start is the earliest a task can start based on dependencies and other project constraints. **Early finish** is the earliest a task can finish.

DO THE MATH

You base these calculations on a standard formula plus the other adjustments noted previously. In the software project, the schedule from date is April 8, 2002, the project start date. There are no project nonwork days but there are corporate holidays of May 27, July 4, September 2, October 14, November 25, and December 24 through January 1, 2003. There are no must dates or milestones at this time, and there is no resource overallocation because of the dependencies.

PROCEED WITH CAUTION

Remember that the schedule created in this hour may still be adjusted, either by constraints or by changes in client requirements.

Let's see how we calculate these numbers. To simplify the math, we will be using only whole days for durations, so task 1.2, which had a duration of .5, will become one day, and task 2.1, which had a duration of 12.5, will have a duration of 13.

The first task in this project is task 1.1. By definition, then, the early start of task 1.1 is April 8, 2002. Early finish is early start plus the duration of two, which brings us to April 10, 2002, minus one to return to April 9, 2002.

Now, why we subtract the one day is often confusing, but think about it this way: We start at the beginning of the workday on April 8, and work all day for our first day of the two-day duration. We also work all day on April 9, and complete the task at the end of April 9. But adding two to April 8 gives us the 10, so we need to subtract one to return to the correct day.

To calculate the early start of 1.2, we add one to the early finish of 1.1. Again, we add the one because the earliest the second task can start is the beginning of April 10. The table that follows lists the early start (ES) and early finish (EF) dates for the entire project.

Note that task 1.3 ends on April 12, but task 1.4 isn't scheduled to start until April 15, 2002. This is because April 13 and 14 are weekend days, so the earliest workday after the 12 becomes the 15.

Task	Duration	ES	EF
1 *Installed Purchasing System*	60	4/8/02	6/28/02
1.1 Survey Potential Systems	2	4/8/02	4/9/02
1.2 Create Short List	1	4/10/02	4/10/02
1.3 Perform Investigation	2	4/11/02	4/12/02
1.4 Develop Investigation Report	1	4/15/02	4/15/02
1.5 Select System	1	4/16/02	4/16/02
1.6 Purchase System	30	4/17/02	5/28/02
1.7 Install System	4	5/29/02	6/3/02
1.8 Test System	5	6/4/02	6/10/02
1.9 Turn Over to Production	4	6/25/02	6/28/02
2 *Trained End Users*	15	6/4/02	6/24/02
2.1 Develop Training	13	6/4/02	6/20/02
2.2 Hold Classes	2	6/21/02	6/24/02

From this forward pass, we get a total project duration of 60 workdays and an elapsed time duration of 77 days.

PERFORM AWARDS PROJECT FORWARD PASS

Let's do the calculations again on the awards banquet project. The schedule from date is the project start date, also April 8, 2002. The corporate holidays are, as noted, May 27, July 4, September 2, October 14, November 25, and December 24 through January 1, 2002. There are no must dates or milestones at this time, but remember the five-day lag time between finalizing the dinner and holding the dinner. There is resource overallocation on tasks 2.11, 2.12, and 2.13, but the three can still be done in three days.

The forward pass of the schedule is given in the following table:

Task	Duration	ES	EF
1 *Winners*	33	4/8/02	5/22/02
1.1 Create Team	1	4/8/02	4/8/02
1.2 Create Selection Process	3	4/9/02	4/11/02
1.3 Develop Nomination Forms	2	4/12/02	4/15/02
1.4 Gather Nominations	15	4/16/02	5/6/02
1.5 Evaluate Nominations	1	5/7/02	5/7/02
1.6 Select Winners	1	5/8/02	5/8/02
1.7 Announce Winners	1	5/9/02	5/9/02
1.8 Create Plaques	10	5/9/02	5/22/02
2 *Banquet*	37	5/9/02	7/1/02
2.1 Determine Potential Dates	1	5/9/02	5/9/02
2.2 Determine Potential Halls	1	5/10/02	5/10/02
2.3 Review Hall Menus	1	5/13/02	5/13/02
2.4 Create Short List of Halls	1	5/14/02	5/14/02
2.5 Dine at Each Potential Hall	1	5/15/02	5/15/02
2.6 Select Hall	1	5/16/02	5/16/02
2.7 Announce Banquet	1	5/17/02	5/17/02
2.8 Send Invitations	9	5/17/02	5/30/02
2.9 Gather RSVPs	15	5/31/02	6/20/02
2.10 Finalize Dining Arrangements	1	6/21/02	6/21/02
2.11 Choose Entertainment	2	5/13/02	5/14/02
2.12 Choose Speakers	2	5/13/02	5/14/02
2.13 Choose Photographer	1	5/13/02	5/13/02
2.14 Hold Dinner	1	7/1/02	7/1/02

This gives us a total project duration of 70 days and an elapsed duration of 84 days.

PERFORM RESTORATION PROJECT FORWARD PASS

Using the same Leetle Toy Company corporate holidays, calculate the forward pass for the restoration project. An answer appears in Appendix A.

Although this lesson uses the traditional method of only whole numbers for the durations in the mathematical calculations (hence the rounding of durations, and the adding and subtracting of one day), most of the major project management software packages now calculate the schedule to the minute if necessary.

Perform Backward Pass

The forward pass gives us the total duration of the project and its scheduled completion date. To find out if any tasks in the project have any extra room to be late, we need to perform a backward pass.

Understand Late Start and Late Finish

Late start is the latest that a task can start without delaying subsequent tasks. You calculate it by subtracting the task's duration from its late finish and then adding one.

Late finish is the latest that a task will finish if everything goes according to plan. By definition, the late finish of the last task in the network equals the early finish of the last task. In finish-start relationships, the late finish of subsequent tasks is the late start of the successor task minus one. On tasks with lead-time, it is the late finish of the successor task minus the lead-time.

STRICTLY DEFINED

Late start is the latest a task can start without delaying the project. **Late finish** is the latest a task can finish without delaying the project.

Understand Float/Slack

Once you have calculated the late dates, you can see if any of your tasks have extra room that would allow the tasks to slip their schedule without hurting the project. This room to slip is called *float* or *slack*. It is calculated as the number of workdays between the early finish and the late finish on each task.

STRICTLY DEFINED

Float is the amount of time that a task can slip without delaying the project. Another term for float is **slack.**

There are actually two types of float:

- Free float is the amount a task can slip without delaying the next task.
- Total float is the amount a task can slip without delaying the whole project.

In simple projects, free float and total float are generally equal, but in projects with several parallel paths, the two can have significant differences. The float that is shown in this lesson is total float.

Do the Math

To start the backward pass on the new purchasing software project, we say that the late finish of task 1.9 is June 28, 2002.

From there on, the backward pass data looks like the following table, with the late start (LS), late finish (LF), and float for the entire project:

Task	Duration	LS	LF	Float
1 *Installed Purchasing System*	60	4/8/02	6/28/02	—
1.1 Survey Potential Systems	2	4/8/02	4/9/02	0
1.2 Create Short List	1	4/10/02	4/10/02	0
1.3 Perform Investigation	2	4/11/02	4/12/02	0
1.4 Develop Investigation Report	1	4/15/02	4/15/02	0
1.5 Select System	1	4/16/02	4/16/02	0
1.6 Purchase System	30	4/17/02	5/28/02	0
1.7 Install System	4	5/29/02	6/3/02	0
1.8 Test System	5	6/18/02	6/24/02	10
1.9 Turn Over to Production	4	6/25/02	6/28/02	0
2 *Trained End Users*	15	6/4/02	6/24/02	—
2.1 Develop Training	13	6/4/02	6/20/02	0
2.2 Hold Classes	2	6/21/02	6/24/02	0

Note that only one task has any float. The early finish on task 1.8 is June 10, 2002 and the late finish is June 24, 2002. This gives us a difference of 14 days, but only 10 of those are workdays, so the float is 10 days. This means that task 1.8 is the only task that can slip without delaying the entire project, and it could slip up to 10 days without hurting the schedule. If it slips more than 10, however, the entire project will slip.

PERFORM AWARDS PROJECT BACKWARD PASS

Let's apply this same technique to the awards banquet project. Late finish equals early finish, or July 1, 2002. The rest of the math looks like this:

Task	Duration	LS	LF	Float
1 *Winners*	33	4/8/02	6/28/02	26
1.1 Create Team	1	4/8/02	4/8/02	0
1.2 Create Selection Process	3	4/9/02	4/11/02	0
1.3 Develop Nomination Forms	2	4/12/02	4/15/02	0
1.4 Gather Nominations	15	4/16/02	5/6/02	0
1.5 Evaluate Nominations	1	5/7/02	5/7/02	0
1.6 Select Winners	1	5/8/02	5/8/02	0
1.7 Announce Winners	1	6/27/02	6/27/02	34
1.8 Create Plaques	10	6/17/02	6/28/02	26
2 *Banquet*	37	5/9/02	7/1/02	0
2.1 Determine Potential Dates	1	5/9/02	5/9/02	0
2.2 Determine Potential Halls	1	5/10/02	5/10/02	0
2.3 Review Hall Menus	1	5/13/02	5/13/02	0
2.4 Create Short List of Halls	1	5/14/02	5/14/02	0
2.5 Dine at Each Potential Hall	1	5/15/02	5/15/02	0
2.6 Select Hall	1	5/16/02	5/16/02	0
2.7 Announce Banquet	1	6/28/02	6/28/02	29
2.8 Send Invitations	9	5/17/02	5/30/02	0
2.9 Gather RSVPs	15	5/31/02	6/20/02	0
2.10 Finalize Arrangements	1	6/21/02	6/21/02	0
2.11 Choose Entertainment	2	6/27/02	6/28/02	32
2.12 Choose Speakers	2	6/27/02	6/28/02	32
2.13 Choose Photographer	1	6/28/02	6/28/02	33
2.14 Hold Dinner	1	7/1/02	7/1/02	0

PERFORM RESTORATION PROJECT BACKWARD PASS

Based on the information provided so far, calculate the backward pass numbers on the restoration project. An answer appears in Appendix A.

DETERMINE THE CRITICAL PATH

The *critical path* of any project is the longest path through the network. Any task on the critical path that misses its original schedule will lengthen the entire project schedule.

STRICTLY DEFINED

The **critical path** is the longest path through the network. By definition, all tasks on the critical path have no float, which means that any increase in the duration on any critical tasks will increase the schedules.

LOCATE THE CRITICAL PATH

In some projects, it is easy enough to identify the critical path simply by looking at the network diagram, but in complicated projects, the critical path contains all the tasks with no float. It is not uncommon for projects to have critical paths that branch into two or three parallel paths at some point in the project.

HIGHLIGHT THE CRITICAL PATH

Once the critical path has been identified, it is normally highlighted in some way. The two most common ways are to shade the critical tasks red or to change the node pattern on critical tasks. In the latter case, this might mean that noncritical tasks have traditional rectangular nodes but that the critical path nodes may be rounded rectangles.

PROCEED WITH CAUTION

 The critical path does not identify the most important tasks in a project; it simply identifies the longest sequence of tasks.

HOUR 11

Creating a Gantt Chart

CHAPTER SUMMARY

LESSON PLAN:

In this hour you will learn about ...

- Reviewing the network diagram.
- Reviewing resource assignments.
- Reviewing the project calendar.
- Reviewing the project schedule.
- Drawing a Gantt chart.

Another very convenient tool for displaying the project schedule is the Gantt chart. Henry Gantt invented the Gantt chart in the late 1800s. Since that time it has been one of the most popular visual tools for both planning and tracking projects. The following sections of this hour provide some background on Gantt charts and explain how to create and use them.

UNDERSTAND A GANTT CHART

In the late 1800s, a Bethlehem Steel employee developed a charting technique as part of his system for improving the efficiency of the plant. Henry Gantt called this process the "Task and Bonus System," and in it he set the foundation for most of today's project management techniques. The most famous, of course, is the chart that still bears his name.

Gantt invented his charting technique to track the estimated duration of tasks versus the actual duration. His intention was to provide process status "at a glance," making it easier for everyone involved to see progress or lack thereof. He did this by designing a horizontal bar chart that listed task names down the left-hand column, and then displayed the corresponding task durations as bars drawn across the appropriate time-scale columns. He used one set of bars for the planned task duration and another set below the planned to represent the actual.

FYI For an enlightening view of Gantt's Task and Bonus System and his charts, track down a copy of one of his original articles published in *Engineering Magazine* and other engineering journals of the time. A favorite is "The Task and Bonus System," *Engineering Magazine,* April 1911.

Where the two sets of bars were equal, Gantt knew that tasks went according to schedule. Any differences showed tasks that had not gone as planned. This is still the power of Gantt charts. They are easy to create, even manually, and virtually anyone can read them.

In this hour we'll look at the steps involved in creating and maintaining a Gantt chart. We'll also look at how this tool helps us to take "reality checks" of our schedule and resource assignments.

PREPARE TO CREATE A GANTT CHART

Before you can draw a Gantt chart of your project, you need to review several pieces of the project plan. The following steps discuss what to review and why:

1. **Review Network Diagram.** Because the Gantt chart shows the proposed schedule graphically, you need to make sure that the dependency relationships noted in the network diagram are still valid.

2. **Review Resource Assignments.** After you've reviewed the network diagram, review the resource assignments, skill levels, and durations to make sure that these are still as accurate as possible.

3. **Review Project Calendar.** Unlike network diagrams, Gantt charts are time scaled with the task bars spanning from the start of the task through the end of the task. Any project nonwork days can be shaded in the chart to help people see where the nonwork periods are in each task.

4. **Review Project Schedule.** You can use the project schedule in two ways when creating a Gantt chart. One is to use the dates calculated in the schedule as the basis for drawing the Gantt bars. Perhaps a better way, however, especially if you manually calculated the schedule, is to use the Gantt charting process to verify your math in the schedule.

JUST A MINUTE

Creating a WBS based on deliverables or roles may yield a Gantt chart that does not waterfall in scheduled dates. While this is fine, some managers prefer to see the tasks cascade. To avoid this, you can create the WBS by phase and then list tasks sequentially within phase.

DRAW GANTT CHART

After you've reviewed the resources, network diagram, and schedule, you're nearly ready to draw the Gantt chart. Just two decisions are left to make. What time scale will you use on the chart, and what *symbology* will you use on the bars?

STRICTLY DEFINED

Symbology is the term used for the graphic symbols expressing the durations of tasks in the project schedule.

Let's look at the choices for these decisions.

DETERMINE TIME SCALE

The time scale on the Gantt chart is critical to the ease of reading the chart, and so it needs to be related to the duration of the project as well as to the average durations of the tasks. Short duration projects, or projects with average task durations of less than five days, are easier to read if the time scale is daily. Medium duration projects, or projects with average durations of less than a month, are easier to read with a weekly time scale. Long projects, or those whose tasks average more than a month, are easier to read with a monthly time scale. Time scales can also be in seconds and minutes, or hourly, quarterly, or annually, but these are much less common.

When you are creating manual Gantt charts, time scales of two days, three days, two months, and so on, are also feasible if the project and task durations would be easier to read in this scale. Unfortunately, most of the project management software packages do not allow this flexibility.

Another possibility with manual charts is an interrupted time scale. Say, for instance, that you have a three-month project with the majority of tasks less than three days in duration. A daily scale would be the easiest to read, but would yield an extended time scale. If only one or two of the tasks are long and the rest are short, you can break the time scale during the long duration tasks if no other work is happening simultaneously.

JUST A MINUTE

Unlike his colleague and mentor Fredrick Taylor, generally considered the father of process improvement research, Gantt believed that workers should be paid bonuses if they finished earlier than their schedule, and regular wages if they finished on or after schedule. He also believed that it was the estimator and supervisor who were at fault if workers did not meet their schedules.

Determine Task Symbology

Once you have decided on the time scale, you need to decide on the bar symbology you'll use. This can vary from simple character representations of the task to very complex symbols and patterns. When you are creating your Gantt chart manually, there is no limit on the symbology, but most project management software packages only allow a limited range of symbologies. Let's look at the more common choices.

The simplest to create is a basic character chart with alphanumeric characters representing the task durations. It would look like this:

	April			May
Task	8–12	15–19	22–26	29–3
1 *Installed Purchasing System*	XXXXXXXXXXXXXXXXXXXXXXXX			
1.1 Survey Potential Systems	XX			
1.2 Create Short List	X			
1.3 Perform Investigation	XX			
1.4 Develop Investigation Report		X		
1.5 Select System		X		
1.6 Purchase System			XXXXXXXXXXXXXX	

When tracking a project, the actual dates would be placed as shown here, where the A's are the actuals:

	April			May
Task	8–12	15–19	22–26	29–3
1 *Installed Purchasing System*	XXXXXXXXXXXXXXXXXXXXXXXXX			
	AAAAAAAAAAA			
1.1 Survey Potential Systems	XX			
	AA			
1.2 Create Short List	X			
	AA			
1.3 Perform Investigation	XX			
		AAAA		
1.4 Develop Investigation Report		X		
		A		

Task	April 8–12	15–19	22–26	May 29–3
1.5 Select system		X		
		AAA		
1.6 Purchase system			XXXXXXXXXXXXXX	
				AAAAAAAAAAAAA

Notice how easy it is to see, even in this simple representation, that the tasks 1.2, 1.3, and 1.5 all ran past schedule.

TIME SAVER

If you don't have a project management software package but don't like the look of the character graphics shown in this hour, you can use a spreadsheet package to create your Gantt chart.

Another common symbology is straight lines with vertical bars at the start and end dates. This can be done with character graphics as shown previously, but is generally done manually in a grid format. The figure that follows shows an example of this type of symbology.

With the major project management software packages, the most common symbology is shaded bars. When both plan and actual are being displayed, there are generally two bars as shown in the character graphics example earlier. If space is a concern, however, an open bar can be used to represent the scheduled task, and a narrower shaded bar can be used in the center to represent the actuals.

Task	April				May				June
ID	8	15	22	29	6	13	20	27	3
1.	├───────────────────────────								
1.1	H								
1.2	H								
1.3	H								
1.4	H								
1.5	H								
1.6	├─────────────								

Sample line symbology as displayed on standard graph paper.

DRAW PURCHASING SYSTEM GANTT

To start the purchasing chart, we first need to consider the time scale. This project runs for about three months, which would make a daily time scale too long. Monthly, however, would be too large a scale, especially considering the fact that many of the tasks in this project have durations of less than a week. This leaves a weekly time scale as the most practical. Because this project starts on April 8, 2002, we'll start the time scale on this date.

In terms of symbology, we have several choices. Because shaded bars are the most common, that's what we'll use. When we start adding actuals as the project progresses, we'll shade the inside of the bar with a different color (see the following figure).

Purchasing Gantt chart with weekly time scale.

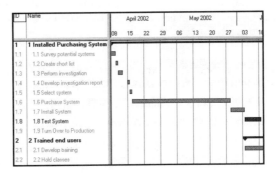

SHOW DISCONTINUOUS TASKS

Most of the tasks we work on are continuous tasks. That is, once we start working on them, we continue working on them until they are complete. When the tasks are displayed on a Gantt chart, they are shown as a continuous bar.

Some tasks, though, such as status meetings, are not continuous, and you may like to note this on the Gantt chart. To do so, you list the task just once, and only draw the bars on the days of the meetings.

JUST A MINUTE

Traditionally, Gantt charts did not show the dependency relationships between tasks. The major project management software packages now enable you to show the relationships if you want, generally with a different line pattern for each of the types of relationships.

SHOW THE CRITICAL PATH

While the concept of a critical path had not been thought of yet when Gantt developed the Gantt chart, today most project managers display the critical path on the Gantt chart by shading the critical tasks in a pattern or color different than the noncritical tasks.

This adds another piece of valuable data to the visual schedule without making it so detailed as to be unreadable.

SHOW TASK FLOAT

Another schedule aspect that can be displayed on the Gantt chart is task float. Float is usually displayed as another bar, of a different pattern, extending from the end of the task through the appropriate number of float days. The float bar is often a solid or dashed line with a vertical bar at the end, like those in the Gantt chart drawn on graph paper shown earlier.

PROCEED WITH CAUTION

 If you like to see ongoing tasks such as status meetings displayed only on their scheduled dates, you will want to verify that any project management software you purchase can handle this requirement.

CHARTING PROJECT MILESTONES

If you have milestones in your project, they can be displayed on the Gantt chart, too. Like float, they should have a symbology different than the tasks, and easily identifiable as milestones. Most often, they are designated by a diamond. The diamond can be solid or shaded so that you can use one pattern for plan and another for actual.

HIGHLIGHT IMPORTANT PROJECT DATES

Other dates commonly highlighted on the Gantt chart include any project nonwork dates, the project start date, finish date, and current date. The nonwork days are usually shaded columns, whereas a simple vertical line generally marks the start, finish, and current dates.

The simple Gantt chart that follows shows examples of discontinuous tasks, critical path tasks, and noncritical path tasks with float, a milestone, and a today line indicating that today is April 22, 2002.

Task	April 8–12	15–19	22–26	May 29–3
1 Sample Character Display	XXXXXXXXXXXX		|XXXXXXXXXX	
	AAAAAAAAAA		|	
1.1 Discontinuous Task	XX	XX	|XX	XX
	AA	AA	|	
1.2 Critical Path Task		CCCCCCCCCC |		
		AAAAAAAAA |		
1.3 Noncritical with Float		XX------|	|	
		AAAA	|	
1.4 Go/No Go Milestone			◊ |	
			♦ |	
				Today

In the "Evaluate the Schedule" section later in this hour I explain how to use task float to evaluate the reality of your project model.

DRAW AWARDS BANQUET GANTT

As we noted last hour, the awards banquet project is scheduled to start on April 8, 2002, and to finish on July 1, 2002. This is a relatively short-duration project, and so a weekly time scale would be appropriate. Task 1.1 starts on April 8 and has a duration of one day, so the bar will span one fifth of the weekly time column.

Plotting each subsequent task based on its dependencies, durations, and resources yields the Gantt chart in the following figure.

Awards Gantt chart with weekly time scale.

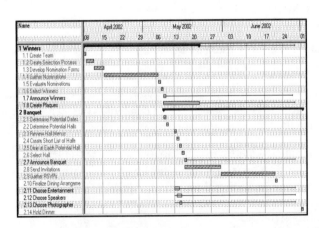

DRAW RESTORATION PROJECT GANTT

Using the network diagram created in the last hour, draw the Gantt chart for the restoration project. An answer is given in Appendix A, "Sample Documents."

SHOW INDIVIDUAL RESOURCE SCHEDULES

A distinct advantage of Gantt charts is that they can also be used to show an individual's or a department's schedule. This way, only a selected portion of the schedule needs to be displayed at once.

The figures that follow show the individual schedules for two of the separate resources in the purchasing system project.

ID	Name	April 2002
		Mon 08	Tue 09	Wed 10	Thu 11	Fri 12	Sat 13	Sun 14	Mon 15	Tue 16
1	1 Installed Purchasing System									
1.1	1.1 Survey potential systems									
1.2	1.2 Create short list									
1.3	1.3 Perform investigation									
1.4	1.4 Develop investigation report									
Analyst1		8.00	8.00	4.00	8.00	8.00	0.00	0.00	8.00	0.00

Resource Gantt chart with daily time scale for Analyst 1 on the purchasing system project.

ID	Name	May 2002	June 2002
		Mon 27	Wed 29	Fri 31	Sun 02	Tue 04	Thu 06	Sat 08	Mon 10	Wed 12	Fri 14	Sun 16	Tue 18	Thu 20	Sat 22	Mon 24	Wed 26	Fri 28
1	1 Installed Purchasing System																	
1.7	1.7 Install System																	
1.9	1.9 Turn Over to Production																	

Resource Gantt chart with daily time scale for Programmer on the purchasing system project.

JUST A MINUTE

While it is tempting to use individual Gantt charts for each of the resources assigned to your projects, resources are generally more effective if the employees can see the total work of the project and see where their work fits in.

EVALUATE THE SCHEDULE

Now that you have an easy-to-read visual image of your schedule, it's time to do a reality check. Let's look at the Gantt charts of the purchasing software and awards banquet projects and see if the schedules accurately model what we believe will be reality.

Let's start with the purchasing software project. While we could tell from the CPM diagram that task 1.8 was the only task with float, what wasn't as obvious was how much longer the instructional design of the training was going to take compared with the testing. If you'll recall, we assigned two testers to the testing task, but only one instructional designer to the training task. To shorten the training task, we could assign another instructional designer. Alternatively, we could remove one of the testers from the testing task. Doing so would still give us five days of float on the testing task.

A revised version of the Gantt chart is shown in the following figure.

Gantt chart for the purchasing system project showing the revised duration of the testing task with only one tester.

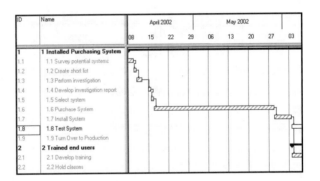

Now let's evaluate how realistic the awards banquet schedule is. Let's start with task 1.7, Announce winners. Notice the float time on this task extends until we hold the banquet. This implies that we really wouldn't have to announce the winners until the banquet, but that we could announce them as soon as we'd selected them. Is this realistic? If we are going to announce the winners before the banquet, we would want that to happen well before the banquet. If we wanted the award winners to be a surprise to all but the winners themselves and the project team, then we wouldn't announce them at all until the banquet.

TIME SAVER

Analyzing how closely your schedule models reality takes some time, but it will save you time in execution if you can locate as many inaccuracies as possible now.

It appears that something is wrong with the way we coded the dependency relationships on this task. If we are not going to announce the winners until the banquet, we should change this dependency to be Finish-Finish and As Late As Possible. That will move the task to occur during the banquet. Better still would be to delete the task because if it is part of the banquet, it is redundant.

If, however, we intended to announce the winners before the banquet, we need to schedule the writing and publishing of the announcement to occur at an appropriate time prior to the announcing of details of the banquet.

When we examine task 2.7, Announce the banquet, we see that this task also has significant float. This, too, is not feasible. We would need to announce the banquet well before the scheduled date and probably before we start sending invitations. If we add a Start-Start dependency relationship between announcing the banquet and sending the invitations, the tasks can start at the same time, but it's assured that the announcement is scheduled well before the banquet itself.

A revised Gantt chart is shown in the following figure.

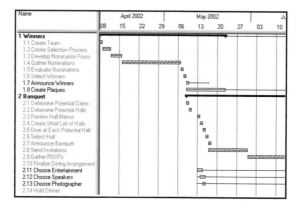

Revised Gantt chart for the awards project.

Four other tasks in the awards banquet project have significant float:

1.8 Create plaques	36 days
2.11 Choose entertainment	34 days

2.12 Choose speakers	34 days
2.13 Choose photographer	34 days

While it would be better for your nerves if these four tasks were done on the early finish dates rather than the late finish dates, they truly could float until the day of the banquet, so they are realistic.

PROCEED WITH CAUTION

When you use color to differentiate between various pieces of a Gantt chart, remember that many people are colorblind and will not be able to tell the difference in the color codes. If you don't know the entire target audience, it would be better to use distinctive patterns than to use the same pattern in different colors.

Understand Resource Histograms

Earlier in this hour we discussed creating individual Gantt charts for each resource or resource group. A closely related concept to this is the resource histogram. In Hour 7, "Creating Your Project Team," I briefly discussed the resource histogram as an available resource-planning tool. In this section we'll look at how to create these charts from your Gantt charts.

Review Resource Overallocation

If you adjusted the project schedule based on resource overallocation, the resource histograms you create from the Gantt charts of that schedule will show the resource assignments as you leveled them. If you did not adjust the schedule based on overallocation, the resource histograms will clearly show this overallocation and enable you to make adjustments now.

Draw Resource Histogram

You start the resource histograms by creating another graph with the same time scale as your Gantt chart. Rather than have tasks listed on the Y-axis, however, you will have a scale of work hours. You draw the resource histograms by taking the Gantt chart and aligning the time scales, and then charting each resource's assignments in a stacked-bar format.

TIME SAVER

Use the resource histograms in your project management software package to analyze your resource allocations. It is faster than reviewing tabular data because you can see both overallocation and under-utilization at a glance.

Let's look at an example in a simple character Gantt chart.

Task	Resource	April 8–12	15–19	22–26	May 29–3
1 Resource Examples		XXXXXXXXXXXXXXXXXXXXXXXXXX			
1.1 Task 1	One	XXXXX			
1.2 Task 2	One	XXXXXXXXXX			
1.3 Task 3	Two		XXXXXXXX		
1.4 Task 4	One		XXXXXXX		
1.5 Task 5	Two		XXXXXXXX		
1.6 Task 6	Two			XXXXXXXX	
1.7 Task 7	One			XXXXXX	
1.8 Task 8	Two			XXXX	

We start out by copying down Resource One's first task as shown here:

```
Resource One           24
                       16
                        8      11111


                     Hours    April                 May
                              8–12   15–19   22–26   29–3
```

Next we copy down Resource One's next task. Three days of this task overlap the first task, so those days are stacked on top of the first. Then there are two weekend days, which are nonwork days and are not plotted, and then the remaining five days of the second task are plotted. This gives us the histogram as shown here:

```
Resource One           24
                       16       222
                        8      11111  22222


                     Hours    April                 May
                              8–12   15–19   22–26   29–3
```

JUST A MINUTE

When resource overallocation is leveled, it may be possible to use float and to not extend the schedule. Usually, however, this is not possible.

Then we add the remaining two tasks, yielding the histogram shown here:

Resource One	24			
	16	222	4	7
	8	11111	22222	44444	777

Hours	April			May
	8–12	15–19	22–26	29–3

Notice that as this sample project is currently scheduled, Resource One would need to work five days of double hours. To eliminate this overallocation, you would need to reschedule the tasks or get an additional resource to take over portions of the tasks that overlap.

We would chart Resource Two's assignments in the same way, yielding the histogram that follows:

Resource Two				
	24			6 8
	16		55	55666	8
	8		33333	33555	66

Hours	April			May
	8–12	15–19	22–26	29–3

Note that this resource is scheduled to work 16-hour days on six days and 24-hour days on two. Clearly, he or she cannot do this, so either the tasks need to be rescheduled or more resources need to help with the work.

A related chart that we discussed earlier is the staffing chart. This histogram shows how all resources are allocated to the project. The major advantage of this type of chart is to help you decide how many people you would need to meet a specific deadline.

TIME SAVER

To see if more resources would help the schedule, simply change the resource assignment to selected tasks rather than divide the work on each task.

Let's look at creating a staffing histogram for the sample project.

You start this chart as you did the individual resource charts: by creating a blank time scale matching that of the Gantt chart. Next you create the hourly scale. For more than one resource, the scale may need to go to 72 hours, or even higher, so leave yourself room to do that.

Resource Staffing

Hours	April			May
40			8	
32		5	6 7	
24		54	55666	8
16	222	33333	44555	77
8	11111	22222	33444	667
	8–12	15–19	22–26	29–3

This chart shows that to get the project done in the time allocated, you would need at least five resources on April 26 and four resources on three other days. If the dependency relationships between the tasks would allow it, you might be able to use a third resource and extend the schedule just a bit.

Experimenting with this reassignment and using these additional graphical charts will help you plan and monitor your projects more efficiently.

Facing Project Risk

Chapter Summary

LESSON PLAN:

In this hour you will learn about ...

- Evaluating risks of the project.
- Evaluating risks to the project, again.
- Developing project contingencies.

Planning for project risk is one of the most important considerations in executing a successful project. In addition, project risk is considered at least twice in the planning process. In the following sections of this hour, you'll learn about two categories of risk to consider when developing your project plan.

Understand Two Categories of Risks

A risk is any potential event that might delay a project, increase its cost, or otherwise harm the project. In today's project management processes, we use the term risk to describe two different categories of concerns about successful completion of the project. These two categories are introduced next and are explained in greater detail in their own sections of this hour.

Risks *of* a Project

The first category of project risk to consider is the risk of completing the project successfully based on your organization's experience with this type of project, the project's size, and other factors. This category of risk is generally considered as part of the feasibility discussion during project initiation and is frequently termed *portfolio risk*.

RISKS *TO* A PROJECT

Risks to the project are the specific events that might occur that could hinder or halt successful completion of the project. These specific events are listed and evaluated, and if the risk of an event is serious enough, we then develop contingency plans for these risks. These risks are usually planned for as part of the project planning processes.

EVALUATE PORTFOLIO RISK

The first risk considerations in any project are the risks *of* the project.

- What may happen to the organization if the project is completed?
- What may happen if it is not?
- What are the odds of successfully completing the project?

You can evaluate this risk in several ways. They range from simple four-quadrant risk matrices to 12-page risk spreadsheets, but they all attempt to evaluate how likely it is that if a project is initiated, it will be successfully completed.

To do this analysis, you need to look at the various risk factors and how they would affect any specific project. The rest of this section discusses these factors and how to use them to evaluate project risk.

DETERMINE RISK FACTORS

When you first start thinking about evaluating your portfolio risk, you need to decide which factors will mean risk to your organization. While the aspects to consider are consistent across organizations, each organization will react to the aspect differently.

For instance, a common risk factor is the number of geographic locations involved in the project. Say that your project will affect five different sites. If your company has little experience working in multiple sites, this will be of high risk to you, whereas in organizations that regularly deal with projects affecting 10 sites, five is a small risk.

These risk factors are often grouped into three categories, including project size factors, stability factors, and experience factors. Let's look at each of these categories and the factors in them, starting with size factors.

Project size can be measured in three main ways: cost, duration, and number of resources. Project costs can range from thousands of dollars to billions of dollars. Larger dollar-value projects tend to be riskier because they represent a higher proportion of investment than other projects. A small change in a small project may cost $1,000, but a small change in a $100 million project may cost millions.

Longer durations make projects inherently riskier because of the concept of horizon planning we discussed in Hour 1, "Understanding Project Management." Creating reliable estimates of cost and time is difficult for longer projects, as is managing the dynamics of the project over a longer time.

More resources make a project riskier because of the increase in communication channels. The potential for misunderstanding of the work increases exponentially. More resources also tend to increase the variety of skill levels of the resources, yielding an increase in potential quality problems.

While these are the primary factors, there are other size considerations, too, such as the number of departments involved, the number of geographic sites affected, the number of stakeholders, and the number of interfaces with other projects. Higher numbers on any of these factors make a project riskier.

Stability factors are those relating to the expected or potential amount of change to the project scope and requirements. Stability factors include a clear definition of project requirements, a clearly identified sponsor, a dedicated sponsor, an influential sponsor, a clearly identified client, and strong client support for the project. Other factors are the project's priority relative to other corporate projects, the amount of changes required by the project, and the stability of the underlying technology.

If any of the first stability factors are not in place, the odds of project success decrease. Lower priority projects, projects that require large changes in corporate policies/procedures, and projects using unstable or untested technology all have more risk.

The last category is experience factors. These include the team members' experience with the type of project, their experience with whatever technology will be used, their experience with each other, their experience with the customer, their experience with potential vendors, and their experience with outside contractors. Lower experience levels make a project riskier.

PROCEED WITH CAUTION

Although we are looking at portfolio risk with the other risk management techniques discussed in this hour, it is usually a feasibility issue considered during project initiation.

CREATE EVALUATION MATRIX

Once you have determined which factors will be considered project risks, you are ready to arrange these factors into a risk evaluation matrix. These matrices are generally organized by listing the factors down the left column, and the various choices for the factors across the top.

DETERMINE EVALUATION WEIGHTS

These risk matrices also commonly include weights for each of the various factors. This enables you to account for organizational differences as noted previously with the example of five sites being a high risk to some and a low risk to others.

Costs may be another area in which different organizations use different weights. A million-dollar project to an organization with annual revenues of only a million would be highly risky. A million-dollar project to a billion-dollar corporation is relatively insignificant.

JUST A MINUTE

Risk management in many industries is now a structured discipline. Check and see if anyone in your organization specializes in this area and can help you evaluate your project.

The table that follows is a blank form showing one possible combination of the factors we discussed previously and some potential weights of those factors. To complete the form, simply choose one of the options and write its number in the choice column. Then multiply the choice by the weight for the factor score. Add each section, and then place the section totals under the appropriate section headers and add them to get the final total. Compare that figure to the numbers in the risk evaluation column to determine if the project has a low, medium, or high risk.

Risk Evaluation Matrix

Section One		Options						
Size Factors	1	2	3	4	Weight	Choice	Score
Project Cost	<10K	10–100K	100–1M	>1M	3		
Duration	<3 mon.	3–6 mon.	7–12 mon.	>12 mon.	2		
Resources	1	2–5	6–10	>10	3		
Departments	1	2–3	4–5	>5	2		
Geographic Sites	1	2–3	4–5	>5	2		
Stakeholders	1–9	10–99	100–999	>1,000	3		
Project Interfaces	0	1	2–4	>4	2		
Section Total							

Section Two		Options						
Stability Factors	1	2	3	4	Weight	Choice	Score
Clear Requirements	High	Med.	Low	None	4		
Identified Sponsor	High	Med.	Low	None	2		
Dedicated Sponsor	High	Med.	Low	None	2		
Influential Sponsor	High	Med.	Low	None	3		
Identified Client	High	Med.	Low	None	2		
Client Support	High	Med.	Low	None	3		
Project Priority	High	Med.	Low	None	3		
Changes Generates	None	Low	Med.	High	4		
Stable Technology	High	Med.	Low	None	3		
Section Total							

continues

Risk Evaluation Matrix   **(continued)**

Section Three Experience Factors	Options 1	2	3	4	Weight	Choice	Score
Project Type	High	Med.	Low	None	4		
Technology	High	Med.	Low	None	2		
Team Makeup	High	Med.	Low	None	2		
Customer	High	Med.	Low	None	3		
Vendors	High	Med.	Low	None	2		
Contractors	High	Med.	Low	None	3		
Section Total							
Risk Evaluation	Size		Stability	Experience		**TOTAL**	
59–117 Low							
118–176 Medium							
177–236 High							

Note that the ranges for low, medium, and high risk are based on the given weight values and will need to be adjusted if you change the weights or if you add or delete factors.

JUST A MINUTE

Some risk matrices use a zero for the value of the lowest risk option, giving you a scale starting with a zero. If this makes more sense to you, feel free to adjust the sample matrix.

EVALUATE THE PURCHASING SOFTWARE PROJECT

Let's see how we might use this table to evaluate the risk of successful completion of the purchasing software project.

Risk Evaluation Matrix

Section One Size Factors	Options 1	2	3	4	Weight	Choice	Score
Project Cost	<10K	10–100K	100–1M	>1M	3	3	9
Duration	<3 mon.	3–6 mon.	7–12 mon.	>12 mon.	2	1	2

Section One Size Factors	Options 1	2	3	4	Weight	Choice	Score
Resources	1	2–5	6–10	>10	3	2	6
Departments	1	2–3	4–5	>5	2	2	4
Geographic Sites	1	2–3	4–5	>5	2	1	2
Stakeholders	1–9	10–99	100–999	>1,000	3	3	9
Project Interfaces	0	1	2–4	>4	2	2	4
Section Total							36

Section Two Stability Factors	Options 1	2	3	4	Weight	Choice	Score
Clear Requirements	High	Med.	Low	None	4	2	8
Identified Sponsor	High	Med.	Low	None	2	2	4
Dedicated Sponsor	High	Med.	Low	None	2	2	4
Influential Sponsor	High	Med.	Low	None	3	2	6
Identified Client	High	Med.	Low	None	2	1	2
Client Support	High	Med.	Low	None	3	2	6
Project Priority	High	Med.	Low	None	3	2	6
Changes Generates	None	Low	Med.	High	4	2	8
Stable Technology	High	Med.	Low	None	3	1	3
Section Total							47

Section Three Experience Factors	Options 1	2	3	4	Weight	Choice	Score
Project Type	High	Med.	Low	None	4	1	4
Technology	High	Med.	Low	None	2	1	2
Team Makeup	High	Med.	Low	None	2	1	2
Customer	High	Med.	Low	None	3	2	6
Vendors	High	Med.	Low	None	2	3	6
Contractors	High	Med.	Low	None	3	1	3
Section Total							33

Risk Evaluation	**Size**	**Stability**	**Experience**	**TOTAL**
59–117 Low	36	47	33	116
118–176 Medium				
177–236 High				

You may want to consider other factors, such as size, stability, and experience, in your organization. Just add them in the appropriate sections.

The total of 116 falls into the low-risk range making this project a low-risk project for the organization. This is a high-end low risk, though, so it is nearly as risky as a medium.

EVALUATE THE AWARDS BANQUET PROJECT

The awards banquet project can also be evaluated with the risk matrix we've created. Let's see how this project would fare.

Risk Evaluation Matrix

Section One Size Factors	Options 1	2	3	4	Weight	Choice	Score
Project Cost	<10K	10–100K	100–1M	>1M	3	2	6
Duration	<3 mon.	3–6 mon.	7–12 mon.	>12 mon.	2	1	2
Resources	1	2–5	6–10	>10	3	2	6
Departments	1	2–3	4–5	>5	2	2	4
Geographic Sites	1	2–3	4–5	>5	2	1	2
Stakeholders	1–9	10–99	100–999	>1,000	3	3	9
Project Interfaces	0	1	2–4	>4	2	1	2
Section Total							31
Section Two Stability Factors	Options 1	2	3	4	Weight	Choice	Score
Clear Requirements	High	Med.	Low	None	4	1	4
Identified Sponsor	High	Med.	Low	None	2	1	2
Dedicated Sponsor	High	Med.	Low	None	2	1	2
Influential Sponsor	High	Med.	Low	None	3	1	3
Identified Client	High	Med.	Low	None	2	1	2
Client Support	High	Med.	Low	None	3	2	6
Project Priority	High	Med.	Low	None	3	2	6

Section Two Stability Factors	1	Options 2	3	4	Weight	Choice	Score
Changes Generated	None	Low	Med.	High	4	1	4
Stable Technology	High	Med.	Low	None	3	1	3
Section Total							32

Section Three Experience Factors	1	Options 2	3	4	Weight	Choice	Score
Project Type	High	Med.	Low	None	4	1	4
Technology	High	Med.	Low	None	2	2	4
Team Makeup	High	Med.	Low	None	2	4	8
Customer	High	Med.	Low	None	3	1	3
Vendors	High	Med.	Low	None	2	3	6
Contractors	High	Med.	Low	None	3	1	3
Section Total							28

Risk Evaluation	**Size**	**Stability**	**Experience**	**TOTAL**
59–117 Low	31	32	28	91
118–176 Medium				
177–236 High				

The total of 91 falls into the low-risk range making this project a low-risk project for the organization.

TIME SAVER

 Entering your risk matrix in a spreadsheet will simplify the mathematics.

EVALUATE THE RESTORATION PROJECT

Based on the information given to this point on the restoration project, evaluate the project portfolio risk. A completed form appears in Appendix A, "Sample Documents."

DETERMINE RISKS TO A PROJECT

While the proceeding sections of this hour discussed the aspects of portfolio risk management, the aspect of risk most commonly associated with projects is the risks *to* a project. That is, once a project has been given an acceptable portfolio risk quotient, what may go wrong in execution to still cause that project to be unsuccessful? These are the risks we'll examine in the following sections.

LIST PROJECT RISKS

To start the risk-evaluation section of project planning, you create a list of potential project risks. You can use a variety of prompts to help you generate this risk list, but perhaps the easiest is to review your other plan components. Specifically, review your project constraints, assumptions, and WBS.

When reviewing your constraints, think of this: If any of these constraints are tightened, what might happen to the project? Remember that in Hour 3, "Starting a Project Plan," we talked about the Technical, Financial, Operational, Geographic, Time, Resource, Legal, and Political constraints of a project. Changes in these areas will be risks to the project.

Four common risks, applicable to almost any project, fall under the technical, financial, resource, and political constraint categories. They are …

- The technology isn't available (or doesn't work as promised).
- The budget will be cut.
- A key team member will leave the project.
- The project sponsor will leave the organization.

Reviewing the specific constraints listed in the plan will help you to discover other risks.

In terms of project assumptions, every assumption has the risk that it is not true. This means that they should also be included in the list.

When you review the WBS, you need to look for specific things that will affect the successful completion of each task.

While creating your list, write down everything that comes to mind, even if it won't seriously affect the project. We evaluate the risks in the next sections. You don't, however, have to try to list every possibility. For small projects, three to seven risks would be sufficient. For medium projects you may want a list of 5 to 10 risks and even for large projects, probably no more than 20.

TIME SAVER

 It will speed up the process of risk evaluation if you come up with an initial list of risks, and distribute it to the team for them to add to.

EVALUATE LIKELIHOOD

Once you have created a list of potential risks, you go back and evaluate those risks on two dimensions. The first dimension is likelihood, as in, how likely is it that this event will happen.

Likelihood is usually evaluated on a scale of 1 to 5 or a scale of 1 to 10. In both scales, one means that the risk event is not likely to happen. The highest number on the scale means that it is almost certain to happen.

You evaluate the likelihood of each risk before moving on to the next step.

EVALUATE EFFECT

After evaluating the likelihood of each risk event, you go back through the list to evaluate the effect of the risk event. Simply put, you decide what might happen to the project if the event really occurs.

Effect is also on a sliding scale of 1 to 5, or of 1 to 10. On both scales, a one indicates that the risk event would have very little impact on the project. The highest number on the scale, on the other hand, means that the event might well stop the project.

The interesting thing about evaluating effect is that it can change depending on where the event occurs in the schedule. For instance, the effect of a key team member leaving at either the beginning or end of a project would not be as high as it would be if that person leaves right in the middle.

If the effect can vary greatly depending on when the event occurs, you may want to list the risk twice on the sheet and include both effect scores.

PROCEED WITH CAUTION

Each contingency in your risk plan will have an associated cost. While we don't specifically discuss contingency costs, you will need to consider them in your risk plan.

CALCULATE SERIOUSNESS

Once you have evaluated likelihood and effect, you just multiply them to calculate seriousness. When you are using a scale of 1 to 5 for each ranking, seriousness will have a value of 1 to 25 (maximum of 5×5). With a scale of 1 to 10, seriousness will have values ranging from 1 to 100 (maximum of 10×10).

The highest numbers in the seriousness column are the risk events for which you will need to develop a *contingency plan*.

STRICTLY DEFINED

A **contingency plan** is a plan to cope with uncertain events and uncertain event outcomes.

DETERMINE PURCHASING SOFTWARE PROJECT RISKS

Let's see how to apply these steps with the purchasing software project. First, we list the potential risks. From this project we had these constraints:

- The new package must run on the existing infrastructure.
- The purchasing system can never be offline, so the current system must run in parallel to the new system until the team is ready to cut over to the new system.
- The DBA may not be available when needed.

The assumptions were as follows:

- The DBA will be available when needed.
- There will be a package that will meet the project requirements.
- The existing computer infrastructure will support the new package.

JUST A MINUTE

The same risk event occurring at different times may require different contingency plans. Each should be noted in your risk plan.

We could turn these into project risk statements this way:

- The DBA will not be available when needed.
- There will not be a package to meet the project requirements.
- The computer infrastructure will not support the new package.
- The computer infrastructure will not support running both the old and new purchasing systems in parallel.

TIME SAVER

While you may think it saves time to develop contingency plans for only the highest ranked risk events, it will save more time in the long run to come up with brief contingency plans for all the risks on your list. That way if these events do happen, you'll be ready with a plan B.

Once we have the listed risks, we can evaluate their likelihood and effect and then calculate seriousness. In the case of the first risk, as this possibility is noted twice, it is probable that it will happen, perhaps a 7 on a scale of 1 to 10. Risk two is not very likely, since accounting systems are among the most numerous types of software packages. Say this is a two. Risk three is also unlikely because with a variety of packages to choose from, at least one should work on the existing infrastructure. Let's give this another two. The last risk, however, is more probable, especially since many computer systems already operate at 80 percent capacity. We'll give this a five.

Next we look at effect. If risk event one happens, it will most likely delay the project but have no other effects. We'll give this a three. Risk two, on the other hand, would have a serious impact, say an eight. Risks three and four would also have serious impacts because both would either require additional hardware or the cancellation of the project. We'll give each of these an eight as well.

We summarize all this in a table similar to that shown here:

Risk	Likelihood	Effect	Seriousness
DBA not available	7	3	21
No package to meet requirements	2	8	16
Package won't run on existing	2	8	16
Old and new can't run parallel	5	8	40

The seriousness calculations tell us that risk four is the most serious and risk one the second most. We'll see what to do with these rankings in the "Develop Contingencies" section later in this chapter.

DETERMINE AWARDS BANQUET PROJECT RISKS

Let's review the constraints, assumptions, and tasks in the awards banquet project and come up with some project risks. The constraints we listed for this project were these:

- The banquet facility must hold at least 200 employees.
- A banquet facility must be available when the selected award winners are available.

PROCEED WITH CAUTION

Remember that while we may list project cancellation as a possible contingency plan, some projects, especially those with legal ramifications, cannot be cancelled.

The assumptions were as follows:

- Employees will submit award nominations.
- At least three employee nominations will be different and for deserving employees.
- Appropriate local banquet facilities will be available.
- 200 of the 250 employees will be able to attend the banquet.

We also had four tasks with a large amount of slack time. These were the plaque task as well as the choosing photographer, entertainment, and speaker tasks. Each has a risk that it might not be completed prior to the banquet.

We would turn these into risks as listed in the table that follows. Note that the major risks to this project are related to the honorees and the awards.

Risk	Likelihood	Effect	Seriousness
No banquet hall available when all honorees available	2	8	16
No outstanding employees to honor	1	10	10
No nominations from employees	3	5	15
Plaques not ready for banquet	2	4	8
More or less than 200 employees attend	7	4	28

DETERMINE RESTORATION PROJECT RISKS

Now that you've listed and evaluated the potential risk events for the purchasing and awards projects, review the constraints, assumptions, and tasks in the restoration project. List the risks and then evaluate the likelihood, effect, and seriousness for each. An answer appears in Appendix A.

DEVELOP CONTINGENCIES

The main reason for listing and evaluating the project risks is to plan what to do if any of these events actually occur. This process is generally referred to as developing contingencies. Three primary coping strategies are employed in these contingencies. The first is to eliminate the risk, the second is to mitigate the risk, and the third is to accept the risk. Each of these coping strategies is discussed in the following sections.

ELIMINATING RISK

While more of a strategy than a contingency, plans that eliminate project risks eliminate the cause of the risk, thereby preventing the risk event from taking place. These are proactive strategies.

As noted earlier, one of the more common risks to any project is the departure of a key team member. An elimination strategy would be to offer to pay the key employees a project completion bonus, give them comp time, or provide other extras to keep them from leaving.

Eliminating risks is generally preferable to mitigating or accepting them because these strategies usually do not affect the project schedule. Most, however, do have associated costs.

PROCEED WITH CAUTION

 When developing contingency plans, you may want to create more than one. That way, if something makes the first plan invalid, you can use the second one.

MITIGATING RISK

Most contingency plans are risk mitigation techniques. That means that they are designed to minimize the effect of the risk event when it has taken place. These techniques are reactive techniques.

A common risk mitigation technique, especially in large, complex projects, is the purchasing of insurance to cover the costs if an event occurs. On internal projects, you would rarely purchase insurance, but you could use other types of insurance such as special budget reserves against cost overruns and/or time reserves against schedule overruns.

In the resource risk mentioned previously, the most frequent mitigation technique is to cross-train other team members. This reduces the reliance on the key team member if he or she does leave.

ACCEPTING RISK

The third coping technique is again more of a strategy than a contingency because in accepting the risk, we choose not to do anything. We don't employ a strategy to eliminate the risk, and if the risk event does take place, we do nothing to mitigate the effect. Accepting the risk of a resource leaving means we would not give him or her incentives to stay nor would we cross-train. This would generally lead to some project delay while another resource gets up to speed but may be the lowest cost option.

PROCEED WITH CAUTION

 As with all the project plan components discussed in this book, the risk plan should be agreed to by the team, sponsor, and major stakeholders.

DETERMINE PURCHASING SOFTWARE PROJECT CONTINGENCIES

Earlier in this hour we identified five potential risks to the purchasing system project. Let's look at the contingencies we might develop for each.

Risk	L'hood	Effect	S'ness	Contingency
DBA not available	7	3	21	Accept schedule delay
No package to meet requirements	2	8	16	Cancel project or change it to develop internally
Package won't run on existing	2	8	16	Select a different package or upgrade hardware
Old and new can't run parallel	5	8	40	Upgrade hardware

DETERMINE AWARDS BANQUET PROJECT CONTINGENCIES

Now let's evaluate the potential contingency plans for the awards banquet. They are listed in the following table.

Risk	L'hood	Effect	S'ness	Contingency
No banquet hall available when all honorees available	2	8	16	Get several alternate dates to work with

Risk	L'hood	Effect	S'ness	Contingency
No outstanding employees to honor	1	10	10	Cancel plans
No nominations from employees	3	5	15	Team prepare own potential list and nomination forms
Plaques not ready for banquet	2	4	8	Get guaranty from engraver or send plaques later
More or less than 200 employees attend	7	4	28	Find a hall that can hold 250 and negotiate fixed per-person price

JUST A MINUTE

Any cost associated with contingencies needs to be added to the project budget.

DETERMINE RESTORATION PROJECT CONTINGENCIES

Using the rankings of risks identified earlier in this hour, develop contingency plans for at least the top three. Think about what you might be able to do on all the risks. An answer appears in Appendix A.

PART III

Executing Your Project

HOUR 13

Doing the Work

CHAPTER SUMMARY

LESSON PLAN:

In this hour you will learn about ...

- Obtaining authority to proceed.
- Setting project baselines.
- Assembling the project team.
- Creating work packages.
- Holding kickoff meetings.
- Monitoring work.
- Developing the team.

In the first half of this book we covered the project initiation and planning processes. In the second half we'll cover project execution, control and closing processes, and wrap up with a discussion of the most popular project management software packages. In the following sections of this hour, you'll learn about the first steps in executing a project.

OBTAIN AUTHORITY TO PROCEED

After you have completed your project plan and your clients and sponsor (and perhaps your team, if already assembled) have read it, made appropriate changes, and agreed to it, you are ready to get the official authority to proceed. In some organizations this is a simple, informal go-ahead from your boss. In other organizations, the authority is a formal, signed document issued by the project sponsor and/or a steering committee.

Regardless of how approvals are granted, make sure you do get approval for the project before you start executing the plan. It is best if this approval is written so that it can be added to your project notebook.

REVIEW THE PROJECT PLAN

Once you have gotten the authority to proceed with your project, you should review your project plan. In many organizations, you may have been waiting a month or more for project approval and some of the components of the plan may have changed significantly since the plan was submitted. This review may be conducted with the project sponsor or with a project team if one has already been assembled, although it is most often performed just by the project manager.

Reviewing and updating the plan enables you to start the project with current information. The specific plan areas to review are listed here and discussed in subsequent sections:

- **Review Project Deliverables.** To make sure that the end deliverables are still valid, review the deliverables list. Add or modify the deliverables as necessary.

- **Review Required Resources.** If you have not had your project team preassigned, review both the number of human resources you need and their corresponding skill levels. You'll also want to review your nonhuman resource requirements to verify both the count and capabilities.

- **Review Project WBS.** To verify the work requirements, review the WBS. If any additional tasks are needed, add them to the appropriate areas. Also, if you had left the WBS at a very high level for planning purposes, you will need to further decompose the higher levels down to individually assignable tasks.

- **Review Project Estimates.** You also need to review the project estimates, both for resource-constrained and time-constrained tasks. On the resource-constrained tasks, verify the resource assignment to each task, especially in terms of the assumed skill level of the resources.

- **Review Project Schedule.** The last aspect of your plan to review is the schedule. If you had added or adjusted tasks, or added or adjusted resources, you will need to recalculate task durations and then recalculate the schedule.

While this hour strongly recommends that you review and revise your project plan before you baseline (see the next section) and start executing the plan, in some organizations no changes can be made to the plan that is approved. Be sure to verify the policies in your own organization before you set your baselines.

SET PROJECT BASELINES

After you have reviewed your project plan components and have made any necessary modifications, you're almost ready to start executing the plan. The only other thing you need to do before you start executing and tracking your project is to set your project *baseline*. That is, you need to save a copy of your project plan so that you can compare your project progress to your plan.

STRICTLY DEFINED

A **baseline** is a stored copy of your original plan used to compare to your actual plan as the project progresses.

Specifically, you'll need to save a hard copy (printout) and a soft copy (computer file) of the project plan itself and any other computer-generated documents, such as the project schedule. You should store all these materials in your project notebook.

If you are using a project management software package for scheduling and tracking, you will want to save a baseline of that project file, too. All the major software packages enable you to take a snapshot of your schedule and save that data in specially designated baseline fields. While the specific fields vary from package to package, they all include a minimum of these fields, per task:

- Baseline start date
- Baseline finish date
- Baseline duration
- Baseline effort
- Baseline cost

If you are using a spreadsheet tool or some other manual or computerized tool that does not save baselines, then you will have to copy these fields to storage fields for tracking purposes.

PROCEED WITH CAUTION

If you are using a project management software package, then once you have created your project baseline you should not rebaseline. The only exception would be if there have been radical changes to the project scope and evaluating against the original plan is no longer reasonable.

SET PURCHASING BASELINE

The purchasing system project has been approved, and you have reviewed the project plan. Since the plan was created, none of the deliverables, resources, WBS, or schedule have changed. To set the plan baseline for this project, we simply save a copy of the approved project plan, including schedule, in the project notebook.

JUST A MINUTE

If you are using a project management software package to calculate your schedule, you will also need to perform the baseline operation in the package. It is also best to save the plan file and schedule to disk and place the disk in your notebook with the hard copies.

SET AWARDS BASELINE

In reviewing the project plan for the awards banquet, the steering committee noticed the cost for a photographer. One of the members has extensive photography experience and has volunteered to do the photography. Remove the photographer as a deliverable and remove this task from the WBS. Then recalculate the costs and schedule and baseline the project plan (see the following figure).

The revised schedule for the awards banquet.

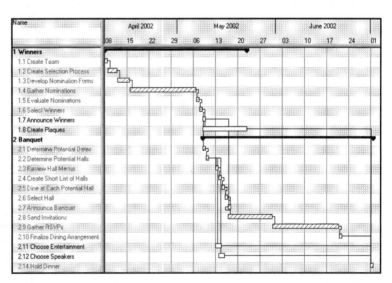

The specific data to be baselined is shown in the table that follows:

Task	Duration	Hours	Cost	Start	Finish
1 *Winners*	34	106.50	$3,708	4/8/02	5/22/02
1.1 Create Team	1	5.00	$160	4/8/02	4/8/02
1.2 Create Process	3	50.00	$1,600	4/9/02	4/11/02
1.3 Develop Forms	2	30.00	$960	4/12/02	4/15/02
1.4 Gather Nomin.	15	2.50	$80	4/16/02	5/6/02
1.5 Evaluate Nomin.	1	6.00	$192	5/7/02	5/7/02
1.6 Select Winners	1	6.00	$192	5/8/02	5/8/02
1.7 Announce	1	6.00	$192	5/9/02	5/9/02
1.8 Create Plaques	10	1.00	$332	5/9/02	5/22/02
2 *Banquet*					
2.1 Potential Dates	1	2.00	$64	5/9/02	5/9/02
2.2 Potential Halls	1	20.00	$640	5/10/02	5/10/02
2.3 Review Menus	1	13.00	$416	5/13/02	5/13/02
2.4 Short List	1	13.00	$416	5/14/02	5/14/02
2.5 Dine at Halls	1	6.00	$462	5/15/02	5/15/02
2.6 Select Hall	1	2.00	$114	5/16/02	5/16/02
2.7 Announce	1	6.00	$192	5/17/02	5/17/02
2.8 Send Invitat.	9	2.00	$484	5/17/02	5/30/02
2.9 Gather RSVPs	15	4.00	$128	5/31/02	6/20/02
2.10 Finalize Arr.	1	1.00	$32	6/21/02	6/21/02
2.11 Entertainment	2	10.00	$720	5/13/02	5/14/02
2.12 Speakers	2	13.00	$1,416	5/14/02	5/15/02
2.14 Hold Dinner	1		$6,000	7/1/02	7/1/02

JUST A MINUTE

If you created your resource costs based on generic resource billable rates, you should change the billable rates to reflect the actual rates of your resources before you baseline.

SET RESTORATION BASELINE

The project plan for the restoration project was approved by both the Leetle Toy Company steering committee and by the board of the nonprofit organization. While it was approved without change, the project start date in the schedule has passed. The new start date is two weeks later. Set the project baseline from the revised schedule calculated from the new start date. An answer appears in Appendix A, "Sample Documents."

ASSEMBLE PROJECT TEAM

Depending on how teams are assigned in your organization, you may or may not already have a project team by this point in the project. If your team is not already designated, this section explains how to assemble your team.

ACQUIRE RESOURCES

Now that your project has been approved for the execution phase, you can acquire your resources as outlined in the resource sections in your plan. If you need to negotiate with other people to gather the resources, you do that now. If you will be using contracted resources, you would write and issue your RFPs, gather the proposals, and select the contractor(s).

JUST A MINUTE

If you're not familiar with issuing RFPs or with evaluating proposals, check with your internal legal department for guidance. If you don't have a legal department, several PM areas such as Information Systems and Contracting have trade guidelines for working with RFPs and proposals.

DEVELOP A CONTACT LIST

An important addition to the communication plan after your team is assembled is the contact list. You should list core team members and other important project contacts. Specific information to note for each person includes the following:

- Full name
- Mailing address
- Phone number

- E-mail address
- Pager number

Other pieces of information that might be convenient to include on this contact list are each person's fax number, work hours, and time zone. You may also want to note their roles on the project, their titles, and the organization for which they work.

For convenience, you might also repeat the contact response times if you've specified them in the communications plan. Some lists note the days, times, and locations of the regularly scheduled status meetings, too.

TIME SAVER

 Keep the project contact list to one page and make it easy for you and your team members to use. Printing it on card stock may also help if the list will be used frequently or if the project has a long duration.

Once you have created and issued the contact list, you may need to update it as team members change offices or as new members arrive and others depart. If the list is not current, team members will call you instead of directly contacting the person they should be contacting (see the following figure).

Role	Name	Mailing Address	Phone	Fax	E-Mail Address	Pager Number	TZ
PM	Sally Manager	123 Any Street, St. Paul	555-888-1289	555-888-1610	SalMan@Leetle.com	800-754-1200	C
*Team Member	Jackie Jons	1567 Broad Street, St. Paul	555-888-1288	555-888-1610	JacJon@Leetle.com	800-754-1199	C
.....							
.....							

TZ/ Time Zone
E   Eastern
C   Central
M Mountain
P   Pacific

Response Times:
Phone   24 hours
E-mail   4 hours
Pager   1 hour

* in front of the role indicates second shift, 3 P.M. to midnight

A sample layout for a project contact list.

CREATE PURCHASING CONTACT LIST

While we won't be creating names and contact information for any of the sample projects, let's look at the key data to include in each one. In the purchasing project, the contact list should start out with the project manager, project sponsor, purchasing department manager, and each team member. As the project progresses, you may need to add the contact information for the vendors on the short list and/or contact information for other customers of the contending products. You would definitely add contact information on the selected vendor once that decision has been made.

CREATE AWARDS CONTACT LIST

For the awards project contact list we would include the project manager, sponsor, the administrative assistant, and the three employee representatives. As the project continues, you would add the banquet manager at the selected facility and may add the plaque shop, photographer, speaker, and entertainment contacts, too. Because only the administrative assistant would contact these people, however, you may not want to add them to the list for everyone.

CREATE RESTORATION CONTACT LIST

From the information in the restoration project, create a contact list for this project. You can use the sample format shown previously or you can create your own. An answer is included in Appendix A.

CREATE WORK PACKAGES

As we noted in Hour 6, "Creating a Work Breakdown Structure," work packages help you to delegate the work to your team members. Now is the time to create those packages for distribution to them.

TITLE THE WORK PACKAGES

Each work package is generally tied to one task in the WBS. The title associated with the package might be the task name itself or it may be titled by the deliverable. It doesn't really matter which titling scheme you use as long as you are consistent and the team understands what you are doing.

TIME SAVER

Titling work packages by task name is generally easier for resources when they are using project management time sheets to track their time because this is what most of the packages use for titles.

ASSEMBLE OTHER RELEVANT DATA

Other pieces to include in the work package are the scheduled start and end dates for the tasks, their duration and effort estimates, and their deliverable(s). Where applicable, you should also note how the team member and others would know when the task is complete, how the quality of the deliverable will be measured, and what standards must be followed.

As with delegating anything, however, unless standards require it, the work package should not include information on how to do the work. The team members should be allowed to decide the best approach to their own tasks. If they ask you for guidance, however, it is fine to advise them.

CREATE PURCHASING WORK PACKAGES

As with the contact list, we won't be creating a complete set of work packages for the examples, but we do want to look at some of the work packages in each project.

In the purchasing project, let's look at the first four tasks:

1.1 Survey potential systems

1.2 Create short list

1.3 Perform investigation

1.4 Develop investigation report

We start the work package by titling the work, and in these examples we'll use both the task number and task name. For the duration, estimated hours, and start and finish dates, we'll use the baseline data. The inputs and deliverables generally come from the deliverable lists in the plan, although intermediary deliverables may not have been specifically stated.

TIME SAVER

 If you are using a project management software package to schedule your project, most can also create the customized work packages for each resource. You will need to add data on inputs, deliverables, and standards per task to use this feature, however.

The work packages might look like this:

Task 1.1: Survey potential systems

Assigned to: Analyst 1

Estimated Hours: 16

Scheduled Start: 4/8/02

Scheduled Completion: 4/9/02

Estimated Duration: 2 days

Inputs: Requirements generated from earlier project and DataPro or similar listings of applicable software.

Deliverable: Comparative information on eight to ten software packages that appear to meet the initial requirements for a new purchasing system.

Task 1.2: Create short list

Assigned to: Analyst 1

Estimated Hours: 4

Scheduled Start: 4/10/02

Scheduled Completion: 4/10/02

Estimated Duration: 1 day

Inputs: Comparative information on eight to ten software packages that appear to meet the initial requirements for a new purchasing system.

Deliverable: List of three to five software packages that appear to BEST meet the initial requirements for a new purchasing system.

JUST A MINUTE

There should be minutes from every project meeting. Because you will be running each meeting, you should not be the person taking minutes. Appoint one of the attendees scribe for each meeting to take and issue the minutes.

Task 1.3: Perform investigation

Assigned to: Analyst 1, Analyst 2, and Analyst 3

Estimated Hours: 16 each

Scheduled Start: 4/11/02

Scheduled Completion: 4/12/02

Estimated Duration: 2 days each

Inputs: List of three to five software packages that appear to *best* meet the initial requirements for a new purchasing system.

Deliverables: Product details on each package that will enable comparing how each product does or does not match each requirement.

Task 1.4: Develop investigation report

Assigned to: Analyst 1, Analyst 2, and Analyst 3

Estimated Hours: 8 each

Scheduled Start: 4/15/02

Scheduled Completion: 4/15/02

Estimated Duration: 1 day each

Inputs: Product details on each package that will enable comparing how each product does or does not match each requirement.

Deliverables: Written report detailing each package's fit with the requirements.

Standards: Each section of the report should use the same format for ease of comparison.

CREATE AWARDS WORK PACKAGES

Now let's create some of the work packages for the awards banquet project. As with the purchasing project, this data is pulled from other pieces of the plan and from your knowledge of the work involved.

Task 1.2: Create Selection Process

Assigned to: PM, Employee committee

Estimated Hours: 50 (total)

Scheduled Start: 4/9/02

Scheduled Completion: 4/11/02

Estimated Duration: 3 days

Inputs: Selected team

Deliverable: Detailed written process for soliciting nominations, evaluating nominations, and selecting at least three winners from the nominated employees.

TIME SAVER

 Meeting agendas should be distributed prior to any meeting so that each attendee can be prepared for the discussions scheduled to take place. This will save time during meetings as well as save the necessity of additional meetings caused when attendees are unprepared.

Task 1.3: Develop Nomination Forms

Assigned to: PM, Employee committee

Estimated Hours: 30 (total)

Scheduled Start: 4/12/02

Scheduled Completion: 4/15/02

Estimated Duration: 2 days

Input: Detailed written process for soliciting nominations, evaluating nominations, and selecting at least three winners from the nominated employees.

Deliverable: Nomination form with blanks for appropriate evaluation data as developed in the process.

Standards: Must be easy to understand and simple to complete and preferably in both a written and word-processing template format.

CREATE RESTORATION WORK PACKAGES

Based on the work breakdown structure, resource assignments, and schedule created so far, create the work packages for the restoration project. An answer is included in Appendix A.

JUST A MINUTE

You still may not know who your specific resources will be when you create your work packages. This is fine but may require some updates to the packages after the specific resources are assigned due to the specific resources' skill levels, other project commitments, and the like.

HOLD KICKOFF MEETINGS

It is best to start off each project with one or two project kickoff meetings. Each would have a different target audience and a different agenda, but the general purpose of each is to clarify the next steps in the execution phase. The meetings and their agendas are described in the following sections.

SCHEDULE KICKOFF MEETINGS

As soon as the project is approved, schedule the kickoff meetings. If possible, try to hold the meetings the same week in which approval is received, but due to schedule and geographic constraints, the meetings may need to take place the following week.

CREATE MEETING AGENDAS

All meetings should have an agenda. The agenda for the kickoff meetings will generally be brief. The purpose is to meet other team members, review the project plan, and firm up the project roles and responsibilities.

HOLD INTERNAL KICKOFF MEETING

The internal kickoff meeting is held with the internal, core project team. It is a brief 15- to 30-minute meeting of all the core members, so they can meet each other and gear up for the project ahead. With this core group you will need to review the communication plan, especially the times and locations of status meetings and due dates for status reports and time sheets. You will also discuss project strategies, especially if the project will involve external clients.

Prior to holding this meeting you will need to decide who are the core team members and what the agenda will be. Specific agenda items for this meeting may include the following:

- Project overview
- Team member introductions
- Role and responsibilities
- Schedule
- Communication plan
- Project strategies

Each of these topics will be covered briefly, so the team should be ready to discuss each item. In addition to sending out the agenda prior to the meeting, you may want to include a copy of the project plan.

JUST A MINUTE

If the members of your full project team are located at dispersed sites, you may need to hold a teleconference or videoconference for the full team kickoff meeting.

Hold Full Team Kickoff Meetings

After the core team has had a chance to get up to speed on the project, you'll want to hold a full team kickoff meeting. This meeting should include all the people who will be working on the project, even those in other departments or companies.

This meeting will be longer than the internal kickoff meeting but should still be less than one hour. The agenda will be virtually the same as the internal meeting but will concentrate on the plan, schedule, and responsibility aspects related to the external team members rather than to the internal members.

Hold Purchasing Kickoff Meetings

Because we can't actually hold any of the kickoff meetings for the example projects, let's look at the attendees and agendas for each.

For the purchasing system, the internal (core) team attendees would be the project manager, the three analysts, the systems programmer, the instructional designer, and the two system testers. The agenda would be the same as previously noted.

PROCEED WITH CAUTION

 Core team members may not want to attend both kickoff meetings, but it is important that they hear all the discussions firsthand. It is also important, though, to keep this meeting to under one hour so that the core team members don't tune out.

For the full team kickoff meeting, the attendees would include the core team plus the project sponsor, the purchasing manager, and perhaps one or two purchasing staff members. The agenda for this meeting would also follow the earlier example but would focus primarily on the communication interfaces between the core group and the other stakeholders and the proposed schedule.

Hold Awards Kickoff Meetings

Because of the strategies used for the awards project, its kickoff meetings would be different than others may be. The core team meeting would be proceeded by senior management meetings selecting the three employee nomination committee members, and so the core meeting would be the first task scheduled in the project WBS. There would be no external kickoff meeting for this project.

HOLD RESTORATION KICKOFF MEETINGS

Based on the data presented so far on this restoration project, determine which kickoff meetings would be required, who would be invited to each meeting, and what the meeting agendas would be. An answer appears in Appendix A.

MONITOR WORK

After you've held the appropriate kickoff meetings, you will monitor the project work as outlined in your work packages. Things to monitor include the start, end, and effort of each task; the quality of the work; the number of deliverables; and the like.

GO TO ▶
Hours 14, "Following Your Control Plans," and 15, "Tracking Your Progress," cover in detail the types of things to monitor throughout project execution.

DEVELOP TEAM

Depending on the team makeup, project duration, and existing skill sets of your team members, you may need to perform some team development activities. Two of the most common are described in the following sections.

CONDUCT TRAINING

Because projects are always generating some type of change, your project team may not have the requisite skill set to work with the changes. In these cases, you may need to provide training for these members. This training can vary from simple mentoring with a more senior person to full-blown one- to two-week sessions.

If there are external costs for the training and it is specific to the project, these costs are added to the project cost. If, however, the training is for general development, such as meeting leading, communication skills, and the like, the training should be charged to the appropriate training budget.

CONDUCT TEAM-BUILDING

To get your team to work together more effectively you might need to conduct team-building exercises. These can range from simple team games to complex team retreats for large, high-profile projects.

For any project, one fun and productive exercise is to create a project identity through developing a project logo and/or project slogan. While this may seem trite to some of your team members, having a distinctive logo and slogan can not only build the team but will help differentiate this project from any other simultaneous projects.

Another team-building strategy may be to *co-locate* the project team members. This improves project communication immensely but may also have detrimental effects as well if team members are frequently moved.

STRICTLY DEFINED

Co-location involves placing all the key team members in close physical proximity with one another.

DEVELOP PURCHASING TEAM

Let's look at some of the development activities that might be appropriate for the purchasing project. As this is a relatively short project, it's unlikely that any of the team members will need training, although the analysts may need coaching on matching requirements to product specifications. Co-locating the instructional designer with the testers may be worthwhile during the development of the training.

DEVELOP AWARDS TEAM

On the awards project, there don't appear to be any development activities required.

DEVELOP RESTORATION TEAM

Based on the data given so far for this restoration project, consider the development activities that may be necessary for successful completion of the project. An answer is provided in Appendix A.

PROCEED WITH CAUTION

While co-location can speed up task handoff and communications, be careful to maintain team members' privacy and workspace requirements. Cramming eight people into a small conference room can make situations worse rather than better.

HOUR 14

Following Your Control Plans

While most people believe that the project executing processes are where the work is done, most project managers acknowledge that controlling the project is the real work. Project control processes go hand-in-hand with project execution processes. In this hour you'll learn how to use your project control plans to keep your projects on track.

USE COMMUNICATION PLAN

The control plan that you will use most frequently is the communication plan. Let's look at some aspects of the plan to review and then discuss how to follow and perhaps update it.

REVIEW COMMUNICATION PLAN

Because one or two months may pass between when you develop your project plan and when the project is approved, you should start the control processes by reviewing all your control plans. In the communication plan, the things to review include the lines of communication, the format for each of the documents, the frequency of communication, and the content.

CHAPTER SUMMARY

LESSON PLAN:

In this hour you will learn about ...

- Using the communication plan.
- Using the change control plan.
- Using the quality management plan.
- Using the procurement plan.
- Using the risk plan.

Follow Communication Plan

GO TO ▶
Creating project status reports is covered in detail in Hour 20, "Reporting Project Performance."

The first step in following your communication plan is to create templates for the regular communications. At a minimum, you'll want a template for your status reports and time sheets. You may also want templates for the agenda for status meetings and minutes of status and working meetings. The agendas for the status meetings should include the specific tasks that will be discussed and an approximate timeframe for each discussion. These individual estimates should be totaled to give an estimated duration for the meeting, which should rarely exceed one hour. Agendas for working meetings can follow similar formats, but the content will vary depending on the specific issue addressed in each meeting.

Depending on the type of project and the interfaces with the various stakeholders, you may also want to create templates for newsletter articles, presentations, and performance reports. The newsletter template would include the page layout, typestyles, and font sizes to use for the various components, and they may also suggest word counts, graphics, and so on. The presentations template would include standard backgrounds as well as typestyles and fonts for title slides, bullet slides, and any other slides you may need in your given project. The template for the performance reports should lay out the graphics that will be used to show the cost of the project, the number of tasks complete, and the resource usage.

If you and your team created a project logo and/or slogan, place this in all your templates. This will enable you to follow standard project formats while giving each individual project its own unique look.

After you create these templates, you then use them as noted in the plan.

TIME SAVER

 You may not have to create from scratch all the templates you'll be using. Templates come standard with most popular word processing, presentation, and project management packages. Just tailor them to meet your needs.

Update Communication Plan

At the beginning of the execution phase, you'll want to update the plan by taking any of the generic resource labels in your plan and changing them to specific individuals. For instance, replace the reference to "sponsor" with the sponsor's name. For "team," you may want to substitute the first names of each team member. Any reference to "stakeholder" may need to be changed to more specific categories such as internal stakeholders, client, and the like.

From time to time throughout execution, though, you may have to make other plan updates. These may include changes to the lines of communications themselves, to the templates you've created, or to any other aspect of the plan.

Use Purchasing Communication Plan

In the purchasing system project, you would place your name as the project manager and change the generic analyst names to the real resource names. If you know who the programmer, testers, and instructional designer are, then you will also update those names.

Once that is done, create the templates for the status reports and time sheets. Since we noted in previous answers that the format for the software comparisons need to be consistent, you may also want a template for the software comparison sheets.

Using the plan, you would issue your status reports, gather your team's time sheets, and distribute other information.

JUST A MINUTE

While you as project manager have the primary responsibility for reviewing, following, and updating your project control plans, your team members and sponsor should also follow the plans and offer suggestions for changes and improvements.

Use Awards Communication Plan

For the awards project, you would also update the generic names with real names, including listing the senior manager as the photographer for the event.

The major communications for this project will be the announcements and the invitations, as well as the regular status reports and time sheets.

Use Restoration Communication Plan

Using the information provided so far, review and update the communications plan in the restoration project. Also determine which communications will require templates and what data each should include. An answer is provided in Appendix A, "Sample Documents."

Use Change Control Plan

The second most highly used plan is the change control plan. As with the communication plan, we start the execution phase by reviewing this plan, and then we follow it and perform any necessary updates to the plan.

Review Change Control Plan

In most cases, the change control plan will not change between projects or between the writing of the plan and the project's approval. Still, you should review the plan before starting the project work, just to make sure.

Follow Change Control Plan

To follow the change control plan, you will gather change requests, evaluate their impact on the five success criteria areas, and then forward the requests to the appropriate levels for approval or denial. Once a decision is made on each change, you will communicate that decision and its effect on the project via the distribution method described in either the change-control or communication plan.

Update Change Control Plan

You will rarely have to update the change control plan. The only thing that may change is the specific sponsor or other individual who needs to approve the changes.

PROCEED WITH CAUTION

 When you are sending changes up the chain of command for approval, this could take a day to several weeks depending on the response time of the sponsor or steering committee. You may need to adjust your schedule to account for this delay.

Use Awards Change Control Plan

The change control plan for the awards project developed in Hour 5, "Developing Project Control Plans," was as follows:

- Changes must be requested on form CC-1, Change Control Request Form.

- The project manager can make changes to the date of the banquet until contract with the facility is signed.
- No changes to the budget can be made without sponsor approval.

You are three weeks into the project, and you have received the following e-mail from the employee selection committee:

"We have found four employees whom we believe qualify for the awards. We would like to select all of them. What do you think?"

What would you do?

First, you'd need to decide if this is a change to the project.

Unfortunately, the change control policy we wrote doesn't give us much guidance here, so let's review the project objectives and/or deliverables. The objective related to the selection is objective one:

- Select up to three outstanding employees to honor within four months.

Because this doesn't say "at least three" it does appear that this is a change to the project.

PROCEED WITH CAUTION

Remember that you do not need to accept all project changes submitted. Changes that will cause unreasonable delay or increased cost can be rejected both by you, when in your discretion area, and by the sponsor or steering committee, too.

Next, we need to document the change on the official form noted in the policy and then evaluate the project impact. It appears that the only impact will be on the number of plaques created, which will add approximately $100 to the project. The policy also states that all changes to the budget must go through the sponsor, so this form would then be forwarded to him for his approval.

If the sponsor approves the change, you would need to update the documentation associated with this change. This would include modifying the project costs as well as the first objective (select up to four) and the deliverables (four plaques). You would then notify the rest of the project team of the change.

USE RESTORATION CHANGE CONTROL PLAN

You are three weeks into the restoration project, and you have received the following memo:

> Hidden in the crawlspace under the stage we have located 37 balusters that appear to have come from the back stair. We would like to use these for the stair restoration. Any suggestions?

First, you need to determine if this is a project change, and if so, how to evaluate it in terms of the critical success factors. You also need to decide who can approve this if it is a change. An answer is given in Appendix A.

USE QUALITY MANAGEMENT PLAN

Another control plan to follow is the quality management plan. Some suggestions for doing so appear in the following sections.

REVIEW QUALITY MANAGEMENT PLAN

The quality management plan listed the quality standards for your project, the steps you'd take to ensure that quality, and those you'd take to control that quality. Prior to starting work on the project you need to review these sections to make sure that they are still relevant to the project. You also need to make sure that you haven't missed any appropriate standards or assurance and control steps.

FOLLOW QUALITY MANAGEMENT PLAN

As you execute the project, you need to perform the quality assurance and quality control portions of your quality management plan. If you discover any processes that are not producing quality projects, you will need to change the processes. If you discover any product or service defects, you will need to correct these, either by fixing the problem or by doing the work again without error.

UPDATE QUALITY MANAGEMENT PLAN

Measuring and evaluating the quality of the products and services against the standards in the plan may uncover other standards that should also be followed. It might show unnecessary standards, too. In both cases, the quality plan should be modified to reflect the new measures.

JUST A MINUTE

If you have quality assurance and/or quality control specialists in your organization, it may be their jobs to monitor the quality of your project. Check on this.

USE AWARDS QUALITY MANAGEMENT PLAN

The Awards project is underway and some of the deliverables have been completed. Your team just finished the final draft of the nomination form and is preparing to distribute it to the entire company. According to your quality plan, what, if anything, should you do before this happens?

The quality management plan we developed in Hour 5 stated the following:

- Selection team will meet in at least three potential banquet facilities to verify quality/quantity of dinners and service.
- Dates and times will be verified with award recipients and facilities.
- All memos, articles, and invitations will be proofread by at least one person other than the writer.

While forms are not specifically listed in bullet three, the intention of that bullet was to proofread everything before it was distributed. This means that at least one person other than the project manager and the selection team—who would all be considered the writer as joint developers of the form—needs to proofread the form. This person should also test the form's ease of use, as this was a standard listed in the work package for the form.

Any errors on the form should be corrected, and any confusing portions of the form should be changed. Then the form needs to be proofed and tested again until it is error-free and easy to use.

You may want to include a proofreading quality control measure for all your projects creating written materials. It is better to catch errors before documents are distributed.

During the form review cycle, you should also update the quality plan. Bullet three should be modified to read as such:

- All documents will be proofread by at least one person other than the writer and not distributed until error-free.

You may also want to add a fourth bullet that addresses the ease-of-use standard mentioned in the work package but nowhere else in the plan. One version might be as follows:

- The nomination form will be easy to use and to understand, measured by the fact that the data is requested in a logical sequence, that the blanks on the form allow enough space for the requested data, and that the form can be completed within 10 minutes.

Use Restoration Quality Management Plan

Using the data presented so far on this project, how would you apply the quality plan to the rebuilding of the rear stair discussed in the change control exercise? An answer is provided in Appendix A.

Use Procurement Plan

The fourth control plan is the procurement plan. If your project plan included this optional component, you will need to review the plan at the beginning of the execution phase, and then follow it and perhaps update it as the project continues. Each of these actions is described in the following sections.

Review Procurement Plan

After the project has been approved, you need to review the procurement plan and make sure it is still in line with what is now known about the project. This is especially true if you are going to procure consulting services and/or expensive products. You need to make sure these are still required and that the specifications are clear.

TIME SAVER

If you will be frequently using vendors, and if your organization does not have a standard vendor contract or letter of agreement, then it will be worth your time to have one developed that you can use for other future contracts.

FOLLOW PROCUREMENT PLAN

To follow your procurement plan, you execute the work specified in it. If you will be using an RFP to solicit products or services, this is when you would write and distribute it. If you were holding a bidding briefing meeting, you would prepare materials for the meeting. If you are placing notices in the newspapers or online, you would also do this during execution of your plan.

Once your announcements for bids go out in whatever prescribed format, you would then gather the various proposals, evaluate them, compare them, and select the appropriate vendor(s). You will then contract with the selected vendor(s).

You will also follow your procurement plan, and any vendor contract when processing invoices, vendor time sheets, status reports, and the like. Some of these materials may be controlled through the communication plan as well as the procurement plan.

Any materials created or received in regard to procurement should be dated and then filed in your project notebook. This includes the following:

- The RFP or other bid announcements.
- Originals of all proposals.
- Originals or copies of all contracts.
- Contractor reports.

UPDATE PROCUREMENT PLAN

As you work through the entire project plan, you may find that portions of the procurement plan need to be updated. If so, make the changes and recirculate the updated plan.

PROCEED WITH CAUTION

Some organizations require that the original contracts be filed in their legal departments. Prior to doing so, however, make sure you have kept copies and filed them in your project notebook. This makes it easier for you to verify contract terms and also provides you with a backup in case anything happens to the originals.

USE AWARDS PROCUREMENT PLAN

The awards procurement plan stated the following:

- Selection team will identify at least three potential facilities and get menus and price lists from each.
- Selection will be made based on price as well as on quality measures noted.
- Invitations will be printed internally.
- Plaques will be purchased from the same vendor as last year's awards.
- All vendors will submit invoices after rendering of services to be paid within 30 days.

In reviewing this plan, we notice that it failed to include information on procuring speakers, entertainment, and the photographer. Prior to executing the tasks related to these contracts, we would want to add a bullet that reads as follows:

- Selection team will identify at least three potential speakers and entertainment options and then get pricing and availability from each.

The existing bullet two covers how the appropriate vendors would be selected. Note that we no longer need to include the procurement of the photographer because we have a volunteer. If you were concerned about the quality of the volunteer's work, however, it is perfectly acceptable to leave the photographer-related task in your project plan and evaluate him as dictated in the quality and procurement plans.

JUST A MINUTE

Some organizations require written contracts with all vendors, while others allow less formal letters of agreement, and still others allow a handshake agreement. Make sure that you understand the type of contracts your organization and your vendors require.

USE RESTORATION PROCUREMENT PLAN

Based on the data given in the restoration exercises so far, explain how you would use the restoration procurement plan to hire contractors and suppliers. An answer appears in Appendix A.

USE RISK MANAGEMENT PLAN

Although we did not introduce the risk management plan in the hour on project control plans, this plan really is a control plan. Like the four previous control plans, the risk management plan needs to be reviewed, followed, and updated throughout project execution.

REVIEW RISK MANAGEMENT PLAN

When you start executing each project, you should review your risk management plan. You do so to look for missing risks as well as to refamiliarize yourself with the risks and contingencies already noted. You should also periodically review this plan because risks will change throughout the life of the project.

FOLLOW RISK MANAGEMENT PLAN

Unlike the other control plans discussed in this hour, you only follow the risk management plan if the risk events listed in the plan actually occur. If they do, reevaluate the contingency you developed for that risk event and make sure it is still a viable counteraction. If so, then follow the contingency plan, and then make all the changes to the WBS, deliverables, costs, and schedule necessitated by the contingency.

PROCEED WITH CAUTION

In most cases, following a project contingency plan is considered a change to the project, and it will need to go through the project change control process.

UPDATE RISK MANAGEMENT PLAN

The risk management plan is one of the few control plans that may need regular updating. As the project progresses, certain events will no longer be risks, and other events will become more serious. You may also find new risks that hadn't been considered, and you'll need to evaluate them and develop contingencies just as you did with the original plan.

Remember that as risk events occur and you follow the contingency plans, these actions may introduce new potential risk events or increase the odds that another risk event will occur, too. When this is the case, you need to update the risk management plan to reflect these changes.

USE PURCHASING RISK MANAGEMENT PLAN

The risks identified for the purchasing system were as follows:

- DBA not available
- No package to meet requirements
- Package won't run on existing infrastructure
- Old and new can't run parallel

Not included as a risk is that the selection of an appropriate package might not be possible with the tasks and deliverables as outlined in the plan. This should be added to the risk plan, with a contingency to accept the changes in the schedule created by additional work.

USE AWARDS RISK MANAGEMENT PLAN

The risks we noted in the awards banquet project included the following:

- No banquet hall available when all honorees available
- No outstanding employees to honor
- No nominations from employees
- Plaques not ready for banquet
- More or less than 200 employees attend

GO TO ▶
Because the completion plan is followed when you are wrapping up your project, you do not follow it in the execution phase but rather in the completion phase, which is discussed in Hour 21.

We had not included the idea that there may be more than three honorees, so we would add that to the plan, with the contingency of accepting the additional awardees, which is what we did.

USE RESTORATION RISK MANAGEMENT PLAN

Review the risk management plan for the restoration project and see if there are any missing risks, or if any of the risks would be evaluated differently as the project progresses. An answer is in Appendix A.

PROCEED WITH CAUTION

Remember that as you make changes to your control plans, you should be noting these changes with revision numbers and dates to track the changes.

REVIEW AND UPDATE COMPLETION PLAN

The last control plan was optional, but if you included a completion plan in your project plan, you will need to review it, and perhaps update it. Although this is the last plan that you will use in your project, it is best to review it when you start executing the project. This way, if you find any errors or omissions, they can be corrected as soon as possible. We will discuss following the plan in Hour 21, "Finishing the Work."

HOUR 15

Tracking Your Progress

CHAPTER SUMMARY

LESSON PLAN:

In this hour you will learn about ...

- Collecting task dates.
- Monitoring milestones.
- Collecting actual effort.

One of the driving forces behind Gantt's creation of his "Task and Bonus System" and his Gantt charts was to easily track project progress. Tracking project progress is important for two reasons. First, it tells you where you are in the current project. Perhaps more important, though, it enables you to collect the metrics you need to more effectively plan your next project. In the following sections of this hour, you'll learn what type of data to track, how to collect it, and how to use it in evaluating your project progress.

COLLECT TASK DATES

If you track nothing else on your project, you should track dates. These dates are considered "actuals," that is, the dates on which tasks actually started and completed.

Ideally, actual dates are stored in separate columns in a project management package or on separate bars in a manual Gantt. This will enable you to compare the baseline dates to the actual dates and to still have a calculated schedule.

The following sections describe what to track and why.

RECORD TASK START DATES

GO TO ▶
Tracking actual costs is covered later in Hour 17, "Monitoring Costs."

If you are just going to track project progress, you'll need to track project-related dates. Even if you are not using time sheets to track effort, each resource should note the date he or she starts work on each task assigned to him or her.

You then take these dates and enter them into the project schedule. If you are using a project management software package, you will enter these dates in the actual start field. If you are manually tracking your project, either on paper or in a spreadsheet package, you'll want to create a separate column for the actual start dates.

JUST A MINUTE

While some project management packages enable you to track down to the minute, recording just the start and finish dates is sufficient for most projects.

RECORD TASK FINISH DATES

GO TO ▶
The comparison between estimated duration and actual duration of each task will be discussed in more detail in Hour 18, "Evaluating Project Status."

You should also have your resources note the completion date of each task. If you are not using time sheets, these dates are often reported on the weekly status reports.

As with the start dates, you would enter the dates you are given into actual completion date fields, either in your project management package or in your manual record.

CALCULATE DURATION

After a task has been completed, you can calculate the actual task duration. This is simply the difference between the completion date and the start date on each task. This calculation will enable you to compare your estimated duration to the actual duration of each task.

PROCEED WITH CAUTION

Many of the most popular project management software packages calculate scheduled and actual durations as elapsed time, not as workdays. Beware of this when comparing your durations. A two-day task scheduled to start on a Thursday and end on a Friday will have an actual duration of four days if it starts on Friday and finishes on Monday.

COLLECT PURCHASING TASK DATES

The analysts working on the purchasing system project have started working on the project. Analyst 1 started task 1.1 on April 10, 2002 and completed it on April 12, 2002. She started and completed task 1.2 on April 15, 2002. She started task 1.3 on April 16, but analysts 2 and 3 didn't start task 1.3 until April 17.

This gives us two completed tasks so far, with durations calculated as follows:

Task	Resource	Actual Start	Actual Finish	Actual Duration
1 *Purchasing System*		4/10/02		
1.1 Survey Potential	Analyst 1	4/10/02	4/12/02	3
1.2 Create Short List	Analyst 1	4/15/02	4/15/02	1
1.3 Perform Investigation	Analyst 1	4/16/02		
	Analyst 2	4/17/02		
	Analyst 3	4/17/02		

COLLECT AWARDS TASK DATES

The Awards project got underway on April 8, 2002, with a meeting between you, the project manager, and the senior vice presidents of the various divisions of Leetle Toy Company. In this meeting, each vice president gave you the names of three people in their areas who might be interested in serving on the committee. It took you the rest of the day and most of the following to get the team together and arrange for a meeting on April 15.

In the meantime, you started thinking about the process, and in the meetings on April 15 through April 17 you were able to agree to the process and develop the nomination form. The dates and calculated durations are as follows:

Task	Resource	Actual Start	Actual Finish	Actual Duration
1 *Winners*		4/8/02		
1.1 Create Team	PM	4/8/02	4/9/02	2
1.2 Create Process	PM	4/12/02	4/16/02	5 (3WD)

continues

continued

Task	Resource	Actual Start	Actual Finish	Actual Duration
1.2 Create Process	Team 1	4/15/02	4/16/02	2
	Team 2	4/15/02	4/16/02	2
	Team 3	4/15/02	4/16/02	2
1.3 Develop Forms	PM	4/16/02	4/17/02	2
	Team 1	4/16/02	4/17/02	2
	Team 2	4/16/02	4/17/02	2
	Team 3	4/16/02	4/17/02	2

COLLECT RESTORATION TASK DATES

The project started on May 1, 2002, and has been running for five weeks. Actual dates for each task are given in the following table.

Code	Task	Start	Finish
1	*Project Definition*	5/1/02	
1.1	Define Project Scope	5/1/02	5/9/02
1.2	Create Project Plan	5/9/02	5/13/02
2	*Analysis and Design*	5/14/02	
2.1	Structural Analysis	5/14/02	
2.1.1	Hire Struct. Engineer	5/15/02	5/15/02
2.1.2	Get Engineer's Report	5/16/02	5/29/02
2.1.3	Make Go/No Go Decision		
2.2	Architectural Designs	6/4/02	
2.2.1	Hire Architect	6/5/02	

Calculate the durations on the completed tasks. An answer appears in Appendix A, "Sample Documents."

PROCEED WITH CAUTION

Remember that the durations calculated by your project management software packages and by a spreadsheet subtracting dates will give you elapsed time durations. Some managers prefer that you report on workday durations instead, so you may need to manually subtract the nonwork days from your durations.

MONITOR MILESTONES

As you collect your actual start and end dates and durations, this will have an effect on your schedule. Tasks on the critical path that finished early may improve the schedule and those finishing late may delay the schedule. Both of these things may affect your project milestones. In this section we discuss how to recalculate the schedule based on the actuals and evaluate the changes to the project milestones.

RECALCULATE SCHEDULE

When the actual start and end dates and durations of tasks don't match the baseline schedule, a new schedule must be calculated. In actuality, you will recalculate your project schedule every week as you gather the actuals and evaluate their effect on the schedule.

If you are manually recalculating the schedule, you start the calculations with the actual start date of the first task in the project. For durations, you use the actual durations recorded and then use the estimated durations on tasks that have been started but not finished or that have not been started. Following this math on another forward pass will give you the revised schedule for your project.

If you are using a project management package to track your project, simply enter in the actual start and finish dates your team members have given you. The tool will then recalculate duration and recalculate the schedule.

PROCEED WITH CAUTION

Don't panic if you miss a milestone or two in your projects. This is virtually inevitable. Still, you should consider what happened to cause you to miss a milestone so that your chances are less that you'll miss additional ones.

RESET MILESTONES

You may find that the new schedule based on actual dates may cause your milestones to slip. If the milestones are several weeks out, it is likely that you can make up the slippage and get back on track, but this isn't always the case. There will be times when you will miss milestones, and there will also be times when some of those milestones will need to be renegotiated and reset.

MONITOR PURCHASING PROJECT MILESTONES

We had not set any specific dates as milestones in the purchasing system project, but we still need to see what the effect of the actual dates and durations will be. To do this, we need to recalculate the schedule starting with the actual dates given in the previous section.

GO TO ▶
There will be some milestones that cannot slip. Strategies for getting a project back on track are discussed in Hour 19, "Getting Projects Back on Track."

Note that Analyst 1 started her task 1.3 on April 16, but that Analysts 2 and 3 didn't start until April 17. This gives a total projected duration for the task of three days even though the separate resources can each complete their own portion of the task in two days. These discrepancies are noted in the duration column in parentheses.

Some of these dates are actuals, and some are revised schedule dates. The actuals are underlined.

The revised schedule now looks like this:

Task	Resource	Actual Start	Actual Finish	Actual Duration
1 *Purchasing System*		4/10/02	7/4/02	60
1.1 Survey Potential	Analyst 1	4/10/02	4/11/02	2
1.2 Create Short List	Analyst 1	4/15/02	4/15/02	1
1.3 Perform Investigation	Analyst 1	4/16/02	4/17/02	2 (3)
	Analyst 2	4/17/02	4/18/02	2
	Analyst 3	4/17/02	4/18/02	2
1.4 Develop Report	Analyst 1	4/18/02	4/18/02	1 (2)
	Analyst 2	4/19/02	4/19/02	1
	Analyst 3	4/19/02	4/19/02	1
1.5 Select System		4/22/02	4/22/02	1
1.6 Purchase System		4/23/02	6/3/02	29
1.7 Install System	Program.	6/4/02	6/7/02	4
1.8 Test System	Tester 1	6/10/02	6/21/02	10
1.9 Turn Over	Program.	7/1/02	7/4/02	3
2 *Trained End Users*		6/10/02	6/28/02	15
2.1 Develop Training	Instr Des.	6/10/02	6/26/02	13
2.2 Hold Classes		6/27/02	6/28/02	2

The total change to the schedule at this point is six days because this project was originally scheduled to complete on June 28 (see the following figure). We'll discuss these discrepancies in more detail in subsequent lessons.

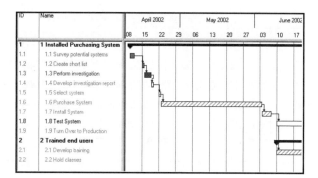

The revised schedule for the purchasing project.

MONITOR AWARDS PROJECT MILESTONES

The actuals for the awards banquet will also affect its schedule, so we need to recalculate the schedule on this project, too. We did not put any specific milestones in this project, either, but we can see how the schedule has changed in the table and figure that follow.

Task	Actual	Actual	Actual
1 *Winners*	4/8/02	5/23/02	34
1.1 Create Team	4/8/02	4/9/02	2
1.2 Create Selection Process	4/12/02	4/16/02	3
1.3 Develop Nomination Forms	4/16/02	4/17/02	2
1.4 Gather Nominations	4/18/02	5/8/02	15
1.5 Evaluate Nominations	5/8/02	5/8/02	1
1.6 Select Winners	5/9/02	5/9/02	1
1.7 Announce Winners	5/10/02	5/10/02	1
1.8 Create Plaques	5/10/02	5/23/02	10
2 *Banquet*	5/10/02	7/2/02	37
2.1 Determine Potential Dates	5/10/02	5/10/02	1
2.2 Determine Potential Halls	5/13/02	5/13/02	1
2.3 Review Hall Menus	5/14/02	5/14/02	1
2.4 Create Short List of Halls	5/15/02	5/15/02	1
2.5 Dine at Each Potential Hall	5/16/02	5/16/02	1

continues

continued

Task	Actual	Actual	Actual
2.6 Select Hall	5/17/02	5/17/02	1
2.7 Announce Banquet	5/20/02	5/20/02	1
2.8 Send Invitations	5/20/02	5/31/02	9
2.9 Gather RSVPs	6/3/02	6/21/02	15
2.10 Finalize Dining Arrangements	6/24/02	6/24/02	1
2.11 Choose Entertainment	5/14/02	5/15/02	2
2.12 Choose Speakers	5/15/02	5/16/02	2
2.14 Hold Dinner	7/2/02	7/2/02	1

The revised schedule for the awards banquet.

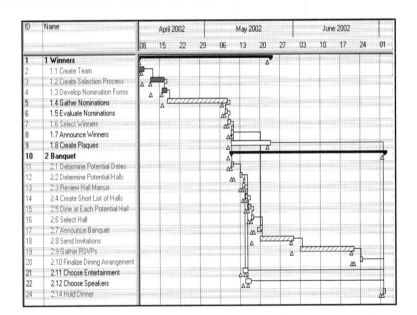

On long or complex projects, when you are updating the sponsor or the casual stakeholders, you will most likely want to report progress against milestones and not each individual task. It's usually only the project team that is concerned with progress at the task level.

MONITOR RESTORATION PROJECT MILESTONES

Now that we have actual dates for the restoration project, we need to recalculate the schedule and see what the effect is on the project milestones. An answer is provided in Appendix A.

COLLECT ACTUAL EFFORT

Although many organizations don't collect actual effort on tasks, this is really the only way that you will be able to build your own database of metrics. Without these metrics, you will not improve the accuracy of estimates, which generally means that you will not be able to improve the accuracy of any of your project schedules.

With metrics, you still cannot guarantee that estimates are accurate, but they are much more likely to be so, especially on tasks that are repeated during many similar projects. Some project managers have been able to get estimates accurate to plus or minus 10 percent of the actuals, which is, by many definitions, as close as you can ever get to on time and within budget.

Another reason to collect this effort data, especially on time and material contracts, is to accurately track the cost of a project. While the start and end dates provide enough information to recalculate schedules, variable cost is based on the actual effort spent on a task.

The following sections discuss how to gather and use this data.

PROCEED WITH CAUTION

 If your organization does not already track time in some way, convincing people that time tracking is necessary will be difficult. You may need to work together with other project managers and functional managers to convince employees and the rest of the management team that time tracking is critical to improving project execution over time.

ISSUE PROJECT TIME SHEETS

The first thing you need to do to start tracking time is to issue project time sheets. If you are using a project management package, time sheets can be generated directly from the package. If you are using an automated time accounting system, many of them can interface both with your accounting systems and with your project management systems. But even if you need to use a spreadsheet package, you should create time sheets for your projects. They can be printed and distributed, or they can be reviewed online.

It is generally better that the time sheets be tailored to each resource. That is, the time sheet should list only the tasks assigned to the individual resource. That way, each resource does not have to wade through everyone's tasks. On long projects, it is also better to list only those tasks that are to be worked on during that current time period. Again, this keeps the time sheets shorter and easier to use.

COLLECT PROJECT TIME SHEETS

You can collect time sheets manually or online. The advantage to manually written time sheets is that you can store each resource's time sheet in the project notebook with the rest of the project data. The disadvantage is that someone then has to key the data into the time accounting, spreadsheet, or project management package that you are using for scheduling and tracking. This someone is usually you or, more rarely, a project coordinator working for you.

TIME SAVER

If you are collecting data online, you don't need to print and distribute time sheets. You can have your team members view their time sheets online and also enter their time online.

There are disadvantages to using an online time sheet, too. In some organizations, even though the time sheets are online, it is still the project manager or a project coordinator who does the data entry. This still requires some way of getting the data from the resources to the person doing the data entry.

Having each resource enter his or her own time directly into an online system is the most efficient time accounting method, but many resources balk at the job, so you will have to do more work convincing them of the long term payoffs.

REVIEW TIME SHEET ACCURACY

Regardless of how you collect and enter time, you will need a way to verify the accuracy of the time. This is generally done with a two-step posting system. In the first step, preliminary data is entered into the system into some type of pending actual fields. Then, after you review the data, you issue a "posting" command that copies the pending data into the cumulative actuals fields.

Another issue of concern on time sheets is that the resources report what actually happened and not what they wanted to happen. For instance, say you have a resource assigned to five tasks with estimated hours as follows:

Task	Estimate
Task 1	15
Task 2	5

Task	Estimate
Task 3	3
Task 4	6
Task 5	2

PROCEED WITH CAUTION

If you believe that your resources are apt to make up actuals, make sure that you discuss the importance of tracking time accurately in at least one project meeting. Then make it easy for the team members to accurately track their time.

Now, presume that the resource has been diligently tracking his or her hours and has recording actuals as noted in the following table.

Task	Estimate	Actual
Task 1	15	5
Task 2	5	15
Task 3	3	6
Task 4	6	3
Task 5	2	2

What will he or she report on the weekly time sheet? Be honest.

Figuring that the total is the same anyway, if the resource believes it is more important to perform to estimates, he or she will report as shown in the following table.

Task	Estimate	Actual
Task 1	15	15
Task 2	5	5
Task 3	3	3
Task 4	6	6
Task 5	2	2

This does not help with improving estimates on the next project. It is critical that resources know that the most important part of tracking is that the actuals are accurate, and not that they match the estimates. In fact, when estimates and actuals do match, it is likely that the resource is lying about the actuals.

COLLECT PURCHASING ACTUAL EFFORT

In the purchasing project, the team members have been working on the project for a week, and we want to gather the effort. The three analysts have turned in these time sheets:

Analyst 1 Task	4/08/02	4/09/02	Date 4/10/02	4/11/02	4/12/02	Total
1 *Purchasing System*						
1.1 Survey Potential			7	5		12
1.2 Create Short List						
1.3 Perform Investigation						

Analyst 1 Task	4/15/02	4/16/02	Date 4/17/02	4/18/02	4/19/02	Total
1 *Purchasing System*						
1.1 Survey Potential						
1.2 Create Short List	6					6
1.3 Perform Investigation		5	6			11

Analyst 2 Task	4/15/02	4/16/02	Date 4/17/02	4/18/02	4/19/02	Total
1 *Purchasing System*						
1.1 Survey Potential						
1.2 Create Short List						
1.3 Perform Investigation		6	5	2		13

Analyst 3 Task	4/15/02	4/16/02	Date 4/17/02	4/18/02	4/19/02	Total
1 *Purchasing System*						
1.1 Survey Potential						
1.2 Create Short List						
1.3 Perform Investigation			4	3	8	15

We will see how to use these actual effort numbers in later lessons.

FYI A popular time accounting package on PCs is Timeslips from Timeslips. For more information on this package, check out the following Web site at www. timeslips.com/products/default.asp.

COLLECT AWARDS ACTUAL EFFORT

We also want to track the effort on developing the awards banquet. This will improve our metrics for the next banquet project. The time sheets submitted per resource are shown here:

Project Manager Task	Date 4/08/02	4/09/02	4/10/02	4/11/02	4/12/02	Total
1 *Winners*						
1.1 Create Team	4	5				9
1.2 Create Process					3	3
1.3 Develop Forms						

Project Manager Task	Date 4/15/02	4/16/02	4/17/02	4/18/02	4/19/02	Total
1 *Winners*						
1.1 Create Team						
1.2 Create Process	4	4				8
1.3 Develop Forms		2	5			7

Team 1 (and Team 2 and Team 3) Task	Date 4/15/02	4/16/02	4/17/02	4/18/02	4/19/02	Total
1 *Winners*						
1.1 Create Team						
1.2 Create Process	4	4				8
1.3 Develop Forms		2	5			7

Because tasks 1.2 and 1.3 were done in meetings, the time for the team members is the same. The project manager had some time on task 1.2 from the previous week because he had started thinking about the process prior to the meetings.

COLLECT RESTORATION ACTUAL EFFORT

In the restoration project, you are in a different situation than you normally are on projects because you are subcontracting the actual work to a variety of artisans. The actual effort numbers for the tasks in this project, then, will be your time as project manager and not as artisan or contractor.

The artisans themselves and the contracting companies would collect their own effort numbers. They would rarely share these numbers with you because they would most likely have bid a fixed price on the jobs.

You, though, should track the tasks that are assigned to you as project manager, regardless of the type of project.

Your six weeks of time sheets are shown here. We will evaluate the effects of these actuals in Hour 18, "Evaluating Project Status."

Project Manager Task	Date 4/29/02	4/30/02	5/01/02	5/02/02	5/03/02	Total
1 *Project Definition*						
1.1 Define Scope			3	2	1	6
1.2 Create Plan						
2 *Analysis/Design*						
2.1 Structural A.						

Project Manager Task	Date 5/06/02	5/07/02	5/08/02	5/09/02	5/10/02	Total
1 *Project Definition*						
1.1 Define Scope	1	1	2	1		4
1.2 Create Plan				3	2	5
2 *Analysis/Design*						
2.1 Structural A.						

Project Manager Task	Date 5/13/02	5/14/02	5/15/02	5/16/02	5/17/02	Total
1 *Project Definition*						
1.1 Define Scope						
1.2 Create Plan						

Project Manager Task	5/13/02	5/14/02	Date 5/15/02	5/16/02	5/17/02	Total
2 *Analysis/Design*						
2.1 Structural A.						
2.1.1 Hire Eng.			4			4
2.1.2 Get Report				4		4
2.1.3 Go/No Go						

Project Manager Task	5/20/02	5/21/02	Date 5/22/02	5/23/02	5/24/02	Total
1 *Project Definition*						
1.1 Define Scope						
1.2 Create Plan						
2 *Analysis/Design*						
2.1 Structural A.						
2.1.1 Hire Eng.						
2.1.2 Get Report			1			1
2.1.3 Go/No Go						

Project Manager Task	5/27/02	5/28/02	Date 5/29/02	5/30/02	5/31/02	Total
1 *Project Definition*						
1.1 Define Scope						
1.2 Create Plan						
2 *Analysis/Design*						
2.1 Structural A.						
2.1.1 Hire Eng.						
2.1.2 Get Report			3			3
2.1.3 Go/No Go						

Project Manager Task	6/03/02	6/04/02	Date 6/05/02	6/06/02	6/07/02	Total
2 *Analysis/Design*						
2.1 Structural A.						
2.1.1 Hire Eng.						
2.1.2 Get Report						
2.1.3 Go/No Go						
2.2 Architectural						
2.2.1 Hire Arch.		1	3			4

PROCEED WITH CAUTION

Some organizations require that their team members enter their time in three separate systems: one for the accounting packages, one for the personal/payroll packages, and one for the project management packages. This is a sure way to encourage employees to take the easy way out and lie about their time.

TIME SAVER

If you have two or three systems that do not automatically interface and you want accurate time accounting data, write a system to do the interface. It takes time up front to develop the system, but it will save you time and accuracy in the long run.

HOUR 16

Updating Your Project Plan

CHAPTER SUMMARY

LESSON PLAN:

In this hour you will learn about ...

- Reviewing and changing requirements.
- Reviewing and changing WBS tasks.
- Reviewing and changing deliverables.
- Reviewing and changing scheduled tasks.

Once you've started working on your project, it will invariably change. Your requirements may change, the WBS may change, or your deliverables may change. Even if none of these change, your schedule undoubtedly will. In this hour, you'll learn how to update your project plan to reflect these changes.

REVIEW AND CHANGE REQUIREMENTS

Following your control plans, especially the change and quality control plans, will help you stay on track with delivering products and services that meet your original requirements. But what if something happens that causes the requirements themselves to change? Because one measure of project success is in meeting the project requirements, it is important to periodically review those requirements and make any necessary updates.

What types of things may change in your project requirements as the project progresses? Obviously, any infinite number of specific requirement changes may take place, but they do tend to fall into three categories of requirement changes:

- Missing requirements
- Infeasible requirements
- Extraneous requirements

Let's look at each category in a little more detail.

Make sure you review potential changes to project requirements with the project sponsor and your team, especially when you are considering removing requirements. They will generally be better able to determine which are infeasible and which are extraneous.

EVALUATE MISSING REQUIREMENTS

As the project progresses, you and your team may discover that there were implied project requirements that were never documented. Because these may require additional work, and in some cases require rework, it is important to add these to the project plan as soon as possible.

EXAMINE INFEASIBLE REQUIREMENTS

When you created your project initiation document, you addressed project feasibility as well as project costs and benefits. The project plan you created was based on this project initiation document and on other data uncovered while doing additional project research. Once the project is approved, though, and work starts, you may find that certain project requirements are no longer feasible given the existing project parameters.

For instance, you may have a requirement for color printing that adds an additional $10,000 to the cost of a software package. Based on other changes to the project, this may no longer be feasible, both in terms of functionality or cost. In a construction or building restoration project, a requirement may have been for a slate roof. But once you investigate the project more thoroughly, you find that acquiring enough slate for the roof will add $20,000 to the project cost and will delay it for two months while enough slate of the proper color can be gathered and shipped. This may make a slate roof infeasible now.

JUST A MINUTE

Remember that any of the changes discussed in this hour should go through your project change control process to make sure that all the relevant parties agree to the changes and understand the effect of the changes. This process was developed in Hour 5, "Developing Project Control Plans," and reviewed in Hour 14, "Following Your Control Plans."

Uncover Extraneous Requirements

Requirements that have become infeasible are not extraneous. In previous examples, we still need to print somehow, and we still need to roof the building, just not in the way originally imagined. Extraneous requirements are those that we no longer need at all. Examples of this may be the elimination of a patio or a hot tub or some other feature that will not be replaced with something else.

Change Awards Requirements

In Hour 14 we had a change to our plan that we honor four employees instead of three. This represented changes in the deliverables but really wasn't a requirement change. What would be considered a change in requirements would be changing the size of the banquet facility, changing the banquet to be lunch rather than dinner, and so on.

Change Restoration Requirements

In reviewing the restoration requirements and the rest of the project plan, see if there are any missing, extraneous, or infeasible requirements. An answer is given in Appendix A, "Sample Documents."

Review and Change WBS

Performing portions of the project work may uncover more work that was missed in the original WBS. Simple tasks of less than an hour that might be considered "to do" items of larger tasks in the plan are just performed anyway without creating separate tasks for them, but there may be cases where an entire branch of the WBS was inadvertently left out. Also, an assumption may prove false, which would require more work to be added.

Both of these situations will mean a change to the WBS to insert the missing tasks. You will then also have to estimate these tasks and insert them into the network to schedule them.

JUST A MINUTE

When you add new tasks to the WBS and then estimate and schedule them, you need to baseline those new tasks. Be careful, however, not to rebaseline the original tasks.

Although any changes to the WBS are generally additions, this isn't always the case. Sometimes you may have specified work in the WBS that is no longer necessary. In those rare cases, you would remove the tasks, adjust the network, and recalculate the schedule.

Change Purchasing WBS

In reviewing the purchasing WBS, you notice that the product selection is being made based purely on the written data given by the analysts in their report. While this data can guide the selection of a vendor package, it is likely that the sponsor will want other evaluations of each package as well.

Additional tasks might include interviews with three clients of each of the packages, client visits to one site using each package, and in-house tests of each package.

Each of these tasks can be estimated and tracked and are not work components contained or implied in any of the existing tasks in the plan. With sponsor approval, they should be added to the plan, estimated, inserted into the network, and scheduled.

The revised purchasing project WBS now looks like this:

Task

1	*Purchasing System*
1.1	Survey Potential Systems
1.2	Create Short List
1.3	Research Candidates
1.4	Interview Clients of Each System
1.5	Perform Site Visits
1.6	Perform In-House Tests
1.7	Develop Report
1.8	Select System
1.9	Purchase System
1.10	Install System
1.11	Test System
1.12	Turn Over

2   *Trained End Users*

2.1   Develop Training

2.2   Hold Classes

JUST A MINUTE

Not all project managers renumber the task ids of original tasks when new ones are added to the plan. Because we are using the WBS code as an id, the codes would need to change to show the task's relative position in the WBS. If you were using a numbering system that allowed letters, then you could letter the new tasks as 1.3a, 1,3b, and so on.

Another approach to the WBS would be to make the new tasks subtasks of the develop report task. That approach would yield a WBS that looks like this:

Task

1   *Installed Purchasing System*

1.1   Survey Potential Systems

1.2   Create Short List

1.3   Perform Investigation

1.4   Analysis Report

1.4.1 Interview Clients of Each System

1.4.2 Perform Site Visits

1.4.3 Perform In-House Tests

1.4.4 Write Report

1.5   Select System

1.6   Purchase System

1.7   Install System

1.8   Test System

1.9   Turn Over to Production

2   *Trained End Users*

2.1   Develop Training

2.2   Hold Classes

This approach eliminates the need to renumber the tasks and still provides for the additional work. As was the case when you originally created this WBS, either approach is fine. It depends on how you and your team prefer to look at the WBS.

GO TO ▶
To review creating and organizing tasks into a WBS, reread Hour 6, "Creating a Work Breakdown Structure."

GO TO ▶
To review the four types of dependency relationships, refer to Hour 9, "Creating a Network Diagram."

For each of these tasks, we need to create estimates. While it will take only an hour or so to interview the clients in task 1.4.1, setting up the interviews for each will cause some delay, so we will give ourselves five days to perform this task even though the effort will be about 18 hours. Site visits will also take time to arrange and execute. We'll allocate five days for this, too, with 24 hours of effort. The in-house tests will take even longer. We'll allocate at least 10 work days and 24 hours of effort. We'll leave the write-report task at the 24 hours of effort we had before.

Because we may eliminate candidates based on the results of interviews and/or site visits, we will assign dependency relationships as finish-start between each new task. These are summarized in the following table:

Task	Duration	Effort	Dependency
1.4 Analysis Report			
1.4.1 Interviews Clients	5	18	1.3
1.4.2 Perform Site Visits	5	24	1.4.1
1.4.3 Perform In-House Tests	5	24	1.4.2
1.4.4 Write Report	1	24	1.4.3

CHANGE AWARDS WBS

Task 2.8, Send Invitations, is really multiple subtasks. As noted in the quality plan, the invitations need to be proofed. Prior to that, they need to be designed, layed out, and to have a draft printed. After the invitation is proofed, it can be sent to the printer, printed, and then stuffed in envelopes, labeled, and mailed.

If each of these subtasks can be individually estimated and tracked, then you might want to add them to the awards WBS. At this point, however, the work package for this task makes it clear that these subtasks need to be completed to consider the task completed, so we will leave the WBS as is.

CHANGE RESTORATION WBS

Based on the actuals noted in Hour 15, "Tracking Your Progress," and the restoration project information discussed to date, analyze the restoration WBS to see if there are any missing or extra tasks. An answer appears in Appendix A.

REVIEW AND CHANGE DELIVERABLES

The details of your deliverables are likely to change during your project, especially in longer projects. Some deliverables will no longer be necessary and some deliverables will need to be added. Both of these may require changes to the WBS or may have been caused by changes to the WBS. Deliverable changes are generally caused by forgetting some products or services; sometimes deliverables are not needed and can be removed from the list.

CHANGE PURCHASING DELIVERABLES

The WBS changes discussed in the previous section will necessitate some changes in the deliverables. As stated in Hour 3, "Starting a Project Plan," the deliverables for this project were as follows:

- Survey of potential systems
- Short list of systems to investigate further
- Investigation results of each system
- Selected system
- The installed purchasing system
- Trained end users
- New purchasing process

By bullet number three we had meant the written report on each system, which is still the deliverable we'll select from, but we have some additional intermediary deliverables:

- Minutes of interviews with clients
- Site-visit reports
- In-house test results

These additional intermediary deliverables will be inputs into the final recommendation report.

JUST A MINUTE

Changes in the WBS and/or in the deliverables will generally require changes to the resources' work packages, too. Make sure you update these.

Change Awards Deliverables

The change request noted in Hour 14 necessitated a change to the deliverables. At this point, no additional changes to the deliverables appear to be necessary.

Change Restoration Deliverables

Review the restoration project plan and the changes noted in the previous sections to determine if there are any missing or extraneous deliverables. An answer is shown in Appendix A.

Review and Change Schedule

In Hour 15, we discussed the changes to the schedule caused by the tracking of actuals against the plan. The changes to the schedule discussed in this hour are changes to the schedule caused by other things. The two most common are changes to the calculated *estimate to complete* and changes necessary to fix *dependency violations* (see the "Dependency Violations" section later in this chapter).

STRICTLY DEFINED

Estimate to complete is the amount of work effort remaining on a task. A **dependency violation** is an error in the schedule in which the actual date or hours entered cause the early start dates calculated in the schedule to miss the dependency conditions coded.

Update Estimates to Complete

Because the whole point of creating a project network diagram and schedule is to model reality as closely as possible, it is important to regularly evaluate the model based on the latest progress. One thing that can frequently change is the amount of time remaining on a task. This is called the estimate to complete. Let's look at this field in more detail.

JUST A MINUTE

Although this hour refers primarily to the use of the "estimate to complete" field with resource-constrained tasks, it can be used with time-constrained tasks, too. So if delivery schedules slip from 30 days to 60 days and you've already waited 20 days, the new estimate to complete for this task would be 40 more days.

Estimate to complete can be a calculated field or a field that you or your resources enter. Say you originally estimated that the effort on a task was 40 hours. Your resource has worked 22 hours on that task to date. This leaves a new estimate to complete of 18 hours. So, when you update your project schedule, this is the number you would use to calculate a duration and then schedule in your forward pass.

But let's say that your resource tells you that 18 hours is not enough to successfully complete the task. He or she really needs 31 more hours. This 31 becomes your new estimate to complete and is now the value you use when calculating the schedule.

Estimates to complete may be revised up or down, but in most cases they go up, which will generally extend your project schedule.

DEPENDENCY VIOLATIONS

Dependency violations are caused when you enter actual information into a schedule that conflicts with the existing early start dates. While this may be a data entry problem on occasion, a mismodeling of the dependencies in your network generally causes it; that is, you have entered dependency relationships between tasks in your project that are not the true relationship between the tasks.

In most cases, you have said that two tasks have a typical finish-start relationship—that the predecessor must finish before the successor can start. But then work starts in the predecessor task, and you find that work can start on the successor task, too. So, the resource starts work on the successor, and as soon as you enter that start date, you have a dependency violation.

While you don't have to fix dependency violations, you really should. The more closely your network and schedule model reality, the higher your chances of completing the project successfully will be. And fixing the problem is relatively simple. Just change the dependency relationship to allow the tasks to overlap, since that is how you performed them.

Each of the major project management software packages displays these dependency violations in different ways. One of them highlights the text on the two tasks in violation. Another highlights the Gantt bars of the tasks in violation. Still another gives you a calculation error message but does not highlight the Gantt display in any way (see the following figure).

An example of a
dependency viola-
tion error message
from Microsoft
Project.

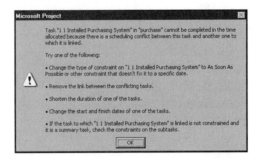

Keep in mind that if you are not using a project management package to generate and track your schedules, you may never see dependency violations, which could mean that you would not meet your schedule. You would need to manually compare your early start dates to your actual dates to make sure this hasn't happened.

CHANGE PURCHASING SCHEDULE

Let's look at how the actual effort reported in Hour 15 on this project affects the estimate to complete on each task. A summary of the actuals to date for resource Analyst 1 is shown here:

| Analyst 1 | | Reporting Period | | | | |
Task	4/08/02	4/15/02	4/22/02	4/29/02	5/06/02	Total
1 *Purchasing System*						
1.1 Survey Potential	12					12
1.2 Create Short List		6				6
1.3 Perform Investiga.		11				11

Analyst 2 charged 13 hours to task 1.3 during the week of 4/15/02, and Analyst 3 charged 15 hours during that same week.

None of the resources have reported completing task 1.3, so the actuals and estimates would look like this:

Task	Resource	Baseline Effort	Actual Effort	Estimate to Complete
1.3 Perform Investiga.	Analyst 1	16	11	5
	Analyst 2	16	13	3
	Analyst 3	16	15	1

If any of the resources believed that they had more work left than indicated by the calculated estimate to complete, they should note that. For purposes of this exercise, we'll presume that Analyst 3 has increased the estimate to complete to six hours.

The new schedule, complete with additional WBS tasks, is shown in the following figures.

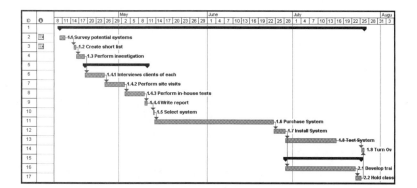

The revised schedule for the purchasing project.

Name	ID	April 2002					Total Actuals (Hours)	Pending (Hours)	ETC (Hours)	Start	Finish
		Mon 08	Tue 09	Wed 10	Thu 11	Fri 12					
1 Winners										5/8/02	5/10/02
1.5 Evaluate Nominations	PM						1.25	1.50		5/8/02	5/8/02
	Team1						1.25	1.50			
	Team2						1.25	1.50			
	Team3						1.25	1.50			
1.6 Select Winners	PM						1.25	1.50		5/9/02	5/9/02
	Team1						1.25	1.50			
	Team2						1.25	1.50			
	Team3						1.25	1.50			
1.7 Announce Winners	PM						1.25	1.50		5/10/02	5/10/02
	Team1						1.25	1.50			
	Team2						1.25	1.50			
	Team3						1.25	1.50			
2 Banquet										5/10/02	5/20/02
2.1 Determine Potential Dates	PM						0.50	0.50		5/10/02	5/10/02
	Team1						0.50	0.50			
	Team2						0.50	0.50			
	Team3						0.50	0.50			

A sample time sheet leaving space for the resource to update the estimate to complete field.

TIME SAVER

 Many project managers put the estimate to complete field on each resource's time sheet. That way, if they need to correct it, they can do so directly on the time sheet. You can allow for this both in manual and online time-accounting systems.

Change Awards Schedule

According to the time sheets from Hour 15, the first three tasks in the awards project are complete. The forms have been made available to the employees, and at this point, the team is just waiting for the nominations to be submitted. This means that the schedule has not changed from that given in Hour 15.

Change Restoration Schedule

The actuals charged to this project in Hour 15 do not indicate any changes needed in the estimate to complete values of any of the tasks with time charged, but we would have a problem with this project with the actuals as noted. Figure out what this problem is and how we might fix it. Then evaluate the effect on the project. An answer is provided in Appendix A.

PROCEED WITH CAUTION

Although the major project management packages enable you to enter actuals and work remaining based on a field called "Percent Complete," you get a much closer model of reality if you don't use this field and if you don't allow your resources to, either. Project tasks often go quickly to 90 percent complete and stay there for months. You and your team should enter actuals, and if the calculated estimates to complete are no longer valid, change them.

PART IV

Controlling Your Project

CHAPTER SUMMARY

LESSON PLAN:

In this hour you will learn about ...

- Tracking project costs.
- Calculating earned value.
- Using earned value to determine project status.
- Calculating the cost of work remaining.

Because one of the major success measurements is completing a project within budget, it's logical that one of the primary tools used to evaluate project progress considers project cost. In this Hour, we will look at how to track project costs and how to use them to determine progress.

TRACK PROJECT COSTS

Although many organizations don't track project costs, there are three good reasons to do so. First, tracking costs can help you to keep within budget on the current project. Second, it can help you to keep on schedule in your current project. Last, it can help you to better estimate future projects. The following sections discuss how to track your project's fixed and variable costs.

TRACK FIXED COSTS

Depending on the accounting system you use, you might track fixed costs in one of two ways. Organizations that work with purchase orders may charge the cost to the project as soon as the purchase order is cut because this is usually when the project account is charged. In other organizations, the project is not charged for a cost until the product or service is paid for, that is, until a check is issued.

If your project financing is connected directly to your accounting system, make sure that you understand when the project account will be charged. Checks for products and services might not be issued until months after a purchase order goes out. If you are charged when you're not expecting to incur the charges, your project may look ahead of or behind schedule.

If your project management package does not interface with your accounting systems, or if you are using a spreadsheet package or other method of tracking, tracking fixed project costs is still straightforward. Every time you order a product or service, record the order price. Then, when you pay for the product or service, record that, too. What you pay is the actual fixed cost, but tracking the cost as soon as you incur it (order something) can help you to anticipate project cash flow needs.

Wherever possible, the costs should be associated with specific tasks within specific timeframes. Many of the software packages can accrue the cost on a task over the task's duration as well as apply the cost at the beginning or at the end of the task. You should use the method closest to the way you will actually spend the money. If you are paying for a product or service in equal payments over the duration of the task, then you'll want to select the constant payment accrual method. The software will take the dollar amount you specified and divide it into equal payments over the duration of the task.

On the other hand, if you pay for something when you order it, then this cost would be placed at the beginning of the task. And if you pay at the end of a task, then that is where the cost should be placed. This will affect some of the math determining whether or not you are on schedule.

The accrual method used for applying your actual costs should match that used in your baseline schedule, or your project may inaccurately look ahead of or behind schedule.

Track Variable Costs

To track your variable costs, you need to track your resource use. We discussed how to do this in Hour 15, "Tracking Your Progress," for people resources, but keep in mind that you would track the use of nonpeople resources the same way. The resource use is then multiplied by the rate per use to give you the actual variable cost.

TRACK PURCHASING PROJECT COSTS

Let's look at how the actual effort reported in Hour 15 on this project affects the cost on each task. A summary of the actuals to date for the project is as follows:

GO TO ▶
Refer to Hour 8, "Developing Project Estimates," to remind yourself about resource rates.

Task	Resource	Actual Effort	Actual Cost
1 *Purchasing System*			
1.1 Survey Potential	Analyst 1	12	$384.00
1.2 Create Short List	Analyst 1	6	$192.00
1.3 Perform Investigation	Analyst 1	11	$352.00
	Analyst 2	13	$416.00
	Analyst 3	15	$480.00

No fixed costs have been charged yet to the project.

JUST A MINUTE

If you will be tracking variable costs in a project management software package, make sure you have assigned each resource an estimated rate and recalculated the project cost before you baseline the project. Otherwise, your projects may inaccurately look ahead of or behind schedule.

TRACK AWARDS PROJECT COSTS

The only costs incurred to date on the awards banquet project are the resource costs. Based on the actual hours reported earlier, the costs to date for this project are shown in the following table.

Task	Resource	Actual Effort	Actual Cost
1 *Winners*			
1.1 Create Team	PM	9.0	$288.00
1.2 Create Process	PM	11.0	$352.00
	Team 1	8.0	$256.00
	Team 2	8.0	$256.00
	Team 3	8.0	$256.00
1.3 Develop Forms	PM	7.0	$224.00
	Team 1	7.0	$224.00
1.3 Develop Forms	Team 2	7.0	$224.00
	Team 3	7.0	$224.00

TRACK RESTORATION PROJECT COSTS

The progress on the restoration project is moving along as reported in Hours 15 and 16. Based on the actual hours and the fact that all the estimated fixed costs for the project were also the actual costs, calculate the actual fixed and variable costs on the restoration project. An answer appears in Appendix A, "Sample Documents."

CALCULATE COST OF WORK PERFORMED

The costs that we calculated in the previous sections are usually referred to as the Actual Cost of Work Performed, or the ACWP. This is one of the values we need in order to perform a cost and schedule analysis, known as *earned value*. In this section, we look at some other related cost fields and set the stage for performing an earned value analysis later in this hour (refer to the "Understand Earned Value" section).

STRICTLY DEFINED

Earned value is a cost and schedule analysis tool designed to help you evaluate whether or not your project is on schedule and within budget. To perform this analysis, you need to calculate a variety of costs also defined in this Hour.

USE BUDGETED COST OF WORK PERFORMED

The first thing we need to do to set the stage for an earned value analysis is to determine the As-of date for the actuals we've reported. This is generally the Friday or Sunday date of the last time sheets that have been recorded. In the time sheets we've used for the awards project, the last Friday date was 4/19/02. The Sunday date associated with that time sheet would be 4/21/02.

If you don't work on the weekends, using either date will give you the same values for the earned value fields, but if you do have weekend work and your time sheets run Sunday through Saturday, the As-of date would actually be the Saturday date.

Once you have determined the date to use for your As-of date, you are ready to start calculating the rest of the earned value fields. As with the CPM math, many project management software packages will calculate these earned value fields for you, but you need to understand how to perform the math yourself. This is especially true if you are using spreadsheets or other packages to track your projects.

Each of the earned value fields is calculated at two levels. They are calculated per task to see how each task is doing. Then each task's value is summed to see how the overall project is progressing.

Let's see how we do this with the purchasing project. We have time sheets through April 19, 2001, for this project, so we would want to compare our baseline through this date. The table that follows shows the tasks that should have had work performed on them according to the baseline schedule. It also shows the baseline cost of each task per resource.

Task	Resource	Baseline Work	Baseline Start	Baseline Finish	Baseline Cost
1 *Purchasing System*			4/8/02	6/28/02	$3,040
1.1 Survey Potential	Analyst 1	16	4/8/02	4/9/02	$512
1.2 Create List	Analyst 1	4	4/10/02	4/10/02	$128
1.3 Perform Investig.	Analyst 1	16	4/11/02	4/12/02	$512
	Analyst 2	16	4/11/02	4/12/02	$512
	Analyst 3	16	4/11/02	4/12/02	$512
1.4 Develop Report	Analyst 1	8	4/15/02	4/15/02	$256
	Analyst 2	8	4/15/02	4/15/02	$256
	Analyst 3	8	4/15/02	4/15/02	$256
1.5 Select System			4/16/02	4/16/02	
1.6 Purchase System			4/17/02	5/28/02	

The BCWP is the baseline cost of all the work completed through the As-of date. To determine this, we need to review the actuals to date. The actual dates are those underlined in the table that follows:

Task	Resource	Actual Start	Actual Finish	Actual Duration
1 *Purchasing System*		<u>4/10/02</u>	7/4/02	60
1.1 Survey Potential	Analyst 1	<u>4/10/02</u>	<u>4/11/02</u>	2
1.2 Create Short List	Analyst 1	<u>4/15/02</u>	<u>4/15/02</u>	1
1.3 Perform Investig.	Analyst 1	<u>4/16/02</u>	4/17/02	2 (3)
	Analyst 2	<u>4/17/02</u>	4/18/02	2
	Analyst 3	4/17/02	4/18/02	2

Because only tasks 1.1 and 1.2 are completed, these are the only tasks that would have a BCWP, as shown in the following table:

Task	Resource	BCWP
1 *Purchasing System*		$640
1.1 Survey Potential	Analyst 1	$512
1.2 Create Short List	Analyst 1	$128

Sometimes calculations for BCWP are prorated through the As-of date on uncompleted tasks, but traditionally the calculations are performed on completed tasks only, so in this hour we will be using the latter method.

USE BUDGETED COST OF WORK SCHEDULED

The next earned value field to look at is the *Budgeted Cost of Work Scheduled*, also known as BCWS. This field tells us the baseline cost of all the tasks scheduled through the As-of date.

Task	Baseline Cost
1 *Purchasing System*	$3,040
1.1 Survey Potential	$512
1.2 Create List	$128
1.3 Perform Investigation	$1,536
1.4 Develop Report	$768

Because there were no baseline costs associated with tasks 1.5 and 1.6, the BCWS would be $2,944.

STRICTLY DEFINED

The **Budgeted Cost of Work Scheduled (BCWS)** is an earned value field, calculated as the baseline cost of what (according to the baseline schedule) should have been performed to date.

USE ACTUAL COST OF WORK PERFORMED

The *Actual Cost of Work Performed*, or ACWP, is the actual cost of work performed through the As-of date. As we noted in the earlier sections on tracking costs, this is a cumulative value for cost of all work, not just on tasks that have been completed. The totals per task are shown as follows:

Task	Actual Cost
1 *Purchasing System*	
1.1 Survey Potential	$384.00
1.2 Create Short List	$192.00
1.3 Perform Investigation	$1,248.00

Once we have calculated these three earned value cost figures, we will be able to do some comparisons to see how we are doing on the schedule and the budget.

Before we do that, though, let's see how we would calculate these three numbers in the awards and restoration projects.

STRICTLY DEFINED

The **Actual Cost of Work Performed** (**ACWP**) is an earned value field, calculated as the actual cost of the work performed to date.

CALCULATE AWARDS WORK PERFORMED COSTS

We noted the actual cost of the awards project tasks earlier in this hour; in previous hours, we discussed the baseline values for cost. These are summarized in the table as follows:

Task	Base. Start	Base. Finish	Base. Cost	Actual Start	Actual Finish	Actual Cost
1 *Winners*						
1.1 Create Team	4/8/02	4/8/02	$160	4/8/02	4/9/02	$288
1.2 Create Process	4/9/02	4/11/02	$1,600	4/12/02	4/16/02	$1,120
1.3 Develop Forms	4/12/02	4/15/02	$960	4/16/02	4/17/02	$896
1.4 Gather Forms	4/16/02	5/6/02	$80			

From these numbers we can determine the BCWP, BCWS, and ACWP. The BCWP of task 1.1 is the baseline cost of $160, 1.2 is $1,600, and 1.3 is $960. Task 1.4 is not complete, so it has 0 BCWP at this point in time.

BCWS of 1.1 is also $160, 1.2 is $1,600, and 1.3 is $960. Since 1.4 was scheduled to start already, and the 2.5 effort hours were scheduled in the first week, the BCWS of this task is $80.

ACWP is the same as the column labeled actual cost: $288 for task 1.1, $1,120 for task 1.2, and $896 for task 1.3. No time or fixed cost has been charged to 1.4, so its ACWP is 0.

CALCULATE RESTORATION WORK PERFORMED COSTS

Based on the data presented in the answers to the restoration project in Hours 15, 16, and 17, calculate the ACWP, BCWS, and BCWP for the restoration project. An answer is provided in Appendix A.

UNDERSTAND EARNED VALUE

We've already discussed many of the earned value calculations. In this section we'll look at how to apply these calculations to determine if we are on schedule and on budget. We do this by calculating two more values named schedule variance and cost variance. Let's look at how we calculate these values.

UNDERSTAND SCHEDULE VARIANCE AND COST VARIANCE

Schedule variance is used to determine whether or not our projects are on schedule. It is the difference between the BCWP and the BCWS calculated with the following formula:

$$SV = BCWP - BCWS$$

A negative value means that we are behind schedule because we scheduled more work than we actually performed.

GO TO ▶
In Hour 18, "Evaluating Project Status," we look at other ways to evaluate project status, including some ratios often considered to be part of earned value.

Cost variance is used to determine whether or not our projects are on budget. It is the difference between the BCWP and the ACWP, calculated with the following formula:

$$CV = BCWP - ACWP$$

A negative value means that we are over budget because we spent more money than we were scheduled to spend.

USE PURCHASING EARNED VALUE

Now that we have the BCWP, BCWS, and ACWP for the purchasing project, we can use them to calculate the variances and see how we're doing on the schedule and budget. The table that follows shows the values for the numbers:

Task	SV	CV	BCWP	BCWS	ACWP
1 *Installed System*	−$1,536	−$1,184	$640	$2,176	$1,824
1.1 Survey Potential	$0	$128	$512	$512	$384
1.2 Create Short List	$0	−$64	$128	$128	$192
1.3 Perform Investigation	−$1,536	−$1,248	$0	$1,536	$1,248

These numbers show that, overall, the installed system tasks are running behind schedule (−$1,536) and over budget (−$1,184). This is somewhat deceptive, though, because we haven't prorated the budgeted cost of work performed on the nearly completed task 1.3. Still, this accurately shows that we are behind schedule on task 1.3, although we are not really over budget on this task. We were on schedule with tasks 1.1 and 1.2, under budget on task 1.1, and over budget on task 1.2.

TIME SAVER

Create and save a customized view in your project management package that displays the earned value fields. This way you won't need to create one every time you want to look at the values.

USE AWARDS EARNED VALUE

Now let's see what the schedule variance and the cost variance tell us about the status of the awards project. The values are noted in the table that follows:

Task	SV	CV	BCWP	BCWS	ACWP
1 *Winners*	−$80	$416	$2,720	$2,800	$2,304
1.1 Create Team	$0	−$128	$160	$160	$288
1.2 Create Process	$0	$480	$1,600	$1,600	$1,120
1.3 Develop Forms	$0	$64	$960	$960	$896
1.4 Gather Nominations	−$80	$0	$0	$80	$0

At this point the entire project is slightly behind schedule (−$80) and under budget by $416.

USE RESTORATION EARNED VALUE

Calculate the cost variance and schedule variance for the restoration project and evaluate what these mean in terms of your schedule and your budget. An answer appears in Appendix A.

CALCULATE COST OF WORK REMAINING

GO TO ▶
Hour 24, "Choosing a Project Management Package," reviews some of the most popular project management software packages, including whether or not they calculate earned value.

Another aspect of cost that we can explore is the cost of the remaining tasks. As with the actual costs, these costs are divided into the fixed costs remaining and the variable costs remaining. Each of these is described in more detail in the following sections.

DETERMINE FIXED COST REMAINING

The fixed cost remaining on most of the tasks in your project will be easy to determine because most fixed costs are incurred either at the beginning or the end of a task. For tasks that incur cost at the beginning, the cost is remaining if you haven't started the task. Similarly, on tasks where the cost is incurred at the end, the cost is remaining if the task has not finished. The fun comes in, though, with tasks that have progress payments, that is, those where you pay a fixed amount at different periods throughout the duration of the task. For these tasks, you'll need to subtract the payments to date from the total cost to get the cost remaining.

The purchasing system has had no fixed costs so far, so the fixed cost of the software package is still remaining. The team has not determined what package to buy, if any, so this is still an estimated fixed cost of $50,000 to $200,000. This cost would be the *Estimate at Completion* because there have been no actual fixed costs to date.

STRICTLY DEFINED

Estimate at Completion (EAC) is the estimate for both effort and cost at the finish of a task. It is the sum of the actuals to date plus the new estimate to complete.

DETERMINE VARIABLE COST REMAINING

Variable cost remaining depends on the scheduled resource use left on the each task. It is calculated by multiplying the estimate to complete for each resource on each task by the resource's rate.

On the purchasing system, we have completed only two tasks, so we have remaining variable costs on all the tasks. They are shown as follows.

Task	Resource	Duration	Remaining Variable Cost
1 *Installed Purchasing System*			
1.3 Perform Investigation	Analyst 1	5	$160.00
	Analyst 2	3	$96.00
	Analyst 3	6	$192.00
1.4 Develop Investigation Report			
1.4.1 Interview Clients	Analyst 1	6	$192.00
	Analyst 2	6	$192.00
	Analyst 3	6	$192.00
1.4.2 Perform Site Visits	Analyst 1	8	$256.00
	Analyst 2	8	$256.00
	Analyst 3	8	$256.00
1.4.3 Perform In-House	Analyst 1	8	$256.00
	Analyst 2	8	$256.00
	Analyst 3	8	$256.00
1.4.4 Write Report	Analyst 1	8	$256.00
	Analyst 2	8	$256.00
	Analyst 3	8	$256.00
1.5 Select System	PM	2	$64.00
1.6 Purchase System	PM	2	$64.00
1.7 Install System	Programmer	8	$256.00
1.8 Test System	Tester 1	40	$2,560.00
1.9 Turn Over to Production	Programmer	8	$256.00
2 *Trained End Users*			
2.1 Develop Training	ID	100	$3,200.00
2.2 Hold Classes	PM	12	$384.00
	Trainees	84	$1,680.00

CALCULATE COST REMAINING

The total cost remaining is the sum of the variable cost remaining plus the fixed cost remaining. This is calculated per resource, per task, and then these individual values are totaled to give us task, phase, and project totals.

On the purchasing system, the estimated fixed cost of the software package would be added to the previous costs.

JUST A MINUTE

If you will be using earned value to monitor the status of your projects, you will want to use a project management software package that calculates these values for you. If you don't have software that can do this, you could use a spreadsheet package to enter the appropriate formulas.

CALCULATE AWARDS COST REMAINING

All seven of the tasks with fixed costs in our awards project are still open, so the fixed cost remaining are as shown in the table that follows:

Task	Type	Cost Remaining
1.8 Create Plaques	Fixed	$300.00
2.5 Dine at Halls	Fixed	$270.00
2.6 Select Hall	Fixed	$50.00
2.8 Send Invitations	Fixed	$420.00
2.11 Choose Entertain.	Fixed	$400.00
2.12 Choose Speakers	Fixed	$1,000.00
2.14 Hold Dinner	Fixed	$6,000.00

While you would calculate the variable cost numbers per resource per task, for simplicity here, we will review them summarized per task. The cost remaining values in the table that follows includes both the previous fixed costs and the calculated variable costs.

Task	ETC Hours	Cost Remaining
1 *Winners*	21.50	$988.00
1.4 Gather Nominations	2.50	$80.00
1.5 Evaluate Nominations	6.00	$192.00
1.6 Select Winners	6.00	$192.00
1.7 Announce Winners	6.00	$192.00
1.8 Create Plaques	1.00	$332.00
2 *Banquet*	92.00	$11,084.00
2.1 Determine Potential Dates	2.00	$64.00
2.2 Determine Potential Halls	20.00	$640.00

Task	ETC Hours	Cost Remaining
2.3 Review Hall Menus	13.00	$416.00
2.4 Create Short List of Halls	13.00	$416.00
2.5 Dine at Each Potential Hall	6.00	$462.00
2.6 Select Hall	2.00	$114.00
2.7 Announce Banquet	6.00	$192.00
2.8 Send Invitations	2.00	$484.00
2.9 Gather RSVPs	4.00	$128.00
2.10 Finalize Dining Arrangements	1.00	$32.00
2.11 Choose Entertainment	10.00	$720.00
2.12 Choose Speakers	13.00	$1,416.00
2.14 Hold Dinner		$6,000.00

If your costs are tracked in your accounting system, it may be able to calculate earned value numbers for you.

CALCULATE RESTORATION COST REMAINING

Based on the numbers presented in the other restoration exercises and answers, calculate the cost remaining on the restoration project. An answer is given in Appendix A.

Hour 18

Evaluating Project Status

Chapter Summary

LESSON PLAN:

In this hour you will learn about ...

- Comparing baseline to actual requirements.
- Comparing baseline to actual deliverables.
- Comparing baseline estimates to actual.
- Comparing baseline schedule to current.

While one of the major tools for evaluating project status is the cost performance statistics we discussed in Hour 17, "Monitoring Costs," there are several other measurements that can tell us whether or not we are on track and can help us revise our schedules. In this hour we'll look at some other considerations in evaluating project status and updating the schedule.

Compare Baseline to Completed Requirements

In Hour 16, "Updating Your Project Plan," we discussed reviewing project requirements. That aspect of requirements' review was to see if anything had changed to make sure the project plan was current. But there is another aspect of comparing baseline requirements to completed requirements that can help us evaluate status.

First, you start this status analysis by reviewing the requirements listed in your baseline plan. Refamiliarize yourself with the requirements and then count the number of requirements in the baseline plan.

Some project management scheduling packages enable you to enter task-related information such as requirements and deliverables in your schedule files. If you add these to your schedule file, this will save you time switching back and forth between your word-processing file and your scheduling file.

Next, review the current requirements. Count the number of requirements in the current version of the plan and then count how many of these were also in the baseline version of the plan. This will give you comparisons for creating the next statistics.

Once you have the counts for current and baseline requirements, you can compare them to the requirements met to date. Say that in the baseline plan you had 12 requirements for the product of your project. After the project started, this number increased to 15 but included all the original 12. At this point in time, you have met five of those requirements. This means you have met 30 percent of the requirements.

COMPARING BASELINE TO ACTUAL DELIVERABLES

Some projects don't lend themselves to tracking completed requirements because, many times, requirements aren't met until the whole project is over. For this reason, tracking by deliverables may make more sense in your projects.

As with requirements, you start to compare deliverables by reviewing and counting the baseline deliverables. Because final deliverables also are not generally completed until the project is completed, you should look at both the intermediate and end deliverables in this review.

Remember that if, in these reviews, you identify unstated deliverables, then you need to add them via the project change control process.

Because, like the WBS and schedule, the project deliverables may change over the duration of the project, you should also review and count the current deliverables.

After you have reviewed and counted both the baseline and current deliverables, you review and count the completed deliverables, comparing this number to those other numbers.

Let's say that your baseline plan listed two end deliverables and seven intermediate ones. Your current plan listed three end deliverables and 10 intermediate ones, and you have completed one final and four intermediate deliverables. So, to date, your final deliverables are 33 percent complete and the intermediate deliverables are 40 percent complete. This yields an overall deliverables percent complete of 38 percent.

COMPARE PURCHASING DELIVERABLES

These were the baseline deliverables for the purchasing system project:

- Survey of potential systems
- Short list of systems to investigate further
- Investigation results of each system
- Selected system
- The installed purchasing system
- Trained end users
- New purchasing process

The last three of these are end deliverables and the other four are intermediate deliverables. The current deliverables include these four additional intermediate deliverables:

- Minutes of interviews with clients
- Site visit reports
- In-house test results
- System recommendation report

JUST A MINUTE

When you are counting your completed intermediary deliverables, don't count status reports, time sheets, or any regularly created deliverables. Just count those intermediary deliverables that are unique.

As noted in the actuals, tasks 1.1 and 1.2 have finished, meaning that the first two deliverables are also complete. This means that two of eight of the intermediary deliverables, and two of the eleven total deliverables have been finished. So, the deliverables on this project are 18 percent complete.

COMPARE AWARDS DELIVERABLES

The deliverables from the awards project included the following:

- A process for selecting winners
- Winner nomination forms
- Completed winner nominations
- Invitations
- Plaques for each winner
- Selected banquet hall
- Dinner for 200 employees
- Selected winners

The last four of these are end deliverables, and the first four are intermediary deliverables. To date, the first three intermediary deliverables have been completed, giving us three of eight completed deliverables. This means that 38 percent of our awards project deliverables are complete.

COMPARE RESTORATION DELIVERABLES

With the information given on the restoration project to date, determine how many of the baseline and current deliverables have been completed. An answer is shown in Appendix A, "Sample Documents."

JUST A MINUTE

Some project management packages will draw actuals out past the current date on Gantt charts if actual hours exceed scheduled hours. Remember that this may not mean the task is really that far ahead of schedule.

COMPARE BASELINE ESTIMATES TO ACTUAL

In Hour 17 we discussed using earned value to compare baseline estimates to actuals. In this section we'll look at some additional comparisons that may be useful for evaluating project status.

CALCULATE PERCENT COMPLETE

A very popular way of comparing estimates to actuals is to use percent complete. This can be a handy reporting feature because most people are more used to dealing with percentages than they are with other methods of comparison.

To calculate percent complete on time-constrained tasks, simply divide the actual duration by the baseline duration. So, a task with a baseline duration of 10 days and an actual duration to date of 3 days is 30 percent complete.

With resource-constrained tasks, you divide the baseline effort estimate by the actual effort to date. A task with 40 baseline hours of effort that has 20 hours of actuals to date is 50 percent complete. This is true regardless of the baseline duration of the task. That is, if that 40-hour task was scheduled with a duration of 10 day and the 20 hours were completed in 2.5 days, the task is still 50 percent complete. This is one of the deceptive aspects of using percent complete as an evaluation of status.

PROCEED WITH CAUTION

 Don't use percent complete as a tracking feature. That is, don't say that a task is 50 percent complete. Tell the tool you're using that you've used x hours and then have it calculate the percent. Otherwise you will not get accurate metrics to use later.

You can also use percent complete to evaluate an entire project. Project percent complete can be calculated three ways. The first is to take the total effort to date and divide by the total baseline effort. The second is to take the total duration to date and divide by the actual duration to date. The third is to take the percent complete of each task and average it.

Say we had a project with the following estimates and actuals:

Task	Baseline Effort	Baseline Duration	Actual Effort	Actual Duration	Percent
0 Project 1		45	10	20	8
1 Task 1	10	5	5	5	50
2 Task 2		10		5	50
3 Task 3	20	10	15	8	75
4 Task 4	15	10			0

Calculating percent complete using an average of the percent complete on all the tasks gives us a percent complete of 43 percent. But taking the total actual duration and dividing it by the baseline duration yields an 80 percent complete; taking the total effort and dividing it by baseline effort gives us 44 percent complete.

EVALUATE PERCENT COMPLETE

Evaluating percent complete on time-constrained tasks is usually straightforward. As in the previous example, a 10-day task with an actual duration of three days is 30 percent complete. This means that the remaining duration on the task is 7 days.

JUST A MINUTE

One way around these discrepancies is to consider percent complete in two ways. In the first way, you evaluate the status based on the baseline duration, actual duration, and duration remaining and come up with a percent complete for duration. In the second way, you consider baseline effort, actual effort, and effort remaining, which gives you an effort-based percent complete. You then report on both numbers.

But what if this time-constrained task also had effort associated with it and the baseline effort was 20 hours. If the effort to date is already 20 hours, some project management packages will calculate this task as 100 percent complete even if those 20 hours took place in only 2.5 days. This is not correct because the time-constraint is still 10 days, of which only 3 have passed.

Percent complete on resource-constrained tasks can also be sticky. Say that a task of 40 hours of effort with one person assigned is scheduled to take 5 days. The person works on the task for 20 hours, and is, in terms of effort, 50 percent complete. But what if the duration on that task so far is 4 days? Will the remaining effort of that task be done in 2.5 days or in 4? To really determine this, you would need to double-check with your resource.

As you can see, working with percent complete is not as straightforward as it appears at first brush. This is especially obvious when we looked at the discrepancies in the percent complete that arise on the total project depending on how we calculate the value. This is because all these calculations ignore the work or duration remaining that we discussed in Hour 17.

Still, using percent complete can provide you with some useful information.

TIME SAVER

Using the discrepancies in percent complete we noted in this section should help you more quickly identify those tasks that need you to raise or lower their estimate to complete.

USE PURCHASING SYSTEM PERCENT COMPLETE

Let's look at how we might use the effort percent complete feature in the purchasing project to help us determine status. We will also factor in the work remaining to make the value more useful.

The table that follows shows the baseline, actual, and remaining effort on the purchasing system tasks.

Task	Percent	Baseline	Actual	Remaining
0 *Purchasing System*	13%	264	57	400
1 *Installed System*	22%	164	57	204
1.1 Survey Potential	100%	16	12	
1.2 Create Short List	100%	4	6	
1.3 Perform Investig.	74%	48	39	14
1.4 Develop Report	0%			90
1.4.1 Interview Clients	0%			18
1.4.2 Perform Visits	0%			24
1.4.3 Perform In-House	0%			24
1.4.4 Write Report	0%			24
1.5 Select System	0%			2
1.6 Purchase System	0%			2
1.7 Install System	0%	8		8
1.8 Test System	0%	80		80
1.9 Turn to Production	0%	8		8
2 *Trained End Users*	0%	100		196
2.1 Develop Training	0%	100		100
2.2 Hold Classes	0%			96

So, as the table shows, the entire project is 13 percent complete in terms of actual versus work remaining. If we were to calculate percent complete compared to baseline, however, the project would be 22 percent complete, which is not accurate in light of the new tasks we added.

JUST A MINUTE

It is this aspect of ignoring major increases in estimate to complete that also causes many project managers to discount the value of using earned value as a project status tool.

Use Awards Banquet Percent Complete

Because the awards banquet project is also primarily resource-constrained, let's look at effort percent complete on this project.

Task	Percent	Baseline	Actual	Remaining
0 Awards Banquet	38%	198.5	72	113.5
1 Winners	77%	106.50	72	21.50
1.1 Create Team	100%	5	9	
1.2 Create Process	100%	50	35	
1.3 Develop Forms	100%	30	28	
1.4 Gather Nominations	0%	2.50		2.50
1.5 Evaluate Nominations	0%	6		6
1.6 Select Winners	0%	6		6
1.7 Announce Winners	0%	6		6
1.8 Create Plaques	0%	1		1
2 Banquet	0%	92		92
...				

From the table we note that the entire project is 38 percent complete, that the Winners summary task is 77 percent complete, and that three tasks are 100 percent complete.

Use Restoration Project Percent Complete

Using the restoration project data presented to date, calculate and evaluate the percent complete on the tasks in work. An answer appears in Appendix A.

JUST A MINUTE

Each of the major project management software packages uses percent complete in different ways, so if you plan on using percent complete in your projects, make sure you understand how your chosen package works with it.

Compare Baseline Estimates to Current Estimates

Earned value is useful for telling you if a project is behind schedule in terms of cost but is not as useful in telling you how late your project will be if you continue on at the pace you are going. And your revised schedule only reflects how late you are now, not how late you will be if you continue to slip. To evaluate this aspect of the project status you need to do some additional comparisons of estimates to current estimates.

DEVELOP BASELINE TO ACTUAL RATIOS

When we develop the ratios we are discussing, we develop them for completed tasks only. On resource-constrained tasks, we look at the actual and baseline effort, and in time-constrained tasks, we look at actual and baseline durations. Say that we had completed and in work tasks as noted:

Task	Status	Baseline	Actual	Actual Baseline
1 Task 1	Complete	200	50	.25
2 Task 2	Complete	100	150	1.5
3 Task 3	In Work	150	50	
4 Task 4	Not	100		

The effort ratios are calculated as Actual/Baseline and would yield the ratios of .25 and 1.5. This means that we have one task that finished in ¼ the effort estimated and one that took 1½ times longer than expected. The combined ratio on the completed tasks is 200/300, or 2/3.

JUST A MINUTE

Earned Value also provides ratios for these types of comparisons. The Cost Performance Index (CPI) equals BCWP/ACWP. The Schedule Performance Index (SPI) equals BCWP/BCWS.

APPLY RATIOS TO CURRENT ESTIMATES

Once you have developed these ratios, you can apply them to the remaining tasks on the project. If task 3 is similar to task 2, then we may need to raise the estimate to complete on task 3 from 100 to 175, which is calculated by this:

Baseline (150) × Ratio (1.5) – Actual

If, however, task 3 isn't similar to either completed tasks, we may want to leave its estimate to complete alone, or we may want to lower it based on the cumulative 2/3 ratio. This would lower it from 100 to 67.

How you use these numbers will vary considerably from project to project, task to task, and resource to resource.

APPLY PURCHASING SYSTEM RATIOS

The ratios on the two completed tasks in the purchasing system are shown in the table that follows:

Task	Baseline	Actual	ETC	Ratio
0 *Purchasing System*	264	57		
1 *Installed System*	164	57		
1.1 Survey Potential	16	12	0	.75
1.2 Create Short List	4	6	0	1.5
1.3 Perform Investig.	48	39	14	
1.4 Develop Report			90	
1.4.1 Interview Clients			18	
1.4.2 Perform Visits			24	
1.4.3 Perform In-House			24	
1.4.4 Write Report			24	
1.5 Select System			2	

The combined ratio of these completed tasks is .90. This implies that we may be able to lower the estimate to complete on the remaining tasks to 90 percent of our estimates. Because this is within our plus/minus 10 percent accuracy range, we would probably just leave these alone for now. We'd reevaluate the remaining estimates when 1.4.1 and 1.4.2 were complete.

PROCEED WITH CAUTION

Make sure that if you use your calculated ratios to adjust the estimates to complete, then the tasks and the resources on the pending tasks are comparable to those on the completed tasks, or you may not be modeling the actual expected progress.

APPLY AWARDS BANQUET RATIOS

The individual task ratios for the awards banquet project are shown in the table that follows.

Task	Baseline	Actual	ETC	Ratio
0 Awards Banquet	198.5	72	113.5	
1 Winners	106.50	72	21.50	
1.1 Create Team	5	9	0	1.8
1.2 Create Process	50	35	0	.70
1.3 Develop Forms	30	28	0	.93
1.4 Gather Nominations	2.50		2.50	
1.5 Evaluate Nominations	6		6	
1.6 Select Winners	6		6	
1.7 Announce Winners	6		6	
1.8 Create Plaques	1		1	
2 Banquet	92		92	
...				

While the individual ratios are 1.8, .70, and .93, the cumulative ratio is .85. You may want to adjust the estimate to complete for the other team tasks. Note, though, that the tasks performed by the Administrative Assistant would not be adjusted at this point because the ratios to date have not involved her work.

APPLY RESTORATION PROJECT RATIOS

Based on the information given in previous exercises, calculate the restoration project ratios and apply them to the estimate to complete fields. An answer appears in Appendix A.

COMPARE BASELINE SCHEDULE TO CURRENT

The ratios developed previously can also be used to compare the baseline schedule to the current schedule. In this case, rather than comparing and updating the estimate to complete field, we review and possibly update the durations.

TIME SAVER

 If your project management package does not calculate these ratios and does not enable you to create your own formulas, you may want to set up a spreadsheet that will do the math for you. This makes your "what-if" analysis easier.

COMPARE PURCHASING SYSTEM SCHEDULES

Let's look at the schedules for the purchasing system project. The durations of the two completed and one in-work task are shown in the table that follows, as is the overall duration figures for the Installed Purchasing System summary task.

Task	Baseline Duration	Current Duration	Ratio
1 *Installed Purchasing System*	59	77	1.3
1.1 Survey Potential Systems	2	1	.5
1.2 Create Short List	1	1	1
1.3 Perform Investigation	2	5	2.5

Note that the duration ratios vary greatly from the effort ratios. The current schedule is 1.3 times greater in duration than the baseline. This seems to be okay, though, because on the completed tasks and the in-work tasks, the ratio is 1.4. So, while the current schedule is longer than we had originally estimated, the new schedule seems in proportion to the completed tasks to date. This may change later, though, so you should continue to monitor this.

JUST A MINUTE

While all these comparisons do take time, on critical and/or long-term projects, it is well worth the effort to keep the project model as accurate as possible throughout the life of the project.

COMPARE AWARDS BANQUET SCHEDULES

Let's see what the schedule for the awards project looks like:

Task	Baseline Duration	Current Duration	Ratio
1 *Winners*	33	37	1.2
1.1 Create Team	1	2	2
1.2 Create Selection Process	3	3	1
1.3 Develop Nomination Forms	2	2	1
1.4 Gather Nominations	15	15	
1.5 Evaluate Nominations	1	1	
1.6 Select Winners	1	1	

Task	Baseline Duration	Current Duration	Ratio
1.7 Announce Winners	1	1	
1.8 Create Plaques	10	10	

The overall ratio on the baseline versus current schedule for the winners' summary task in the awards project is 1.2, so the existing schedule is somewhat longer than the original. In the tasks completed to date, this ratio is also 1.2, so therefore the slippage seems to have been accounted for. If subsequent tasks continue to slip, this ratio may increase.

COMPARE RESTORATION PROJECT SCHEDULES

Based on the information on the restoration project presented to date, compare and evaluate the restoration project schedule. An answer is given in Appendix A.

HOUR 19

Getting Projects Back on Track

CHAPTER SUMMARY

LESSON PLAN:

In this hour you will learn about ...

- Reviewing and changing dependency relationships.
- Reviewing and changing estimates.
- Reviewing and changing resources.

As work progresses on your project, there will most likely be changes that put you on an overbudget or over-schedule pace. When projects start to slip on the schedule and the budget, you can do several things to try to recover. In this hour, you'll learn how to analyze and update your project plan to get your project back on schedule and on budget.

REVIEW AND CHANGE DEPENDENCY RELATIONSHIPS

Dependency violations are clear signs that you may need to change your dependency relationships, but once a project starts to slip, it is a good time to review dependencies to see if changing dependencies can bring a project back on schedule, too. There are three things to look at with dependencies, and they are discussed in more detail in the following sections.

REMOVE EXTRA DEPENDENCIES

When you created your network diagram, you assigned dependencies between the tasks. As we discussed, when you create dependencies, they push out the schedule dates of the successor tasks. So if you have any extra dependencies in your network diagram, they may be artificially extending your schedule. Removing them can bring your schedule back in.

How would an extra dependency get in your schedule in the first place? There are three ways. Sometimes when you are considering dependencies, you think two tasks have a predecessor/successor relationship, but then you change your mind and don't remove the dependencies link. If you are using a project management package, you may just accidentally create a link between two tasks and not notice it. Most often, though, when using a project management package, extra dependencies end up in your network when you clone another project plan, change some tasks in the old plan, and forget to change the dependencies on the new tasks.

ADD MISSING

Believe it or not, sometimes adding in a missing dependency can bring a schedule back in. How can this happen? If your project schedule was elongated by resource leveling, adding in a missing dependency may eliminate the overallocation that pushed out the original schedule. Granted, this is rare. Adding a missing dependency usually extends your schedule, making your project later than it was when you started. Still, it's better to know this sooner rather than later. If you are going to have to renegotiate on your project, clients and sponsors are much more amenable to one large change than they are to several small ones.

ALLOW TASK OVERLAP

The last thing to look at in terms of dependencies is whether or not any of your links coded as finish-start can actually be performed with some lead-time. Say you have a 10-day task that is the predecessor to another 10-day task. If the second task can start when the first is 70 percent complete, then this will save three days on your schedule.

Now, there are two things to watch out for if you add lead-time to your dependency relationships. First, if the same resource is assigned to both tasks, resource leveling will override the lead-time and not allow the two tasks to overlap anyway. Second, if the tasks really can't overlap, you don't want to code lead-time just to make the schedule look like it is back on time. While clients and sponsors may not like hearing that a project is running late, they prefer to have some warning as soon as possible rather than find out just before the deadline.

PROCEED WITH CAUTION

 When using task lead-time, make sure it truly models reality. If the tasks can't overlap, you wouldn't be helping your project any, and you'd lose your credibility.

REVIEW PURCHASING SYSTEM DEPENDENCIES

The dependencies in the purchasing system project are shown as follows:

Task	Predecessor
1.2 Create Short List	1.1 Survey Potential Systems
1.3 Perform Investigation	1.2 Create Short List
1.4.1 Interview Clients	1.3 Perform Investigation
1.4.2 Perform Site Visits	1.4.1 Interviews Clients
1.4.3 Perform In-House Tests	1.4.2 Perform Site Visits
1.4.4 Write Report	1.4.3 Perform In-House Tests
1.5 Select System	1.4.4 Write Report
1.6 Purchase System	1.5 Select System
1.7 Install System	1.6 Purchase System
1.8 Test System	1.7 Install System
1.9 Turn Over to Production	1.8 Test System
	2.2 Hold Classes
2.1 Develop Training	1.7 Install System
2.2 Hold Classes	2.1 Develop Training

There are no extra dependencies or missing dependencies, nor are there any tasks that can benefit from lead-time.

REVIEW AWARDS BANQUET DEPENDENCIES

The dependencies in the awards project are shown as follows:

Task	Predecessor
1.2 Create Selection Process	1.1 Create Team
1.3 Develop Nomination Forms	1.2 Create Selection Process
1.4 Gather Nominations	1.3 Develop Nomination Forms
1.5 Evaluate Nominations	1.4 Gather Nominations
1.6 Select Winners	1.5 Evaluate Nominations
1.7 Announce Winners	1.6 Select Winners
1.8 Create Plaques	1.6 Select Winners
2 *Banquet*	
2.1 Determine Potential Dates	1.6 Select Winners
2.2 Determine Potential Halls	2.1 Determine Potential Dates
2.3 Review Hall Menus	2.2 Determine Potential Halls
2.4 Create Hall Short List	2.3 Review Hall Menus
2.5 Dine at Potential Halls	2.4 Create Hall Short List
2.6 Select Hall	2.5 Dine at Potential Halls
2.7 Announce Banquet	2.6 Select Hall
	1.7 Announce Winners
2.8 Send Invitations	2.6 Select Hall
	2.7 Announce Banquet
2.9 Gather RSVPs	2.8 Send Invitations
2.10 Finalize Arrangements	2.9 Gather RSVPs
2.11 Choose Entertainment	2.2 Determine Potential Halls
2.12 Choose Speakers	2.2 Determine Potential Halls
2.14 Hold Dinner	1.8 Create Plaques
	2.12 Choose Speakers
	2.11 Choose Entertainment
	2.10 Finalize Dining Arrangements

There are no extra dependencies or missing dependencies, nor are there any tasks that can benefit from lead-time.

It is faster to code lead-time in your network when you first create it. This way you don't have to revise the relationships once a project starts.

REVIEW RESTORATION PROJECT DEPENDENCIES

Review the dependency relationships in the restoration project to see if there are any extra or missing dependencies or if any of the tasks can benefit from lead-time. An answer is given in Appendix A.

REVIEW AND CHANGE ESTIMATES

If adjusting the dependencies in your schedule does not bring the schedule back on track, then you can look at your estimates.

EXPEDITE TIME-CONSTRAINED TASKS

The first estimates to look at are those on your time-constrained tasks. If the time constraint is based on a delivery schedule, you may be able to expedite the delivery. For instance, you may have a 30-day delivery delay on a product you ordered. You may be able to pay slightly more to get the product earlier, or, in some cases, you may be able to get the product earlier from an alternate source. This may also incur an additional charge, but it might not, either.

You may also be able to expedite other time-constrained tasks, such as meetings and training sessions. For meetings, by distributing agendas and prework you may be able to finish a one-day meeting in half a day. Training sessions might be shortened to two days from three with prework and homework.

If the time-constrained tasks are machine-related, you may be able to purchase faster machines. For instance, if the time-constrained task involves printing, binding, or sewing, faster machines will complete the task more quickly. The problem, of course, is the added expense. But if the project deadline is more important than the cost, this will help bring your project back on schedule.

UPDATE SKILL FACTORS

When we created our estimates, we adjusted them based on the skill factors of the resources. Maybe when we created an estimate we used an average skill factor, but we actually were able to assign an expert to the task. By lowering the estimate, we may be able to decrease the schedule.

PROCEED WITH CAUTION

Using more highly skilled resources to get the work done more quickly generally increases the project cost, even when using internal resources. This is because their burden rates and/or charge back rates are usually higher.

Say, for instance, that based on an average resource, you estimated a task at 40 hours. An expert might be able to complete this task in 20 hours, thereby getting the task done two or more days earlier. Now, in reality, you generally will have estimated that you'll get an average employee, and you got a novice, raising that estimate from 40 to 60 or higher.

Still, it is better to know this sooner rather than later. As noted earlier, getting all the bad news at once, and as early as possible, is better than being surprised.

UPDATE ESTIMATE TO COMPLETE

We've already mentioned that we need to regularly update the estimate to complete field. When we're looking for ways to get back on track, we examine the progress to date on tasks and see if any of what we have learned so far might speed up later work.

Say, for instance, that the project involves writing documentation on a variety of new products. When we created our initial estimates, we estimated each documentation task as 80 hours. But over the course of the project, we've refined what is needed in the documentation, determined the best way to write the documentation, and created a template to follow. This should enable us to write the documentation on the subsequent products in around 60 hours each.

Analyzing your project tasks this way may help you get your project back on track.

JUST A MINUTE

Keep in mind that although economies of scale and experience on earlier project tasks may help you reduce the estimate to complete on subsequent tasks, it is equally or even more likely that reviewing your estimates to complete will require you to increase them. Again, it is better to know that as soon as possible.

REVIEW PURCHASING SYSTEM ESTIMATES

Let's take a look at the purchasing system estimates and see if there are any tasks to expedite, skill levels to adjust, or estimates to complete to update. The estimates and schedule on the purchasing project look like this:

Task	Base. Dur.	Cur. Dur.	ETC	Start Date	End Date
1 *Installed Purchasing System*	59	79	204.00	4/10/02	7/31/02
1.1 Survey Potential Systems	2	1		4/10/02	4/10/02
1.2 Create Short List	1	1		4/15/02	4/15/02
1.3 PerformInvestigation	2	5	14.00	4/16/02	4/22/02
1.4 Develop Report		16	90.00	4/23/02	5/14/02
1.4.1 Interview Clients		5	18.00	4/23/02	4/29/02
1.4.2 Perform Site Visits		5	24.00	4/30/02	5/6/02
1.4.3 Perform In-House Tests		5	24.00	5/7/02	5/13/02
1.4.4 Write Report		1	24.00	5/14/02	5/14/02
1.5 Select System	1	1	2.00	5/15/02	5/15/02
1.6 Purchase System	30	30	2.00	5/16/02	6/27/02
1.7 Install System	4	4	8.00	6/28/02	7/3/02
1.8 Test System	10	10	80.00	7/5/02	7/18/02
1.9 Turn Over to Production	4	4	8.00	7/26/02	7/31/02
2 *Trained End Users*	15	15	196.00	7/5/02	7/25/02
2.1 Develop Training	13	13	100.00	7/5/02	7/23/02
2.2 Hold Classes	2	2	96.00	7/24/02	7/25/02

The first thing to look at is whether or not we can expedite any of the time-constrained tasks. You may recall that tasks 1.4.1 through 1.4.3 were given five workdays, even though the effort was less than that. We might be able to remove a day or two from these tasks. We'll look at the rest of the tasks first, though, before we change these. Task 1.6, Purchase System, and task 2.2, Hold Classes, are also time-constrained. While we might be able to shorten the class, two-day classes are generally intense already and shortening to one day might not be feasible. This leaves the Purchase System task.

PROCEED WITH CAUTION

If you are going to substitute products to reduce delivery schedules, make sure that the new product meets the project quality requirements and that you follow the project change control policy as discussed in Hour 5, "Developing Project Control Plans."

Now, when we originally created this task, we said it had to be 30 days long because that was the order time. But notice how those days were scheduled. What we intended to be 30 elapsed days was treated as 30 work days, adding 14 days to the schedule. We don't even have to try to get this shipped faster than 30 days; just adjusting the time-constraint to 22 workdays (the average number of workdays in a month) will bring the schedule in.

Because this is such a large change, we will not adjust any of the other time-constrained tasks at this point. We also don't have any estimate to complete adjustments to make at this time because the skill factors that were estimated are the skill factors of the resources we got, and there have not been any economies or lessons learned to take advantage of. The revised schedule is shown in the following figure.

JUST A MINUTE

Remember that not all time-constrained tasks can be shortened even with expediting, better equipment, prework, or substitution. Still, starting with time-constrained tasks can save you from juggling resources if the adjustments do work.

The revised purchasing schedule after the adjustments to the time-constrained tasks.

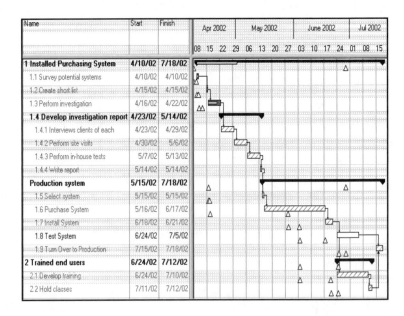

REVIEW AWARDS BANQUET ESTIMATES

The original target date for the awards banquet was July 1, so this project is running one week late (see the following figure). This project has four time-constrained tasks, and they are tasks 1.4, 1.8, 2.8, and 2.9. Note in the previous table that tasks 1.4 and 2.9 have a fixed duration of 15 days, task 1.8 a duration of 10, and task 2.8 a duration of 9 days.

Task	Base. Dur.	Cur. Dur.	ETC	Start Date	End Date
1 *Winners*	33	37	21.50	4/8/02	5/29/02
1.1 Create Team	1	2		4/8/02	4/9/02
1.2 Create Selection Process	3	6		4/12/02	4/19/02
1.3 Develop Nomination Forms	2	2		4/16/02	4/17/02
1.4 Gather Nominations	15	15	2.50	4/22/02	5/10/02
1.5 Evaluate Nominations	1	1	6.00	5/13/02	5/13/02
1.6 Select Winners	1	1	6.00	5/14/02	5/14/02
1.7 Announce Winners	1	1	6.00	5/15/02	5/15/02
1.8 Create Plaques	10	10	1.00	5/15/02	5/29/02
2 *Banquet*	37	37	92.00	5/15/02	7/8/02
2.1 Determine Potential Dates	1	1	2.00	5/15/02	5/15/02
2.2 Determine Potential Halls	1	1	20.00	5/16/02	5/16/02
2.3 Review Hall Menus	1	1	13.00	5/17/02	5/17/02
2.4 Create Short List	1	1	13.00	5/20/02	5/20/02
2.5 Dine at Each Hall	1	1	6.00	5/21/02	5/21/02
2.6 Select Hall	1	1	2.00	5/22/02	5/22/02
2.7 Announce Banquet	1	1	6.00	5/23/02	5/23/02
2.8 Send Invitations	9	9	2.00	5/23/02	6/5/02
2.9 Gather RSVPs	15	15	4.00	6/6/02	6/26/02
2.10 Finalize Arrangements	1	1	1.00	6/27/02	6/27/02
2.11 Choose Entertainment	2	2	10.00	5/17/02	5/20/02
2.12 Choose Speakers	2	2	13.00	5/20/02	5/21/02
2.14 Hold Dinner	1	1		7/8/02	7/8/02

But look at the dates in the schedule. Again, we meant these days to be elapsed, not to be work days. When we adjust these, the project is back on track, as shown in the accompanying figure.

The revised awards banquet schedule after updating the durations.

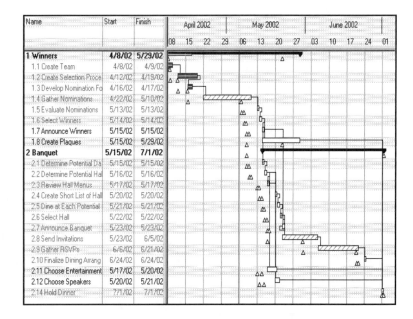

Name	Start	Finish
1 Winners	**4/8/02**	**5/29/02**
1.1 Create Team	4/8/02	4/9/02
1.2 Create Selection Proce	4/12/02	4/19/02
1.3 Develop Nomination Fo	4/16/02	4/17/02
1.4 Gather Nominations	4/22/02	5/10/02
1.5 Evaluate Nominations	5/13/02	5/13/02
1.6 Select Winners	5/14/02	5/14/02
1.7 Announce Winners	5/15/02	5/15/02
1.8 Create Plaques	5/15/02	5/29/02
2 Banquet	**5/15/02**	**7/1/02**
2.1 Determine Potential Da	5/15/02	5/15/02
2.2 Determine Potential Hal	5/16/02	5/16/02
2.3 Review Hall Menus	5/17/02	5/17/02
2.4 Create Short List of Hall	5/20/02	5/20/02
2.5 Dine at Each Potential	5/21/02	5/21/02
2.6 Select Hall	5/22/02	5/22/02
2.7 Announce Banquet	5/23/02	5/23/02
2.8 Send Invitations	5/23/02	6/5/02
2.9 Gather RSVPs	6/6/02	6/21/02
2.10 Finalize Dining Arrang	6/24/02	6/24/02
2.11 Choose Entertainment	5/17/02	5/20/02
2.12 Choose Speakers	5/20/02	5/21/02
2.14 Hold Dinner	7/1/02	7/1/02

REVIEW RESTORATION PROJECT ESTIMATES

Based on the information presented on the restoration project, review the estimates and determine if there are any opportunities to reduce the schedule by expediting dates. An answer is in Appendix A.

PROCEED WITH CAUTION

Remember that a success measurement is no causalities, so don't use overtime excessively or your team member may quit or revolt.

REVIEW AND CHANGE RESOURCES

The third technique for bringing projects back on track is to adjust the resources. The four resource-related techniques are described in the following sections.

ALLOW OVERTIME

If none of the other techniques have worked, the next thing to try is to allow resources to work overtime. Because the existing team is already familiar with the project work, overtime is the preferred way to get more resource time on the project. Sometimes just an hour a day for a week or a half-day on Saturday is enough to bring a project back on schedule.

Most resources understand the occasional need to catch up on work, but be careful not to ask for overtime on a regular basis. Not only does it increase the project cost if the resources get paid for overtime, but it may also lead to burnout, which, in turn, leads to a decrease in efficiency, defeating the purpose.

SWAP RESOURCES

Another resource-related technique is to swap the resource assignments to tasks. For instance, if resource A is assigned to task X and resource B is assigned to task Y, maybe assigning A to Y and B to X will improve the schedule. How could this happen? It may be that either A or B is over-allocated during the scheduling of one of their assigned tasks, and this is elongating the schedule. By swapping the task assignments you may be able to eliminate the over-allocation and reduce the schedule.

Be careful of two things when you swap resources like this, though. First, the two resources need to be equivalent or the estimates will need to change, and this might not help the schedule. Second, it is human nature to wonder what we've done wrong if someone changes an assignment on us. If A and B have already been told which task they will be working on, switching them later will make them wonder why. This may lead to decreased efficiency and effectiveness on the new assignment, again defeating the purpose of swapping them. Explaining the situation to them should help, but still be careful.

PROCEED WITH CAUTION

If you swap human resources on tasks, make sure that you reevaluate the estimate to complete. You need to consider each new resource's availability per day as well as his or her other commitments and skill level.

When cost is a concern and you are running over budget, but not necessarily over schedule, you may also want to use this swap resource technique. In the case of cost overruns, you would actually swap lower cost resources for tasks. These may be either people or materials. Remember that swapping either one may have a detrimental effect on the schedule even if it helps the budget.

PERFORM TEAM OR INDIVIDUAL DEVELOPMENT

Perhaps your project is running late because the team is not functioning as a team. If this is the case, you may want to do some team building activities. We discussed some of these in Hour 13, "Doing the Work." Once the team is functioning more smoothly, you may pick up some lost time. Even if you don't, though, you should not lose any additional time, at least for this reason.

It is also possible that the project is running late because one or more resources does not have the necessary skill to perform the tasks to which he or she is assigned. When this happens, you may need to get skill training for those resources. Generally, the cost of this training is not charged to the project, so it should not affect your project cost.

Once this training has taken place, your resource should be able to perform the assigned tasks more efficiently. While this may not get you back on track, you should not continue to lose time.

TIME SAVER

 Creating generic resources to use for "what-if" analysis will enable you to see if adding more resources will help your project. Make sure, though, that you change the generic resource assignments to real resources once you have decided on the new arrangements.

ADD MORE RESOURCES

The very last thing to try is to assign additional resources to your project. There are several reasons why adding more resources to a project is not always wise. First, any change to the team makeup requires the team to rebuild. This takes time away from actual project work. Second, an increase in team size means an increase in communications, which in turn raises the actual estimates on your tasks. Third, new resources need time to come up to speed. Even expert resources will function like novices until they are comfortable with your project and their tasks. Last, not all tasks can be divided. They need to be done by one individual. And even those that can be divided will start losing payoffs when you assign too many people to them.

Let's see how throwing more resources at a task might work. Say you have a 40-hour task that is divisible. With just one person working on that task eight hours per day, that task can get done in five days. Adding a second person to that task decreases the duration to 2.5 days. Adding a third person yields 1.67 days, a fourth yields 1.25 days, and a fifth yields one day. The table that follows summarizes this.

Estimate	Resources	Duration
40 hours	1	5
	2	2.5
	3	1.67
	4	1.25
	5	1

Now, even if these 40 hours remained constant as we divided the task, there is very little difference between the durations created with three, four, and five resources. They all yield roughly a day. It makes no sense to add the fourth and fifth resources.

JUST A MINUTE

Resist the temptation to assign more resources to your project. It generally does not pay.

Of course, the real problem is that dividing that 40-hour task in two doesn't yield two 20-hour tasks. Even if the resources have the same skill factors and part-time effects, communication alone raises these to 22-hour tasks. With three people, the tasks aren't 13.3 hours each, they are 16 each. With four people, rather than 10-hour tasks you have 14 each, and with five, the tasks are 12 hours each. This gives the durations shown here:

Estimate (Hours)	Resource	Duration (Days)
40	1	5
44	2	2.75
48	3	2
56	4	1.75
60	5	1.5

So, you can see that adding more people doesn't really help. In fact, there is very little difference between adding a second person and adding resources three through five. Remember this when you are tempted to add more people to the project to bring it back on track. Adding a second person to some tasks may be helpful, but rarely does it pay to add more than one.

PROCEED WITH CAUTION

Remember that not all tasks are divisible. You can't make a baby in just one month by assigning nine women to the task.

You may be able to add new resources to the project, not by dividing existing tasks, but by assigning the new resource to an existing task that had been assigned to someone else. This is akin to the swapping resources technique we noted earlier, and so all the pitfalls of doing that apply here as well. And the added complication is that a completely new person will take considerably longer on the task than will the existing resource. Make sure that you increase your estimates to complete to reflect this.

REVIEW PURCHASING SYSTEM RESOURCES

In the table that follows are the resource assignments and their estimates to complete per task:

Task	Resource	ETC
1.3 Perform Investig.	Analyst 1	5
	Analyst 2	3
	Analyst 3	6
1.4 Develop Report		
1.4.1 Interview Clients	Analyst 1, Analyst 2, Analyst 3	6
1.4.2 Perform Visits	Analyst 1, Analyst 2, Analyst 3	8
1.4.3 Perform Tests	Analyst 1, Analyst 2, Analyst 3	8
1.4.4 Write Report	Analyst 1, Analyst 2, Analyst 3	8
1.5 Select System	PM	2
1.6 Purchase System	PM	2
1.7 Install System	Programmer	8
1.8 Test System	Tester 1	80
1.9 Turn Over	Programmer	8
2 *Trained End Users*		
2.1 Develop Training	InstrDesigner	100
2.2 Hold Classes	PM	12
	Trainees	84

In this project, we do have two resource-constrained tasks of over 40 hours: task 1.8, Test System, assigned to a single tester and task 2.1, Develop Training, assigned to a single instructional designer. Task 2.1 has an estimate to complete of 100 hours and a duration of 13 days. Adding a second comparable designer to this task would shorten this task to 7 days.

 FYI An interesting discussion on how adding more resources to a late project usually makes the project later can be found in the classic book *The Mythical Man-Month* by Frederick Brooks. Originally released in 1975, the book was re-released in 1995 through Addison Wesley Longman.

REVIEW AWARDS BANQUET RESOURCES

The table that follows notes the resources assigned to the various awards tasks and the estimates to complete per resource per task.

Task	Resource	ETC
1 *Winners*		21.50
1.4 Gather Nominations	Admin.	2.50
1.5 Evaluate Nominations	PM, Team 1, Team 2, Team 3	6.00
1.6 Select Winners	PM, Team 1, Team 2, Team 3	6.00
1.7 Announce Winners	PM, Team 1, Team 2, Team 3	6.00
1.8 Create Plaques	Admin., Fixed	1.00
2 *Banquet*		92.00
2.1 Determine Dates	PM, Team 1, Team 2, Team 3	2.00
2.2 Determine Halls	PM, Team 1, Team 2, Team 3	20.00
2.3 Review Hall Menus	PM, Team 1, Team 2, Team 3	13.00
2.4 Create Short List	PM, Team 1, Team 2, Team 3	13.00
2.5 Dine at Each	Team 1, Team 2, Team 3, Fixed	6.00
2.6 Select Hall	PM, Team 1, Team 2, Team 3	2.00
2.7 Announce Banquet	PM, Team 1, Team 2, Team 3	6.00
2.8 Send Invitations	Admin., Fixed	2.00
2.9 Gather RSVPs	Admin.	4.00
2.10 Finalize Arrang.	Admin.	1.00
2.11 Choose Entertain.	PM, Team 1, Team 2, Team 3	10.00
2.12 Choose Speakers	PM, Team 1, Team 2, Team 3	13.00
2.14 Hold Dinner	Fixed	

It appears that at this point, nothing would be gained in adding overtime or additional resources or in swapping resources, providing training, or team development.

PROCEED WITH CAUTION

Don't use any of these tricks to artificially reduce the schedule. You'll be much worse off if a project looks on time and ends up late than you would be with renegotiating.

REVIEW RESTORATION PROJECT RESOURCES

Based on the exercises to date, evaluate whether or not any of your tasks might benefit from some changes in resources. An answer appears in Appendix A.

RENEGOTIATE TIME, COST, AND SCOPE

If none of the previous techniques work, then the only thing you can do is renegotiate. You may have to renegotiate an extended deadline, a higher budget, a reduced scope, or some combination of these. On a project at a major food-producing company, the project manager of a late project was allowed to add 10 resources to a project to try to bring it back on schedule. After performing the what-if analysis, though, the project manager found that these 10 resources would only save the project one day and cost an additional $60,000 dollars. The project manager then negotiated a reduction of project scope to get the project done on the original date.

When renegotiating, remember that any decrease in schedule that keeps scope constant will increase cost. Likewise, a reduction of cost with scope constant will generally increase the time. You and your project sponsor will have to decide which factors are the most critical and adjust the others accordingly.

JUST A MINUTE

When renegotiating time, cost, or scope, ask for enough of a change to be sure you can meet the renegotiated numbers. This saves you from having to renegotiate more than once.

HOUR 20

Reporting Project Performance

CHAPTER SUMMARY

LESSON PLAN:

In this hour you will learn about ...

- Creating status reports.
- Developing presentations.
- Writing newsletter articles.

You and your team are not the only ones who are concerned about how your project is going. One of the most critical aspects of project communications involves reporting on your project's performance. These reports help your management, your clients, and your sponsor to understand where the project stands and where it is going. In this hour, you'll learn what data to put in your reports and how to create them.

CREATE STATUS REPORTS

The most common performance report is a status report. The frequency, content, and format of these reports vary greatly from organization to organization, and yet all are designed to make sure everyone involved understands where the project is at any given point in time. The following sections discuss gathering status data and the various formats for status reports.

EVALUATE AUDIENCE

The first step in creating your status reports is to evaluate the audience. As we noted when we created the project communication plan, the different categories of stakeholders will have different needs for status data. In general, the less people are affected by the project, the less detail they will want in the report. So team members will want the highest detail, clients and sponsors less detail, and other stakeholders even less.

GO TO ▶
To review the previous discussions on project communications, see Hours 5, "Developing Project Control Plans," and 14, "Following Your Control Plans."

TIME SAVER

Creating team status reports online can make them easier for team members to create as well as easier for you and other team members to read.

You also want to evaluate the audience in terms of their interest in project status. Why is this important? Remember in Hour 5 when we discussed information-gathering and disclosing patterns? Blind and Closed communicators do not willingly gather information. If we want them to gather status data, we need to make it interesting and relevant to something of concern to them.

The final thing we need to evaluate about the audience is their technical level. People with the background in our project area, even though they may not want detail, will want some technical data in the status reports. It is okay, and often preferred, to use jargon with this group. They understand and expect it. People without the technical background, however, will need status expressed in lay terms.

JUST A MINUTE

If you have difficulty writing status reports or producing other project-related written material, you may want to read some business-writing books or take a business-writing course.

GATHER STATUS DATA

Once you have an understanding of the potential audiences for your status updates, you are ready to start gathering the data. There are three main ways to gather status data from the team. The first is to hold status meetings, the second is to use written or oral status reports, and the third is to use time sheets. Time sheets were discussed in Hour 15, "Tracking Your Progress," and provide you with the nuts and bolts on task dates, completion, and estimate to complete, but they don't provide you with any data on pending problems and the like. For this reason, most project managers require attendance at status meetings or written status reports in addition to the time sheets.

HOLD STATUS MEETINGS

The most common form of status-data gathering is done in status meetings. These meetings are generally held weekly and should include the entire project team. The meeting should be brief, that is, no more than half an hour, and each team member should have time to discuss the status of his or her tasks.

Often issues will surface in status meetings. If they can be handled in less than a few minutes, it is okay to do so, but if they can't be handled briefly, schedule a working meeting for later in the day or the next day. And then invite only the parties necessary to solve the issue. This keeps your status meetings short and to the point, encouraging the entire team to always come to the meeting and to participate.

JUST A MINUTE

If your project team members are not physically located near one another, holding a centrally located status meeting may be difficult. Teleconferencing and videoconferencing may be viable alternatives depending on your organization's conferencing capabilities.

As with all meetings, a scribe should take minutes from the status meeting. This should not be you. Your job is to direct the meeting and to understand what is being said.

During the status meeting, each resource should provide you and the group with the following information:

- Tasks started during the previous time period
- Tasks that were supposed to be started and were not, and why they were not
- Tasks completed during the previous time period
- Tasks that were supposed to be completed and were not, and why they were not
- Work to be started, continued, or completed in the next time period
- The amount of work and/or duration expected on the noncompleted tasks
- Any current problems or pending problems that need addressing

TIME SAVER

You should not take the meeting minutes for status meetings. It breaks your concentration and slows the meeting down. Appoint a team scribe to take all meeting minutes, or have the position rotate.

This data is usually presented by task. That is, you start by asking for information on a specific task and the appropriate resources answer whether or not the task has started, is completed, and so on.

Status meetings can also be used to disseminate status data. This is usually the case when you have a status meeting with the client or sponsor. Rather than asking for data, you explain the project progress to date. Remember when you are preparing for this type of meeting you need to consider the audience as noted. Using jargon with nontechnical people in meetings is just as detrimental as using it in written reports.

Regardless of whether the meeting is with your team or with the project sponsor or clients, you should provide each participant with a meeting agenda. An agenda for a team status meeting might look like this:

Purchasing Project Status Meeting, Monday, June 24, 2002

10:00 A.M., Main Conference Room

At this week's meeting we will discuss the progress on the following tasks.

Task	Resource	Scheduled Start	Scheduled Finish
1.7 Install System	Programmer	6/18/02	6/21/02
1.8 Test System	Tester1	6/24/02	7/5/02
1.9 Turn Over to Production	Programmer	7/15/02	7/18/02
2 *Trained End Users*		6/24/02	7/12/02
2.1 Develop Training	InstrDesigner	6/24/02	7/10/02

Please be prepared to discuss your tasks in less than five minutes each and in the order presented. Thanks!

You would want to then distribute this agenda on the Thursday or Friday prior to the Monday meeting. This gives people the time to prepare.

TIME SAVER

Rather than develop an agenda document for each status meeting, you may want to use the Gantt chart for status meetings. Most of the project management packages enable you to selectively code tasks, so you would highlight just the tasks to be discussed at the meeting. This not only saves you time, but also provides a visual focus for the meeting, which should also decrease meeting time.

CREATE TEAM STATUS REPORTS

Rather than hold weekly status meetings, some project managers prefer to have team members issue written status reports. These are then submitted to you by a deadline, usually noon on the Monday following the As-of date.

From these individual status reports, you would collate and summarize the data and create a team status report. Your summary report would then be distributed to each team member. There are two reasons for this. First, by reading the summary report, each team member can verify your understanding of the data he or she gave you. Equally important, the team members can see how the rest of the project is going. This is especially important if the team members are not in regular contact with one another.

Many organizations have a formal status-report structure, often dictated by their project management methodologies. Whether or not you have a predefined format to use, keep the following in mind to make your status reports more effective. These written status reports should not be extensive or time consuming to create, especially if you also have team members filling out time sheets. They do need to provide you with relevant data, though, especially any current problems or potential problems on the horizon. They can be hard copy, but more frequently today they are e-mailed or filled out online and posted to a status database.

Regardless of the media, written status reports need to provide you with the same data as a status meeting, noted earlier in this section.

JUST A MINUTE

If your team is geographically dispersed and cannot meet together regularly, using written status reports is a good way for you to make sure all the resources stay in the information loop.

A sample blank status report form is shown in the following figure.

An *example of a*
status report form.

LEETLE TOY COMPANY WEEKLY STATUS REPORT

Week Ending Date: _____

Name:	Project:

1. Tasks started this week:

2. Tasks scheduled to start that did not:

    Why did these tasks not start as schedule?

3. Tasks completed this week:

4. Tasks scheduled to complete that did not:

    Why did these tasks not finish as schedule?

5. Plans for next week:

6. Note the task id and new estimate for any tasks requiring changes to the effort estimate to complete or task duration:

7. Note any current or pending problems:

CREATE MANAGEMENT STATUS REPORTS

Management status reports may go to your supervisor, to the project sponsor, or to the steering committee; so, again, the first step is to analyze the audience for these reports. If you are reporting status to higher management and they are not familiar with the project or your jargon, you may need to summarize more.

The purpose of this type of status report is to document where the project stands at a given point in time, so you need to know the time frame on which you are reporting. You also need to know if the report is "to date" or "to date since last report."

In a "to date," or cumulative status report, you report on all the work completed, problems encountered, and other discoveries made throughout the life of the project. For a "to date since last report" status report, you document only information that has changed since your last report. To do this effectively, it's best to have your last report with you, too.

As with most reports, you'll write the first draft of your report, and then proof it and revise it. Once you've made your corrections, you may want to have someone proof it for you, and then correct any additional problems found.

Then you're ready to distribute the report to your audience. You may distribute in hard copy or use some kind of online system, such as Lotus Notes.

JUST A MINUTE

Because most of your status reports are generally written for someone intimately familiar with the project, such as your manager and/or your project team members, it is all right to use technical terms and jargon. These people want all the details, and they'll understand your jargon.

CREATE PURCHASING STATUS REPORTS

It is now June 24, 2002, and the purchasing system project is nearly complete. Here are the minutes of the June 24 status meeting:

Minutes of the Purchasing Project Status Meeting, Monday, June 24, 2002

10:00 A.M., Main Conference Room

Bob James reported that the new system was delivered late. It arrived on June 20 instead of June 17. It will take him two more days to install it.

Ami Nash reported that testing has not started yet because of the shipping delay. Based on the user documentation and the data passed on to her by the on-site reviewers, she has developed the test scripts and is ready to start her testing as soon as Bob is done.

Phil Duvall reported that although the system has not been installed yet, he has been able to review the product documentation and use that to create the tentative outline for the training program. He will continue to work on the course this week and is hopeful that the classes will still be able to be held on July 11 and 12 as currently scheduled.

Recorded by Ami Nash, 6/24/02

Use the minutes to write a brief status report for your boss, Al Bowlen. Presume that this is a weekly update from last week's report. A possible answer appears here:

MEMORANDUM

DATE: June 24, 2002

TO: Al Bowlen

FROM: Jack Dana

RE: Purchasing System Status

As of Friday, June 21, the purchasing system has arrived and is being installed. The installation is scheduled to be completed on June 26. The testing tasks and instructional design tasks have started earlier than scheduled, based on the extensive testing we were able to do during the selection process and the documentation included with the product. The training classes are still scheduled to be held on July 11 and 12.

If you have any questions, call me at 555-6321.

CREATE AWARDS STATUS REPORTS

It is June 24, 2002. The minutes from the weekly status meeting are shown as follows:

Minutes of the Awards Banquet Project Status Meeting, Monday, June 24, 2002

11:00 A.M., Main Conference Room

Sally Levine reported that the final count for the dinner is due at 5:00 today. The RSVP count so far is 213 attending and 36 not attending. That leaves only three invitations outstanding. Of these responses, 156 reserved the chicken selection, 150 the prime rib, and 7 the vegetarian. She will reserve the 213 dinners. She will also confirm the date and time with Dick Metz (Photography), the Side Street Four, and Dr. Phillip Jones.

Recorded by Sally Levine, 6/24/02

A copy of the project actuals to date and updated schedule are attached to the minutes and show that, although the effort was slightly higher than baseline, it did not delay the project.

Based on this data, write a cumulative status report to the Human Resources Manager sponsoring this project.

PROCEED WITH CAUTION

Your team members are not the only ones involved in the project who may be blind and closed communicators. If your boss, your sponsor, or other significant project stakeholder is a blind or closed communicator, written reports are not advised. You should communicate with these people in person to make sure they are getting your messages.

MEMORANDUM

DATE:	June 24, 2002
TO:	Stan Agant
FROM:	Jack Dana
RE:	Awards Banquet Status

A week from tonight, we will be hosting the Leetle Toy Company Awards Banquet. The project team has selected four worthy recipients and has planned an excellent evening for the 213 employees who plan on attending. The dinner will be proceeded by a magician and followed by the awards ceremony. After the ceremony, the classic rock band, the Side Street Four, will provide dance music.

I look forward to seeing you Monday. If you have any questions in the meantime, call me at 555-6321.

Note that this briefly summarizes the event and adds the latest information, which is the current RSVP count. If this cumulative report were going to someone not already intimately familiar with the project, more background information would be required.

CREATE RESTORATION STATUS REPORTS

It is June 24, 2002, and you have just completed a meeting with the architects. While there, you received this oral progress report:

"We have completed the drawings of the existing building and are wrapping up the plans for the restoration. We will have something for you to review early next week."

Based on this, write a cumulative status report for the preservation organization. An answer appears in Appendix A, "Sample Documents."

If you created a project logo or slogan, put this on your slide background. This will help your audience to identify your project in other media, too.

DEVELOP PRESENTATIONS

In addition to status meetings, you may have to do occasional project presentations. These are often done before steering committees, boards, or other groups of project stakeholders. This section explains some of the steps involved in creating status presentations.

- **Evaluate audience.** As always, start by evaluating the audience for your presentation. The more diverse the background of the audience members, the more general you will need to keep your presentation. If they have little inherent interest in your project, you will have to make your presentation entertaining as well as informative.

- **Design standard background.** To give your presentation a consistent look, you should design a standard background. Although the popular presentation software packages come with predefined backgrounds, taking the time to develop a custom background is worth it. Most people know and are tired of the backgrounds that ship with these packages. A customized look will help them pay attention as well as emphasize your project.

- **Design slide layouts.** After you have developed your standard background, you need to design the layouts for your slides. You will most likely need a title slide layout and a bullet list slide layout, but depending on your presentation content, you may need other layouts, too. These layouts will set your typefaces, sizes, and format, again, so that your presentation will be consistent.

You may have corporate standards that you must follow for presentations. That is, there may be standard backgrounds, fonts, logo sizes, colors, and screen layouts to use. Make sure you check on this before creating your first project presentation.

- **Create slides.** Before you start creating the actual content of your slides, it is helpful to think about how many slides you will need. On average, each slide takes two to five minutes to present. This means that in an hour-long presentation, you would have 12 to 30 slides. This gives you a ballpark number to shoot for and helps to evaluate the detail you have time to go into.

- **Practice presentation.** After you have developed your presentation, you need to practice delivering it. This will let you verify that your presentation won't exceed the time limit. It will also help you to polish the delivery and become familiar with the content and order of the slides.

You may find after practicing the presentation that you need to rearrange or remove some slides. Do so, and then practice the presentation again until your delivery is as smooth as possible.

CREATE PURCHASING PRESENTATIONS

There is a company meeting coming up on June 28, and your sponsor has asked you to give a 20-minute talk on the new purchasing system. He wants you to include a brief overview of the project purpose, the steps taken to date, the project status, and the future implementation dates. Design the presentation for this status update.

PROCEED WITH CAUTION

While the earned-value calculations are useful to you for evaluating status, most people do not understand them. Try to present your status information without using the earned-value fields, or at least not by name.

The audience is the entire company, so we know that only a few will know the history of the project and also that only a few will understand the technical terminology. We also know that most will want summary-level information, so we don't want to detail the process or the task start and finish dates or to give them any of the earned-value statistics.

We have only 20 minutes, and it is important not to exceed the allotted time. This means we will probably need 8 to 10 slides. While we won't design the entire presentation, let's sketch out the content of each slide. We'll start with a brief history of the project, review the selection process, and then discuss the upcoming training, implementation, and cut-over dates. Slides could be divided into two major categories. The titles, content, and timing might include the following:

1. Project Description
   - Business Need—From plan—1 minute
   - Project Goal—From plan—1 minute
   - Project Sponsor—From plan—1 minute
   - Project Approval—How handled and date—2 minutes
   - Project Team—From plan—2 minutes
   - Project Approach—From plan—2 minutes

2. Project Review
   - Start Date—From schedule—1 minute
   - Vendors Considered—From plan—2 minutes
   - Selection Process—From plan—2 minutes
   - Selected Vendor—From plan—1 minute
   - Current Status—From status—2 minutes
   - Implementation Schedule—From schedule—2 minutes

3. Questions?

TIME SAVER

If you are asked to give more than one presentation on your project, you may be able to use some of the slides in multiple versions of the presentation. This saves you from having to develop each presentation from scratch.

This arrangement would give us 13 slides, 12 providing information and the thirteenth asking for questions. The estimated total time is 19 minutes without the questions. If you wanted to minimize the number of slides, then business needs and goals and some of the other slides may be combined.

CREATE AWARDS PRESENTATIONS

For the awards banquet project, the senior executives presenting the awards will do the only presentation. You may be asked to help describe the project process but not to do the actual presentation.

CREATE RESTORATION PRESENTATIONS

The annual meeting of the preservation group that you are helping with the restoration is June 27. They have asked you to bring them up-to-date on the progress of the restoration. They are especially interested in when they can start using the facility but would also be interested in any unique aspects of the restoration to date.

Based on this and the other information presented so far, outline a presentation for the annual meeting. An answer appears in Appendix A.

WRITE NEWSLETTER ARTICLES

Another common method of disseminating project status to large groups of stakeholders is through newsletter articles. These may be done monthly or quarterly depending on the project duration and visibility. This section describes how to create effective newsletter articles.

JUST A MINUTE

Make sure that in considering your audience, you also evaluate the current impressions of your project. It may be that, in addition to presenting project status, you need to review some of the project benefits and business needs to help win positive opinions of the project.

EVALUATE AUDIENCE

As with meetings and presentations, the first step in writing an article is to evaluate the audience. Generally, the audience will have little knowledge of the project, little knowledge of project-related jargon, and little interest in the project. Your article will need to be brief yet informative and interesting.

FOLLOW NEWSLETTER STANDARDS

If your article will be in a corporate newsletter or in a trade association newsletter, it is likely that you will have to follow standards for length, format, or illustrations. You may also have to follow sentence length and reading level guidelines. If so, make sure that you get these early and follow them so that your article will be published.

DRAFT ARTICLE

Once you know about the intended audience and any standards you have to follow, review your project status reports and the project plan, and then develop the article. You may want to start with an outline and then write a draft. Review the draft and make corrections and then ask someone else to proof the article for you. This is part of the quality plan in the awards banquet project, but it is good practice anytime.

PUBLISH ARTICLE

When your article has been polished and proofed, it is ready to be published. An in-house newsletter or trade publication may ask you to proof *galleys* before the newsletter is printed and distributed to the rest of the organization.

STRICTLY DEFINED

Galleys are pre-print versions of a publication showing how the text and graphics will appear in the final copy.

CREATE PURCHASING ARTICLES

In addition to presenting at the company meeting, you have been asked to write a brief article for the company newsletter. This article should contain virtually the same information as the presentation. A possible version is shown as follows:

New Purchasing System Premiering Mid-July

In December of 2000, Harold Johnson, manager of the Purchasing Department, approached the steering committee about the possibility of replacing the purchasing system. His main concern was that the current system often causes a purchasing turnaround time of up to 10 days, yielding unnecessary inventory purchases.

In March 2001, the steering committee approved the investigation into and replacement of the existing purchasing system with one that could reduce purchase order turnaround to three days and would cut the purchase of excess inventory by 10 percent. They authorized the formation of a project team, which I head. We investigated more than 20 products on the market and prepared a short list of the top three packages that would meet our needs. We then researched each of these packages and chose Purchase Plus from BPS as the best package for our needs.

We are currently installing the package and developing an in-house training course for the purchasing employees. The training will take place in mid-July, and the new system will be up and running shortly after that.

If you would like any additional information on the project, give me a call.

If you are being asked to give multiple presentations and/or to write frequent articles discussing your project, you may need to delegate the creation of these. This will free up your time to concentrate on the delivery of the project. You will still want to carefully proof and approve of all presentations and articles, though.

CREATE AWARDS ARTICLES

We had two articles noted as deliverables in our project plan. The first article was to announce the winners, and the second was to announce the banquet. The banquet hall, Santonios, was selected on May 23, so the banquet can be announced in the June company newsletter. A possible article is shown as follows:

Awards Banquet Slated for Monday July 1

At 6:00 P.M. on July 1, 2002, we will be gathering at Santonios restaurant to celebrate the wonderful year we've had. We will be singling out and honoring four employees for their valiant efforts, but we will really be thanking every one of you for jobs well done.

You will be receiving personalized invitations shortly. Please plan on joining us for a fun-filled evening of magic, awards, song, and dance.

CREATE RESTORATION ARTICLES

The quarterly Leetle Toy Company newsletter would like for you to write a brief article on the progress of the restoration project you are managing. Because this is an employee newsletter, you'll want to mention the benefits to the company as well as to the preservation group. The article should run approximately 300 words. An answer appears in Appendix A.

PART V

Closing Out Your Project

Hour 21
Finishing the Work

Chapter Summary

LESSON PLAN:

In this hour you will learn about ...

- Following the completion plan.
- Closing project accounts.
- Celebrating achievements.

When your deliverables are complete, the project is nearly over, but there is still important work to be done to close the project. In this hour, you'll learn what to do to formally finish the project. Even if you did not write a completion plan and include it in your project plan, you should still follow the steps in this hour to complete your project.

Follow Completion Plan

In Hour 5, "Developing Project Control Plans," we discussed the project control plans. One of the most important ones for certain types of projects was the project completion control plan. If you wrote a completion control plan when you created your project plan, this is where you'll follow it. If not, you should still follow the steps explained in the sections in this hour.

Review and Update Completion Plan

About a week before you believe you will finish your project, you should review your completion plan. If anything has changed since you originally wrote the plan, then you need to update the plan and circulate the changes to the project sponsor and your team. This ensures that everyone understands the closeout processes that you intend to follow.

If you did not originally write a completion plan, you might want to write one now and circulate it to the appropriate stakeholders.

Verify Deliverables Are Complete

The first step in closing the project is to verify that you are, in fact, finished. You do this by reviewing your project deliverables, comparing them to the deliverables listed in your project plan, and making sure that each matches the quality and completeness requirements also noted in the plan.

If there are deliverables that are not yet complete, then you and your team need to go back and finish them. If you find any quality problems in the completed deliverables, then you need to go back and fix them.

It may take additional time and/or cost to finish the deliverables or to fix quality problems. Sometimes this is accounted for in your schedule as a separate task, or it may have been accounted for in the original estimates for the tasks associated with each deliverable.

Even if you did not allocate enough time or budget for this rework, you need to perform it. Why? Because you should not proceed to the next step unless your deliverables meet the appropriate quality and completeness measurements. Turning over substandard products is often worse than not delivering anything at all.

JUST A MINUTE

If a project product is being phased in at different locations or in different departments, you may turn over some deliverables earlier than others. In this case, the project would not be complete until the deliverables have been turned over to all areas.

Turn Over to Client

After you and your sponsor are satisfied that the deliverables are complete and that they meet the quality standards, you turn the products and/or services over to the client. In a software project, this is when the new software package goes "live," that is, when the users start to use it for production. In a training development project, this is where the pilot test has been completed and the training department starts offering the course on a regular basis. In a building project, this is where the client mortgages and moves in to the new or restored building.

Note that with service projects or with an event project, turnover is slightly different. You don't generally turn an event over to the client. You plan it and run it for them and present them with the results (income, evaluations, and so on) after the event has taken place. With services, you provide the service and present summaries of the results.

PROCEED WITH CAUTION

If the project involves a product that may require ongoing support, make sure that your completion plan notes how that support will be handled. This is especially important when other areas will be doing this ongoing work. Otherwise, you will be asked to continue supporting and maintaining your project product.

There may be times when the deliverables are complete but the client is not ready to accept them. Conflicts with other projects, vacations of key clients, and other events may cause this to happen. If this does occur, you simply wait to deliver the products/services until the client is ready to receive them. While this delays the project, turning products over when clients are not ready may negatively affect the long-term project success.

In very rare cases, the client may totally reject your project's products or services. Hopefully the quality, communication, and change control plans you used minimized the odds of a complete rejection of the product(s), but this could happen. Generally this happens because of major changes in corporate directions that have little to do with the quality of your product. Still, these changes affect your product's applicability to the new environment.

For instance, a major implementation of new accounting systems was canceled just prior to delivery because the company had been sold and the new parent company required completely different accounting software capabilities. While this is disappointing, to say the least, it is also reality.

CLOSE CONTRACTS

When a project has contracts, these need to be closed according to the terms in the contract. In general, the contract ends when the contractor has submitted a final invoice and you have paid it. But double-check your contract, or discuss this with your contracts department to verify how closing contracts works in your organization.

PROCEED WITH CAUTION

Although finishing a project early is generally a good thing, make sure to double-check your contracts. Some require you to pay full price even if the contract ends early.

Pay Final Invoices

Paying the final invoice is the last financial obligation in your project. Invoices need to be paid according to the schedule in your completion plan and in the contract. If invoices are paid later than the contract requires, your project may incur unnecessary additional charges. And some of these late payment charges can be high enough to send your project over budget at the last minute. This is one of the few additional costs we can avoid, making it important to do so.

Provide Warranty/Support

If your project product or service was something that might require warranty or support, you should have included a predefined warranty/support period in your completion plan. Warranty/support periods can range from a week to six months depending on the project.

The warranty portion of the agreement generally covers any quality-related problems with the project product. In a software project, for instance, it may include fixing minor bugs or making minor screen changes and the like. In a building project, it may be retaping the drywall seams that cracked on drying, tightening a loose plumbing fitting, and so on.

The support portion of the warranty/support agreement may include answering questions by phone for a week after implementation. It may also provide 30 days of on-site support to answer questions. If a project involves training, then the support may include additional training for new employees added after the initial project training. Note that the tricky part of this is that training may be provided as part of the support for only 30 days, and then the clients are on their own. This is tricky because they tend to forget this.

In rare circumstances, warranty/support may actually involve the removal of the product. With software projects, this may mean taking the new system out of production and returning to the old system. With building projects, this may mean moving back out of the building once the project is complete.

The project sponsor and clients need to understand and agree to the warranty/support provided. They need to know exactly what is included and what other things would be considered aspects of a new project or some other type of fee-based support. This is why the terms should be specified in the project plan right from the start of the project.

If warranty/support issues were not included in your initial plan, write them up and circulate them to the appropriate stakeholders. Then, preferably, have the stakeholders sign them and return them to you prior to the actual completion of the project.

JUST A MINUTE

Typical warranty/support periods run 30 days after the end of the project and cover minor changes/improvements in a product, telephone answers to brief questions, and the like. More extensive work generally requires new projects.

Use Purchasing Completion Plan

We did not include a completion plan for the purchasing project, so we will need to make sure we follow the steps listed earlier.

We need to start out with a review of our deliverables to make sure they are of quality and are complete. The seven intermediary deliverables were completed at the appropriate places earlier in the project, so we are concerned only with the final deliverables at this point. They were …

- The installed purchasing system.
- Trained end users.
- New purchasing process.

JUST A MINUTE

If your project products are being turned over in stages, you may want to create separate WBS tasks for the delivery of each stage. This way you'll be able to schedule and track each one separately right from the project start.

The purchasing system has been installed and tested, the users have been trained and the new purchasing process is in place, so all that remains is to turn the system over to production.

The purchasing department is ready to accept the deliverables, so we can go ahead and turn the system over to production. Once we do that, we will provide for 30 days warranty/support to answer questions and perform minor system changes. Because we contracted with the purchasing system vendor for this product, we most likely would not pay the final invoice until this warranty/support period was over and we were positive the system was working correctly in our environment.

Use Awards Completion Plan

The awards completion plan stated that …

> The project will be considered complete when all outstanding invoices have been received and paid, and the sponsor has written one last article on the banquet for the employee newsletter.

To follow this, you would make sure that all the vendors submit timely invoices so that they can be paid quickly, preferably within a month of the banquet. Then you need to make sure that the sponsor writes a final article in the company newsletter. If the sponsor needs help with the article, he may call upon you. This would be considered warranty/support service for this project. If group photographs were taken and need to be distributed to all employees, this might also fall under the warranty/support umbrella. If, however, this was going to take a significant amount of time, it may actually be added to the project as a closeout task.

Note that in this case, the deliverables are largely completed prior to the event and that the turnover to the client is done by holding the event. Conferences, retreats, weddings, and other event projects would work the same way.

Use Restoration Completion Plan

Review the restoration completion control plan and outline the specific steps you would take to follow the plan. If any of the steps previously discussed were not included in your completion plan, explain how you would handle each. An answer appears in Appendix A, "Sample Documents."

JUST A MINUTE

Projects run for trade organizations or other nonincorporated nonprofit groups may require their own bank accounts. When this is the case, make sure you close these bank accounts or it is likely that you will continue to be charged bank fees, adding unnecessarily to the project cost.

OBTAIN PROJECT SIGNOFF

Once the deliverables have been turned over and the warranty/support period is over, it is time to perform the administrative closeout steps. These include closing the project accounts, preparing the final actuals, and obtaining sponsor signoff. Each of these is discussed in more detail in the following sections.

CLOSE ACCOUNTS

After all the invoices are paid, you can close the project accounts. Accounts tracking fixed costs should be closed so that no checks can be cut against the project. The variable cost accounts should also be closed as soon as your resources are finished. This way they can't charge any more time to the project.

PREPARE FINAL ACTUALS

When the accounts have been closed, you know that no more costs or time can be charged to the project. This is the time to prepare a tally of the final actuals. Included in this would be the actual start and finish dates for the project, the actual duration and effort amounts, and the actual fixed and variable costs. This data should be stored in your project notebook because it will be needed for creating your final project report and for evaluating your project.

PROCEED WITH CAUTION

 If you are working with a project management software package and using it to track your project dates, you will not be able to account for the discrepancy in dates between turning deliverables over to the client and actual project closeout unless you have included project closeout tasks in your WBS. While some project managers express concern over these types of tasks appearing in a WBS, they have to be there if you are going to track them through the software package.

OBTAIN SIGNOFF

The last step in completing your project is to obtain project signoff. This is when the sponsor formally accepts the results of the project and signs a written document so stating. This document may be signed by routing the signature page, by meeting with the sponsor, or in a wrap-up lessons-learned session.

This signoff document should contain the following pieces of information:

- Project Name
- Project Completion Date
- Sponsor Name
- Project Manager Name
- Signature line for Sponsor
- Signature line for Project Manager
- Date line for Sponsor to date signature
- Date line for Project Manager to date signature

If project signoffs must go through a higher-level steering committee, this form will need to include appropriate signature and date blanks for each committee member, too.

Other pieces of information that might be convenient to list on this form include the following:

- Project goal
- Affected departments/clients
- Project final deliverables
- Project team members

These may help you to categorize the project later when you are looking for similar past projects to use as a basis for future ones.

Why do we need this final signoff document? Although it doesn't happen frequently, there will be times when, down the road, the client and/or sponsor may decide that the product you gave them was, in fact, not what they wanted. For example, perhaps you installed a new order entry system. The requirements were that the system be able to handle Web orders, phone-in orders, and mail-in orders with check or credit-card payments. Two months after the system is in, a walk-in customer wants to pay cash, and the system won't handle it. The department head complains. This is a valid complaint, but clearly this is something that should have been tested. Both parties are at fault for neglecting to do so.

JUST A MINUTE

In some organizations, the project signoff document must be signed before the project accounts can be closed. Make sure that you check and see whether or not this is the case in your organization.

In building projects, owners often change their mind on fixtures or other installed products or become dissatisfied with the quality of something that was supplied. Again, these may be valid complaints, but the time to fix these things is during the warranty/support period, not after the project has closed.

So, the sponsor's signature on this signoff document certifies that they did agree to, and accept, the deliverables at the project end (see the following example signoff). While this may not cancel the need to rework portions of the product, or even to start over from scratch, everyone knows that the product was appropriately approved of when implemented.

LEETLE TOY COMPANY PROJECT SIGNOFF SHEET

Project Name:	Project Manager:
Start Date:	Completion Date:
Project Duration:	Sponsor:
Project Goal:	
Project Deliverables:	
Team Members:	
Clients/Affected Departments:	
By signing this document I acknowledge that I have delivered all the stated deliverables at the agreed to quality levels	By signing this document I acknowledge that I have received all the stated deliverables at the agreed to quality levels.
Project Manager Signature:	Sponsor Signature:
Date:	Date:

An example of a blank signoff form that could be used in any of your projects.

You and your project sponsor should both sign the document. As with the other formal project documents, this project signoff document is filed in your project notebook.

CELEBRATE

An important component of each project is the end of the project celebration. This can be as simple as pizza and wings for the team or as lavish as a formal dinner dance for your team members and their significant others. The type of celebration tends to be linked to both the project duration and the project budget. That is, the longer a project and/or the more the project costs the organization, the more expensive the celebration tends to be. The simple lunch party is most common, and generally follows mid-sized projects. The lavish dinner party is more rare, generally following especially long, hard projects.

Regardless of the type of party, the celebration enables you to thank the team for their hard work. This provides an emotional closure for everyone. They can then move on with more vigor to the next project(s). And by keeping the cost to one tenth to two tenths of a percent of the project budget, few people would complain.

JUST A MINUTE

The entire project team, not just the core team, should be invited to the project celebration. This is especially important if some of the team members are off-site and don't always have the opportunity to meet face-to-face with the rest of the team.

OBTAIN PURCHASING PROJECT SIGNOFFS

After the purchasing system has been running for its 30-day period of warranty and support, it is time to close out the project. You would close the software account as a project account, but most likely would open it as some type of ongoing maintenance account, too, that will handle future upgrades to the product. The project signoff would be handled by the project sponsor and may also include the signoff of the purchasing manager as chief client. A sample of the signoff form for the purchasing project is shown in the following figure.

LEETLE TOY COMPANY PROJECT SIGNOFF SHEET

Project Name: Purchasing System Replacement	Project Manager: Jack Dana
Start Date: 04/10/02	Completion Date: 08/19/02
Project Duration: 92 Workdays	Sponsor: Alan McNichol, VP Finance
Project Goal: To provide a new purchasing system for the company which will reduce purchase order turnaround to three days and will cut the purchase of excess inventory by ten percent.	
Project Deliverables: O The installed purchasing system O Trained end users O New purchasing process	
Team Members: Bob James, Ami Nash, Phil Duvall, Cindy Johnson, Jack Andrews, Joe Allen	
Clients/Affected Departments: Primarily Purchasing, but all departments that use the purchasing system	
By signing this document I acknowledge that I have delivered all the stated deliverables at the agreed to quality levels	By signing this document I acknowledge that I have received all the stated deliverables at the agreed to quality levels.
Project Manager Signature: Jack Dana	Sponsor Signature: Alan McNichol
Date: 8/22/02	Date: 8/22/02

An example of an executed signoff form for the purchasing software project.

JUST A MINUTE

The cost of the project party may come from the project budget or may come from a department's operating budget. Make sure you know what your organization's policy is for project celebration expenditures.

The final actuals for the project are noted as follows and would be stored in your project notebook.

Task	Actual Effort	Actual Cost	Actual Start	Actual Finish
1 Installed System	234	$7,488	4/16/02	8/19/02
1.1 Survey Potential	12	$384	4/10/02	4/10/02
1.2 Create Short List	6	$192	4/15/02	4/15/02
1.3 Perform Investig.	39	$1,248	4/16/02	4/22/02

continues

continued

Task	Actual Effort	Actual Cost	Actual Start	Actual Finish
1.4 Develop Report	102	$3,264	4/23/02	5/15/02
1.4.1 Interview Clients	23	$736	4/23/02	4/29/02
1.4.2 Perform Visits	24	$768	4/30/02	5/6/02
1.4.3 Perform Tests	27	$864	5/7/02	5/13/02
1.4.4 Write Report	28	$896	5/14/02	5/15/02
1.5 Select System	2	$64	5/15/02	5/15/02
1.6 Purchase System	2	$64	5/16/02	6/17/02
1.7 Install System	10	$320	6/18/02	6/24/02
1.8 Test System	74	$2,368	6/24/02	7/5/02
1.9 Turn Over	5	$160	7/15/02	7/18/02
1.10 Provide Warranty(s)			7/19/02	8/19/02
2 *Trained End Users*	181	$4,784	6/24/02	7/12/02
2.1 Develop Training	85	$2,720	6/24/02	7/10/02
2.2 Hold Classes	96	$2,064	7/11/02	7/12/02

OBTAIN AWARDS BANQUET SIGNOFFS

After the banquet has been held and all the outstanding invoices have been paid, it is time to perform the three final closeout steps for the awards banquet project. You would close the accounts, obtain signoff, and develop the actual times and costs.

PROCEED WITH CAUTION

If the cost of the project celebration is coming out of the project budget, you must pay for the celebration before you can close the project accounts.

The final actuals for the awards banquet project are shown as follows:

Task	Actual Effort	Actual Cost	Actual Start	Actual Finish
1 *Winners*	95	$3,440	4/8/02	5/29/02
1.1 Create Team	9	$288	4/8/02	4/9/02
1.2 Create Process	35	$1,120	4/12/02	4/19/02
1.3 Develop Forms	28	$896	4/16/02	4/17/02

Task	Actual Effort	Actual Cost	Actual Start	Actual Finish
1.4 Gather Nominations	6	$192	4/22/02	5/10/02
1.5 Evaluate Nominations	12	$384	5/13/02	5/13/02
1.6 Select Winners	2	$64	5/14/02	5/14/02
1.7 Announce Winners	1	$32	5/15/02	5/15/02
1.8 Create Plaques	2	$464	5/15/02	5/29/02
2 Banquet	56.50	$10,198	5/15/02	7/2/02
2.1 Determine Dates	2	$64	5/15/02	5/15/02
2.2 Determine Halls	9	$288	5/16/02	5/16/02
2.3 Review Hall Menus	4	$128	5/17/02	5/17/02
2.4 Create Short List	4	$128	5/20/02	5/20/02
2.5 Dine at Each Hall	7.50	$490	5/21/02	5/21/02
2.6 Select Hall	1	$32	5/22/02	5/22/02
2.7 Announce Banquet	1	$32	5/23/02	5/23/02
2.8 Send Invitations	4	$578	5/23/02	6/5/02
2.9 Gather RSVPs	5	$160	6/6/02	6/21/02
2.10 Finalize Dining	1	$32	6/24/02	6/24/02
2.11 Pick Entertainment	10	$520	5/17/02	5/20/02
2.12 Choose Speakers	8	$756	5/20/02	5/21/02
2.14 Hold Dinner		$6,990	7/1/02	7/2/02

Note that you wouldn't really need a signoff form for this type of project. The product was a one-time event and is unlikely to cause recurring problems even if the event itself did not go well. Still, it is best to follow the same procedures for all your projects, regardless of the product(s) of that project. This means that for even these types of projects, you should obtain the appropriate formal signoff.

OBTAIN RESTORATION PROJECT SIGNOFFS

Performing these three steps in the restoration project indicates that the project is officially over. Several parties are involved in approving the completion of the restoration project. Determine what data should appear on the restoration signoff document, who should sign the document, and how the signatures would best be gathered.

The restoration project made use of project accounts, Leetle Toy Company accounts, and preservation organization accounts. Determine what accounts would be closed and what actual data should be recorded after the signoff documents have been signed.

The restoration project celebration can be held with just the project team and/or with the preservation group. Determine the venue for the project party and for the larger preservation group party.

An answer is included in Appendix A.

TIME SAVER

You can often save time by combining the project signoff and celebration with the lessons-learned session discussed in Hour 22, "Evaluating Your Project."

Hour 22

Evaluating Your Project

Chapter Summary

LESSON PLAN:

In this hour, you will learn about ...

- Conducting project surveys.
- Performing a lessons-learned session.
- Writing a project summary report.

Wrapping up one project generally leaves you champing at the bit for the next. But before you move on, you should take the time to evaluate this project to see how you might improve subsequent ones. This gives closure to this project and, more important, provides you with valuable lessons for the next project. In this hour, you'll learn what aspects to evaluate and how to document the evaluation for future reference.

Conduct Project Surveys

Now that your project is finished, you want to take some time to evaluate how it went. While you'll already know how you did in terms of cost and time, measuring quality and customer satisfaction is important, too. It is also a good idea to understand how the process worked, from both the client and team perspectives. You can evaluate these aspects by conducting project surveys.

Conduct Client Surveys

You can measure customer satisfaction by surveying the clients. On some projects, you may even do multiple surveys, one approximately two weeks after the project is finished and then another six months after project completion.

Product surveys are different than project surveys and are usually done immediately after the product has been delivered or the service was provided. Product surveys may also have follow-ups six weeks after the end of the project.

Client surveys can be performed in two ways. First, you can conduct interviews with selected clients. This is generally preferred, if feasible. It gives you the face-to-face contact with the client, and it also opens the door for true dialogue about both the project and the product produced.

If you believe that the clients will answer your questions honestly in a group environment, you can save time by conducting the interviews with multiple clients in the same meeting.

Some questions to ask include the following:

- What were your expectations for this project?
- Were these project expectations met? If not, why not?
- Was project information communicated to you in a timely manner? If not, why not?
- Were project-related meetings you attended a valuable use of your time? If not, why not?
- What did you see as the project manager's role in this project?
- Was he or she effective in this role? If not, why not?
- Are you satisfied with the end product(s) of this project? If not, why not?
- Do you believe this project was successful? Why or why not?
- Do you have any other project-related comments you'd like to share? If so, what are they?

It may be possible to perform multiple survey interviews at one time by holding a meeting with several clients. This will save you interview time. The drawback, however, is that many people clam up in a group environment and may be unwilling to give you the type of feedback you need. It may also be difficult for you to track who is saying what, and often the individual perspectives are as important as the data. Last, meetings with multiple clients just don't have the same personal follow-up feel that may help you build better long-term relationships with these clients.

If conducting client interviews is not realistic, though, you can send written survey forms. These are generally not as effective as the interviews for several reasons. First, it is hard to design a good written survey instrument. The questions listed previously can lead to additional follow-up questions when you are talking with the client, but when you are creating a written instrument, you need to anticipate answers and provide alternative questions. You also need to be careful with the phrasing of the questions. In an interview, you can explain a question if the client misunderstands it, but in a written survey, you do not get this second chance.

PROCEED WITH CAUTION

 Although using client interviews is the best way to gather information, some methodologies may require written surveys. They may even prescribe the actual survey document. Make sure you check to see whether or not your methodology includes guidelines for surveys. If it does, you'll need to follow them.

Written surveys may also be ineffective because it is hard to get honest written responses. In a meeting a person can comment "off the record," but a written response is always on the record. Your most valuable input is often that given "off the record."

Third, collecting and analyzing the data is more complicated. You have to read through each form and interpret what someone meant by every comment. In an interview, if you don't understand an answer, you can simply ask for clarification. Then you note the answer in your own words.

Still, at least on long term and/or high visibility projects, you should attempt to do some type of follow-up with the client, even if it is a written survey. The questions previously noted can provide the basis for a written survey, too.

Conduct Team Surveys

It is also important to understand how the team felt about the project, especially when you will be working with specific team members again on future projects. Because you are concerned at this point with evaluating the process, the questions to ask the team members are virtually the same as those you ask the clients. Refer to the previous section for those questions.

JUST A MINUTE

Although client surveys are generally done in interviews, team surveys are most often conducted with written surveys. Team members know one another and the project manager well enough to be brutally honest, even in writing.

Some additional team-specific questions you may want to ask include the following:

- Was the deliverable of each work package clear? If not, what could be done to improve clarity on subsequent projects?
- Did the project manager pay an appropriate amount of attention to the progress of your work? Not enough? Too much? What makes you say this?
- Was the administrative overhead required of you (time sheets, status reports, and so on) appropriate for the project?
- Did the project manager appropriately involve you in the project plan development process? If not, what makes you say this?

Team surveys are usually written and are generally distributed and collected prior to the lessons-learned session. This is so that they can be incorporated into the lessons to be discussed in that session.

Conduct Purchasing Surveys

The client surveys would be conducted as interviews with the purchasing manager and most likely two or so of the seven clerks trained on the system. Team surveys would be distributed to and collected from all three analysts, the systems programmer, the tester, and the instructional designer. Although a vendor, not a client or true team member, you may also want to interview the primary vendor contact on the selected system. This may help you deal more effectively with other vendors and their representatives on future projects.

Conduct Awards Surveys

Because the client for this project is the company itself, with all the employees as stakeholders, conducting the follow-up surveys for this project will be different than it was with the purchasing project. You would conduct product surveys the night of the banquet, and the project client survey would be conducted with the Vice President of Human Resources, the project sponsor.

Team surveys would go to the entire team, including the administrative assistant and each of the members of the selection committee. As noted on the purchasing system, it may also be helpful to conduct a brief interview with the banquet manager at the selected hall, as well as with the magician, the band leader, and the photographer, to get the vender perspective on the project.

CONDUCT RESTORATION SURVEYS

Based on the information given to date, determine whom you would include in client and team surveys and how each of these surveys would be conducted. An answer appears in Appendix A, "Sample Documents."

PERFORM A LESSONS-LEARNED SESSION

Another project evaluation technique is the *lessons-learned session*. In this session you and your team document what went well on the project, what has room for improvement, and what affected your project that was out of your control. The primary reason for conducting a lessons-learned session is to be able to improve the next project. The secondary purpose, though, is to debrief the last project and prepare to move on to the next one. In this regard, lessons-learned sessions are very much like the project celebrations. And in fact, some organizations combine the two. They hold a two-hour meeting where the first hour of the meeting is devoted to the celebration and then the second to the lessons learned.

STRICTLY DEFINED

A **lessons-learned session** is a post-project meeting with the entire team to review various aspects of the recently completed project. The purpose of this meeting is to document lessons so that subsequent projects can benefit from that knowledge. This meeting may also be called a "project-review meeting."

The lessons-learned meeting should include the entire team, including contractors and team members who work off site. Because these last two types of team members often have unique project-related problems, it is important to get their input. As with the celebration, it also gives them the opportunity to see the rest of the team.

In some organizations, this session also includes the client and/or the sponsor. The good thing about this is that the sponsor can come and officially close the project by signing the closing document. The drawback, though, is that the team may be less likely to discuss the things that did not go well in front of him or her. You will know your team and sponsor well enough by this time to judge whether or not this would be the case.

A popular format for discussing and documenting project lessons learned is to create a matrix of characteristics that fall under the headings of "Good, Bad, and Ugly." Some organizations prefer not to use these terms for headings, however, so be sure to follow whatever standards have been established in your organization.

The actual lessons-learned debriefing is performed this way. A scribe is appointed to write the comments on a white board, flip-chart, or overhead so that all the participants can see what is recorded. Each team member is asked to name something that went well in the project. These are recorded in the list. If there are duplicates, this is noted by placing tick marks next to those that are repeated.

For instance, if someone says they liked that the status meetings stuck to the appropriate agenda, and three more people agree, this item would have three tick marks indicating that it was mentioned four times. Other types of things that may go into the good column include relationships with clients, relationships within the team, and quality of deliverables.

After the team members have posted everything that they thought was good and given themselves a virtual pat on the back, then it's time to look at things that could be improved. Now, the funny thing about this part is that you may get some people to list an item here that others listed in the good column. When this happens, it is important to get their reasons for thinking it was bad, not good.

GO TO ▶
Additional information on evaluating the trends in your lessons learned and on how to improve future projects is provided in Hour 23, "Applying Your Lessons Learned."

Some examples of things that show up on the bad or "needs improvement" list include estimates to complete, modeling of the dependency relationships, availability of key resources, and team communications. Obviously, these vary from project to project.

You continue to list the things that can be improved until everyone is satisfied that the list is complete. Hopefully this list is shorter than the good list, but unfortunately, that is not always the case.

The last things to list are the problems that plagued your project that were out of your control. You may never have one of these to list, but is more likely that once in a while you will have at least one thing to list here. Some possibilities in this category include a natural disaster, illness of a major project member, a budget cut, a resources cut, and a vendor going out of business. The company being sold, which terminated the project noted in Hour 21, "Finishing the Work," would also fall in this category.

If this is your first project using this particular lessons-learned method, this is where you would stop the listing process. If, however, you have performed at least one other project, then the next step is to pull out the list of items from the last lessons-learned session and compare them.

You start the comparison with the current list of good items. Looking at the first item in this list, you would see where this item fell on the last list. If an item is good on this list and was good on the previous list, then you can pat yourselves on the back again because this item was good twice in a row. If the item was in the "needs-improvement" list last time, this is even better. It shows that you have improved from the last project.

You do this review for each item in the current good list and mark the item with either a "g" or a "b" for "good" or "bad" (or a "w" or "n" for "went well" and "needs improvement") to show which list it was in the last time. If an item did not appear at all on the previous list, you would not make any notations.

After you have gone through the items in the good list, you move on to the "needs-improvement" list, and you repeat the process. For every item in the "needs-improvement" list, you note which list it was in the last time. If it was in the "needs-improvement" list last time and this time, then you have a pattern developing. You will need to analyze it and see what might be the underlying cause of the problem. Specifics on this evaluation of lessons learned are covered in Hour 23.

TIME SAVER

If you have a computer and projector available in your meeting room, your lessons-learned comments can be directly recorded into the computer. This saves time and errors when transcribing them later.

If an item on the bad list in the current project was on the good list of the last project, then you may have an even greater problem. What happened to cause this item to go from good to bad? Often it has something to do with key resources leaving the project, but there are other things that can cause an item to switch to the needs-improvement list, too. You'll need to explore this so that it can move back to the good list on the next project.

GO TO ▶
To review how to create a risk management plan, go to Hour 12, "Facing Project Risk."

Now, what about those items, if any, in the out-of-your-control list? Hopefully they will never show up again in subsequent projects, but you can't guarantee this. For this reason, any items in this list should be added to the risk-management plan for subsequent projects. The odds are low that the event will occur again, but you'll feel very silly if it does and you hadn't developed a contingency plan for it the next time. The little effort it takes to create the contingency plan is worth it.

CONDUCT PURCHASING LESSONS LEARNED

Let's see how this might work with the purchasing project. The items that went well were …

- The product investigations went smoothly.
- The client site visits were worthwhile.
- The on-site test of the selected system was invaluable.
- It took less time to test the system than expected.
- It took less time to develop the training than expected.
- The systems programmer was available when needed.
- There were only minor problems during the warranty/support period.
- The training classes went smoothly.
- The client is happy with the new system.

Now let's look at the things that need improvement:

- Several tasks were left out of the original WBS.
- There was no baseline estimate for the actual holding of the training classes.
- Not including the system, costs were 50 percent higher than expected.
- The project duration was three weeks longer than expected.

Luckily, there were no events that affected the project that were out of your control.

CONDUCT AWARDS LESSONS LEARNED

Based on the actual data presented so far for the awards banquet project, list the lessons-learned items. The things that went well include …

- The project was delivered under budget.
- The project was delivered on time.
- The volunteer photographer was good.
- The magician selected was good.
- The band selected was good.
- The food was good.

And under needs improvement ...

- More people attended than anticipated.
- More awards were given than originally anticipated.

PROCEED WITH CAUTION

If team members are likely to turn the lessons-learned session into a finger-pointing session, have them create individual lists of items in each category and forward them to you. Then take these lists and compile them into a master list that is presented at the meeting. This should depersonalize many of the comments and enable you all to discuss the issues more rationally.

Conduct Restoration Lessons Learned

Based on the actuals given in the last answer and the other known facts of the restoration project, create the item lists for the lessons-learned session. An answer is given in Appendix A.

Write Project Summary Report

Most organizations require a final status report that summarizes the entire project. Even if your company doesn't require a summary report, it's a good idea to create one for the following reasons: It provides you and other project managers with a convenient overview of the project; it forces you to perform a final project analysis; and, it can be a terrific sales tool for future projects.

These reports don't have to be long. For medium-duration projects, three to five pages is often enough to cover everything you need to cover. Let's take a look at what should go into the summary report.

WRITE PROJECT OVERVIEW

There are two detail sections in a project summary report. The first section explains the background of the project and can be thought of as the project overview. It includes a history of the project, the start and end dates, goals, deliverables, team members, sponsor, and major departments involved. This information is generally presented in a paragraph, not a table format.

Think of this section as a condensed version of your project plan formatted slightly differently and with a different purpose. The plan was written to specify the details for project approval and evaluation guidelines, whereas this is designed to recap why and how the project was done.

This data is also similar to the data you may have included on your signoff form. If so, you can use that as a source document.

WRITE PROJECT ANALYSIS

The other detail section in your project summary report is the project analysis section. This section compares the project baselines to actuals, explains the differences, and summarizes the lessons learned. It is also generally in paragraph format, although the data may be presented in a final table or Gantt chart.

TIME SAVER

If you take extra time writing the introductory paragraphs in your overview and analysis sections, you'll find that you can also use them in the executive summary nearly verbatim. This is okay to do because the target audience for each section is generally different. Even when people read both portions, they usually don't mind the redundancy.

WRITE EXECUTIVE SUMMARY

If your report is five pages or more in length, it is customary to include an executive summary at the front. Although the executive summary will be placed first in your summary report, it should be the last thing you write. This brief section (about one to two pages) covers the project overview and analysis at a very high level. It presents the project in a nutshell version that is useful to you in refreshing your memory of the project in the future, but it is also valuable for the project sponsor and other project managers who don't need detailed information.

PROCEED WITH CAUTION

In some organizations, conducting the lessons-learned session, performing the satisfaction surveys, and writing the project summary report are considered part of the project. If this is the case, then the project accounts are not closed until all three of these activities are complete.

WRITE PURCHASING SUMMARY REPORT

The summary report for the purchasing project should recap the salient points of the project as noted. Because this was a short duration project, the summary report would probably only be one to two pages. When summary reports are that brief, there is no point including an executive summary.

Here is a portion of the project summary report:

PROJECT SUMMARY REPORT
NEW PURCHASING SYSTEM PROJECT
Jack Dana, Project Manager

The new purchasing system project was first conceived in late 2001. The existing system had a turnaround time of up to 10 days and often caused unnecessary inventory purchases. Harold Johnson, manager of the Purchasing Department, believed that a new system could reduce purchase-order turnaround to three days and reduce the purchase of excess inventory by 10 percent. This became the goal of the project.

The project started on April 10, 2002, and completed on August 19, 2002. This spanned 92 workdays. During this time we investigated the more than 20 products on the market and prepared a short list of the top three packages that would meet our needs. We then performed detailed research on each of these packages and chose Purchase Plus from BPS as the best package for our needs.

We also installed and tested the product and developed training for the system. The training was held on July 11 and 12 for seven members of the purchasing department. The system was turned over to production on July 18 and was followed by a relatively uneventful 30-day warranty/support period.

...

The rest of the report would cover the deliverables and lessons learned and wrap up with a review of the baseline versus actual information.

The project summary report is your last chance to toot your own horn (and your team's), so rather than just produce reports of dry facts, enliven them with good writing.

Write Awards Summary Report

We are also ready to write a summary report for the awards project. It will be even shorter than the purchasing report, so again, no executive summary is needed. For simplicity, let's look at the analysis section of this report.

PROJECT SUMMARY REPORT
AWARDS BANQUET PROJECT
Jack Dana, Project Manager

The awards banquet project ...

The project was scheduled to start on April 8, 2002, and complete with the holding of the banquet on July 1, 2002. These ended up being the actual start and finish dates, too.

The baseline budget for the project was $14,792 and the actual cost was $13,638, so the project came in under budget. Most of the reduction in cost was due to hiring a band and magician rather than a band and keynote speaker.

Both the Leetle Toy Company management and the employees were satisfied with the banquet itself, although the management will be doing a six-month follow-up to see if achievements have remained high. The results of this survey will be appended to this document at that time.

Attached is a table listing the baseline start, baseline finish, baseline effort, and baseline cost columns as well as the actual start, actual finish, actual effort, and actual cost columns.

Note that this project finished both on time and under budget. Don't feel bad, though, if some of your projects don't. Remember that meeting requirements, having satisfied customers, and having no casualties are also measures of success and may be more important in the long run than the first two.

Note, too, that we included the mention of a follow-up survey. This is good to note for your own information and also for others who may be reading the document months after the project completes.

If your organization is a vendor of project-driven services or products, project summary reports can be wonderful sales tools. They demonstrate not only the variety of projects you have completed, but also document your project methodology and demonstrate your capabilities.

WRITE RESTORATION SUMMARY REPORT

You are ready to wrap up the restoration project. Based on the data presented, write the restoration project summary report. Remember that there are really several audiences for this report: the Leetle Toy Company executives and employees and the Board of the preservation group and all its members. Although the previous projects just listed what to cover, write a complete summary report for the restoration project. An answer appears in Appendix A.

Hour 23
Applying Your Lessons Learned

Chapter Summary

LESSON PLAN:

In this hour you will learn about ...

- Reviewing previous lessons for trends.
- Adjusting future projects.
- Archiving your project notebook.

One of the two reasons for tracking projects is to get better at managing the next one. But to do this, we also need to evaluate the data and apply what we've learned. In this hour, you'll learn what patterns to look for in your data and how to use this to improve your next project.

Review Previous Lessons for Trends

When we documented the lessons learned in Hour 22, "Evaluating Your Project," we noted that it was important to not just write down the current lessons but to see where the items fell on previous lists. This enables us to recognize patterns and, hopefully, to identify remedies for the aspects that need improving. The following sections describe specific deficiencies to look for.

Evaluate Individual Deficiencies

More often than not, many of the problems we note in our projects come from individual skill deficiencies. The project manager may need more project management training, the senior engineer may need to work on her communication skills, or the mechanic may need to understand newer machine techniques.

We can identify these deficiencies by analyzing both the lessons learned and our baseline versus actual numbers. Say that we have a plumber with baseline effort estimates on a task of 20 hours and actual hours of 32. Although this represents actuals that are 60 percent higher than the estimate, this happens on occasion. But let's also say that on the next project, the same plumber, had estimated hours of 25 and actual hours of 45. The actuals in this case are 80 percent higher than the estimates.

JUST A MINUTE

Note that although this lesson focuses on understanding project problems and fixing them in the future, there will be times when you'll want to analyze your lessons learned to duplicate the good outcomes. The process is the same. Uncover the pattern, but repeat it rather than eliminate it.

Something is wrong here, but what? It could be one of at least three things. First, it might be that this plumber is a novice plumber, and we were estimating for an average or skilled plumber. In that case, the deficiency is in the estimator, who needs to estimate more correctly next time.

But this discrepancy may also be in the metrics database, a second possibility. This plumber may be average, and historically, the database may say that 20 hours is average for the type of task in the first project. On researching further, though, you may find that every person who has reported actuals on the task prior to now was an expert. So what you thought was average was really expert, and again, the estimates need to be adjusted next time.

PROCEED WITH CAUTION

Be careful when assigning team members to training. Many see training as punishment not as enrichment. This is especially true if, to improve the skills of one team member, you decide to bring a class in-house and send the entire team. It is doubtful that this training session will improve anyone's skills and will most likely cause resentment. Sending the needy person to an outside class is much more productive.

The last possibility is that the plumber is an average plumber on most tasks, but on this particular type of task, she is a novice. So, before you assign this particular plumber to another similar task, you should provide her with additional training.

You would analyze all the discrepancies this way.

Evaluate Process Deficiencies

Sometimes the problems in a project were not in the resources but in the project process. One example would be that tasks have not been tracked accurately enough to supply reliable metrics. Large discrepancies between estimates and actuals may point to this. In fact, this could be another problem with the plumber situation noted previously. The only way to fix this is to be more diligent in tracking, which may take three to five projects before the metrics become reliable.

You may also find that communication channels were improperly identified. Either a key stakeholder was missed and hence was not communicated with, or the type of communications with a specific stakeholder group may have been misjudged. Pointers to this type of problem might be requirements-gathering tasks taking longer than they should, deliverables having to be completely reworked, and the like. To fix this, you would need to be more careful in identifying stakeholders and in writing the communication plan.

Slow authorizations or other operational procedures may cause unexpected delays in a project, too. You would notice these in repeatedly missed milestones for go/no go decisions, purchases and deliveries consistently over schedule, and the like. To account for this in subsequent projects, you would either need to ensure that the procedures are more timely or to increase your estimates on these types of tasks to better reflect the reality.

JUST A MINUTE

If your organization has a project management office, there may be an online database for sharing lessons learned across the company. Make sure that you post your lessons there and also review other project managers' lessons to see if anything is applicable to your projects.

REVIEW PURCHASING LESSONS

Let's look now at the lessons learned from the purchasing project and see what might have caused these situations. The lessons noted were as follows:

- Several tasks were left out of the original WBS.
- There was no baseline estimate for the actual holding of the training classes.
- Not including the system, costs were 50 percent higher than expected.
- The project duration was three weeks longer than expected.

Several tasks being left out of the original WBS was a decomposition error on the part of the project manager, sponsor, and team. It was caught just before those tasks needed to be performed, though. To avoid this on the next system selection project, the project manager can use this project as a template. To avoid a similar kind of error in a different type of project, the project manager and team may need to spend more time creating the WBS.

The omission of a baseline value for the participants' time in class was just a data entry error. Again, the PM needs to double-check the estimates more thoroughly before baselining.

The third and fourth difficulties were caused by the first two problems, so they will go away when the first two are fixed.

TIME SAVER

Take the time after each project to analyze your lessons learned. It will save you time in the long run.

Review Awards Lessons

Analyzing the awards banquet may seem like a waste of time in light of the fact that it came in on schedule and under budget, but that was due largely to a change in direction on two expenses that offset the increases in other areas. So, let's look at the lessons learned anyway.

They were …

- More people attended than anticipated.
- More awards were given than originally anticipated.

Both of these things increased expenses. The extra 13 dinners cost $390 and the extra award cost $100. To avoid these potential negative situations in the future, you might want to budget dinners for the whole company. That's the highest possible expense, and it is common to budget on highest versus likely numbers. You might also use weighted average to determine a potential count.

Review Restoration Lessons

Review the restoration lessons and the actual versus baseline data to evaluate the possible causes for each of the detrimental lessons. An answer appears in Appendix A, "Sample Documents."

ADJUST FUTURE PROJECTS

Once you have gathered and analyzed your lessons learned, you are ready to start applying the strategies to future projects. The following sections discuss some of the more common corrections to future projects, but keep in mind that your projects may also require unique solutions.

TRAIN TEAM MEMBERS

Perhaps the most common correction for future projects is to train the team members in the lacking skill. Computer programmers may need to learn new languages, hardware specialists may need to learn the latest maintenance techniques, and telephone technicians may need to learn more about electronics. These are all considered hard skills because the knowledge can be measured by an improvement in efficiency (doing things right) and effectiveness (doing the right things).

JUST A MINUTE

Most organizations have a training specialist or training department that can help you to determine what type of training may be appropriate for your situation. Be sure to consult with them. It will make any training you may want to conduct more productive.

Other types of hard skills would include using computer software packages, typing, plumbing, carpentry, and the like. In any of these areas, people can progress from novice to master in predictable stages and that improvement can be seen and measured.

Yet, many of the skills that are lacking in ourselves and in our team members are soft skills. Not only are soft skills harder to learn, they are much harder to see and measure any improvement. The primary soft skill lacking in team members is communication, but there are dozens of communication-related skills under this one umbrella. Some members may lack presentation skills, some may lack writing skills, some may lack meeting-leading skills, and some may just not understand the importance of communicating. Interviewing is a communication skill. Being assertive without being aggressive is a communication skill. Listening is a key communication skill. A deficiency in any of these areas can severely impact projects.

Unfortunately, as a project manager you will not normally have control over getting training for your resources for these types of skills. The resource's

GO TO ▶
To refresh you memory of work styles, which also affect project communications, refer back to Hour 7, "Creating Your Project Team."

functional manager generally prescribes this training. Still, if you are experiencing difficulties in your projects, odds are that the functional manager is aware of the problem, too, and can be persuaded to help.

PROCEED WITH CAUTION

Be careful how you approach your resources about deficiencies on the project. Focus on the deficiency's effect on the project, not on personal characteristics. If you're not sure how to handle these situations, a good supervisory skills course may help you.

As a project manager, you have to understand that you may be lacking in communication and other soft skills, too. Some general management skills that you will need include leadership, motivation, delegation, and influencing. Brushing up on your personal skills should encourage others to do the same, and even if it doesn't, your increased skill will help you better manage subsequent projects.

Remember though that training is not a panacea, for you or for others. You can't just throw training at people and expect things to improve. You must be very careful that the training intervention matches the real need, or nothing will change. Then you need to continue to practice the new skills. This takes precious time, but as in project planning, the up-front time will save you in execution time in the long run.

PURCHASE ADDITIONAL TOOLS

Often our resources are constrained by the tools at their disposal. To drive a nail, you should have a hammer, not a screwdriver. This is true of other tasks and tools, too. Designing manuals with standard word processors can be done, but the tasks are much easier in a page-layout package. Processing heavy graphics on an outdated computer is also possible but inefficient. Intensive e-mail exchange is more efficient over high-speed connections, not dial-up modems. You get the idea.

But processes can also be tools. Streamlining the number of steps in any process can make entire departments more efficient. So, make sure that you look at what process improvements might be beneficial, too.

Wherever possible, you should make sure that your team members have the right tools for the job. This may mean upgrading to better technology as well as following better procedures. It is not uncommon for a project budget to include the cost of the technology or process improvements. While it increases the cost of the current project, subsequent projects will benefit.

When a change in tools is necessary to increase productivity, be aware that many people have strong attachments to their old tools and may not willingly convert to new ones. Forcing a switch will only exacerbate the problem. You'll no doubt need to prove the worth of the new tool to get them to switch voluntarily.

Refine Communication Methods

Another area for improvement is in the project communication methods themselves. You may want to make time sheets or status reports easier by putting them online. You may want to change the arrangement of data on forms so that they are easier to fill out and understand. You may want to communicate more or less frequently with team members and stakeholders. Any of these things may help the performance of the next project.

Refine Estimating Methods

One of the most common adjustments needed in project planning is an improvement in estimating methods. If you are not using work interruption factors, skill factors, and part-time effect in your estimates, you should start using them. If you are already using them, you may need to evaluate each resource's skill, or you may need to establish better metrics used for creating the standard task estimate on which these build. If the resources themselves are giving you the estimates, you may need to compare these with historical metrics and modify them accordingly.

JUST A MINUTE

If you have been tracking projects through five or more projects and your historical metrics are still yielding inaccurate new estimates, you may find that your resources are not giving you accurate actuals. Reinforce the notion that the accuracy on actuals is more important than meeting the original estimates.

You may also want to consider using weighted average on projects, especially those that are lengthy or likely to change frequently. The weighted average estimate may be more accurate than the most likely.

Another possibility is to purchase a metrics database for projects in your industry. Databases are available for construction-related projects, information systems projects, some manufacturing-related projects, and others. The costs of these databases vary depending on the industry, the size of the database, and the robustness of the representative tasks.

GO TO ▶
To refresh you memory on weighted averages, refer back to Hour 8, "Developing Project Estimates."

The advantage of using a purchased database is that you don't have to wait for three to five projects before you get your own metrics. You are also fairly sure that these metrics represent "average" times on each task because they have been collected oftentimes using literally thousands of resources.

A disadvantage of using purchased metrics is, of course, the initial expense. Another disadvantage is that your tasks may not resemble those in the database closely enough for the metrics to be worthwhile. But if you work in an industry with projects in the millions to billions of dollars, the metrics tend to be stable, and the up-front cost is greatly outweighed by the lowered project costs generally associated with more accurate estimates.

Regardless of whether you tracked your own metrics or purchased them, if they still are not reliably helping you to refine your estimates, you may want to hire a professional estimator. These people specialize in estimating projects and often guarantee their estimates to within 10 percent of actuals.

The cost of an estimator varies depending on your location, the type of project, and the cost of the project. As with purchasing reliable metrics, the savings generated may be well worth the cost of hiring these people, especially on high dollar value and/or high visibility projects.

 Several industries have professional estimators available to help you in developing your estimates. For more information on some of these, check out the trade organizations in your industry. They will be able to point you to the appropriate people.

Because of the nature of estimates, improving your estimates is often the hardest aspect of improving project performance. It may involve quite a bit of trial and error until you can get your definitive estimates into the plus or minus 10 percent of actuals range. Have patience.

ADJUST FUTURE SOFTWARE PROJECTS

Now let's take a look at the types of things we learned on the purchasing software upgrade that would help us on future software projects.

You have been assigned as the project manager of the project to upgrade the general ledger, accounts payable, and accounts receivables systems. Based on what you learned in the purchasing project, what would you do the same? Differently?

Because running system tests of the three contending purchasing systems in-house provided you with not only valuable evaluation information but also helped save time later, you would probably want to repeat that process in this project. You would probably also like to try get the same three analysts assigned to this project, perhaps one per system this time.

Remember that the major problem with this project was that several tasks were not in the original WBS. So, for this accounting systems upgrade project, you will start with the purchasing system WBS and then verify that you haven't missed any tasks. Because the first project was just one system, and this is three, you may want to duplicate the tasks to estimate and then track progress on each separate system. And, you will want to make sure that everything has an effort estimate, if applicable, before you save the baseline.

JUST A MINUTE

As part of the evolutionary process of improving your projects, make sure that you note everything you are trying to duplicate in old projects and what you are trying to change from old projects. This way you'll be able to judge which tactics worked and which didn't.

ADJUST FUTURE EVENT PROJECTS

Your banquet project was so successful that the Leetle Toy Company Management would like you to help organize the annual regional toy fest. Unlike the awards project, though, this event is a major fundraising event for the local toy museum. The Leetle Toy Company donates some funding, and the fest is held on the museum grounds, but participants are charged for attending. Lunch and one souvenir are included per person in the admission charge, and the rest of the events are free.

Using the lessons learned from the awards banquet project, what would you do the same on this project? What would you do differently?

Because this project came in on time and under budget, we would want to apply the things that went well as much as possible. The biggest cost savings on this project were in the adjustments to the services provided the evening of the banquet. We had a volunteer photographer, which saved all the photography expense (presuming that he donated the film and developing, too, since we saw no line items for those expenses).

We also decreased the expense of the entertainment and speaker by getting a band and magician instead. Luckily, these decreased expenses compensated for the increase in awardees and attendees.

So, for this project, we may want to use weighted average estimating for the cost of entertainment as well as for the cost for food and souvenirs for the attendees. You may also want to use weighted average to come up with estimates for the admission fees required to offset these expenses. While this will take you longer to establish the estimates, it will give you four separate cost estimates and a solid idea of the profitability range of the fest.

PROCEED WITH CAUTION

Externally funded projects usually do not have the cost flexibility that internal projects have. So if you are basing the plan of an externally funded project on the plan for an internal one, you'll need to be more cautious in verifying the cost components, especially as compared to the available funding.

ADJUST FUTURE RESTORATION PROJECTS

Based on the lessons learned and actuals versus baseline for the restoration project, discuss what you might do the same and differently in the next restoration project. An answer appears in Appendix A.

ARCHIVE PROJECT NOTEBOOK

The very last thing that you should do with every project is to make sure that all the appropriate documents are stored in your project notebook. This includes all your baseline documents, progress documents, lessons-learned lists, and project summary report. Once you have verified that all the documents are included and are in order, file the project notebook.

Why would you want to do this? Because, surprisingly enough, unless you are a freelance project manager, the types of project you manage will be similar. You never know when you might have a situation in a future project that you know you've already solved in a previous one, but you just can't remember how. Referring to the notebook can save you hours of reinventing the wheel.

JUST A MINUTE

Most often, you will be responsible for archiving your own project notebooks, but if your organization has a project management office (PMO), they may request or require you to archive a copy of your notebook with them. At a minimum, the PMO will want a copy of you project summary report.

HOUR 24

Choosing a Project Management Package

CHAPTER SUMMARY

LESSON PLAN:

In this hour you will learn about …

- Understanding package capabilities.
- Determining software requirements.
- Evaluating hardware capabilities.
- Reviewing software options.
- Working with the popular packages.

In today's businesses, budgets continue to tighten and managers are asked to do more with less. Because of this, keeping our projects on time and on budget becomes critical to the success of not only our individual projects but also to our careers and our companies' profits. Using a project management package can help. Literally hundreds of project management software packages are on the market. But less than 10 of these are the most commonly used packages. In this hour, you'll learn how to select a product to help you manage your projects.

UNDERSTAND PACKAGE CAPABILITIES

A project management software package enables you to schedule and track your projects. Before you can decide exactly what you want from a project management software package, you need to know a little about what they are as well about as their history and their capabilities. These are discussed in the following sections.

UNDERSTAND PACKAGE HISTORY

Although they seem relatively new, project management software packages have been available since the 1970s. The first project management packages ran on large mainframe computers and cost upwards of $100,000 annually. Because of their great expense, they were used mostly by the federal government, government contractors, and large construction firms. These packages had no or limited resource capabilities, could not model dependency relationships other than finish-start, but did have excellent graphics capabilities, for both Gantt charts and network diagrams. They could also track projects, although not all organizations used the tracking features.

 FYI For quick links to some of the more popular software vendors, see dmoz.org/Computers/Software/Project_Management.

In the 1980s, project management packages still ran on mainframes, but throughout the decade, PC packages were becoming available. These first PC packages also had no or limited resource capabilities but had terrible graphics and clunky interfaces. The cost of these packages ranged from around $800 for the PC packages to $100,000 still for mainframe packages. As the cost continued to decline, project management package use spread to nongovernment-related engineering applications and to some information systems, architecture, and training applications.

In the early 1990s, PC packages came into their own, while mainframe packages started to die out. The average cost of today's PC packages ranges from $50 to $10,000, and they are used extensively in the traditional project management industries as well as in most engineering, information systems, facilities, training, and construction departments. They have good resource capabilities today, and their graphics range from acceptable to excellent. They are also being integrated more closely with corporate manpower planning functions, metrics databases, and process management packages.

JUST A MINUTE

 As with any category of software, each project management package has its strengths and its weaknesses. And every project manager has his or her preferences. If you intend to collect meaningful metrics in your organization, it would behoove you to carefully study and test each package and then standardize on a single one.

Understand Process Management Packages

In the late 1980s, companies also started marketing software packages known as process management packages. While project management packages help you to schedule and track a project, a process management package helps you manage the entire project management process. It provides you with templates for common types of projects, suggests the appropriate skill set for each task, and suggests the inter-task dependencies.

Many process management packages also provide estimating metrics databases for a variety of industries, and enable you to use weighted average estimates and skill factors applied to your own collection of metrics. One of the earliest and most popular process management packages was Process Engineer from LBMS. This has now been absorbed in to the Platinum line of software from Computer Associates.

UNDERSTAND PACKAGE CAPABILITIES

While the specific capabilities of packages vary, they all provide a set of standard functions. They enable you to enter your WBS in varying levels of detail and then schedule projects based on time-constrained and resource-constrained tasks, inter-task dependencies, task priorities, and resource availability. They also create and print Gantt and CPM/PERT charts, generally up to E-size wall charts, store your original plan (baseline), enable you to track actual progress on a project, and let you revise the project schedule based on actuals and changes to the plan.

Some packages also calculate Weighted Average, display and print WBS charts, interface with central repositories for resources and project pooling, and enable you to assign resource efficiencies (skill levels) that automatically increase or decrease estimated hours.

PROCEED WITH CAUTION

 Don't introduce a new project management process, new project management package, and new time sheet policies/software all at once. You will overwhelm your people and they will revolt. If possible, introduce the time sheet policies first, then the new process, and last, the project management package to ease the transition.

EVALUATE INFRASTRUCTURE CAPABILITIES

As with selecting any software package, the first thing you need to consider when evaluating project management software packages is which ones will run on your existing hardware and operating system infrastructure. Because most organizations now run some type of IBM-compatible PC hardware and Windows-based software, this is not as big a problem as it used to be when some of the best packages ran only in OS/2 or other less common operating environments. Still, you need to verify that all the packages on your short list can run within your infrastructure constraints.

DETERMINE SOFTWARE REQUIREMENTS

After you know your infrastructure constraints, you can consider your specific project management requirements. Some of the more common are listed for you.

These requirements are divided into basic requirements and advanced requirements. The basic requirements are those that any package you pick should be able to meet. If any of the basic requirements are missing, you may not want to consider that package any longer. The advanced requirements are those that at least one package offers and can save you considerable manual work if they are included in the package. The third section deals not with software requirements, but with vendor attributes that are also important considerations in selecting your software package.

JUST A MINUTE

The fact that many of the Web-based packages have shorter track records does not mean you shouldn't consider them. But you should make sure the tool has all the flexibility and responsiveness you need.

REVIEW PACKAGE BASICS

The requirements listed in this section are those that every product you're considering should be able to handle. A "no" on any of these would most likely eliminate the product from consideration, either from lack of features or from difficulty of use of the feature. Here are the basic requirement questions:

- Is it easy to create and modify the work breakdown structure?
- Is it easy to create and modify resources?
- Is it easy to assign/reassign resources?
- Is it easy to track actual hours?
- Is it easy to schedule projects based on both time-constrained and resource-constrained tasks?
- Is it easy to assign inter-task dependencies?
- Does it allow Finish-Finish and Start-Start dependencies in addition to traditional Finish-Start dependencies?
- Does the program support lead and lag (amounts and percentages)?
- Does it allow task and project priorities?

- Does the product provide customizable organization/shift calendars?
- Does the product provide customizable resource calendars?

JUST A MINUTE

The more popular project management software packages have local, national, and international user groups that have monthly meetings and newsletters and even special conferences devoted just to that product. These groups can be invaluable in optimizing your use of the product. They can give you all the tips, tricks, and workarounds that the vendors aren't apt to.

- Does the product level resources?
- Does the product support multiple project resource leveling?
- Does the product provide multiple ways for creating dependency relationships?
- Does the product draw network diagrams?
- Does the program save at least one baseline?
- Can the information and graphical layouts be tailored and saved?
- Can effort be assigned even on time-constrained tasks?

EVALUATE ADVANCED FEATURES

The following questions address the more advanced features of a project management software package. Not all the popular packages can do all these things, so you may want to weight how important each feature is to you.

Here are the advanced questions to ask:

- Can the program accurately schedule from both project start and from project deadline?
- Can the program schedule tasks using both As Soon As Possible (ASAP) and As Late As Possible (ALAP) methods?
- Does the product have a "shrink to fit" print feature?
- Can the product print to devices as large as E-size?
- Does the program interface with other programs (accounting/tracking)?

JUST A MINUTE

Remember that as the software products continue to evolve, several of the attributes listed here on the advanced list will become standard features.

- Does the product store and calculate estimates by resource efficiency (skill) factors?
- Does the product store resource information centrally?
- Does the product store projects centrally?
- Does the product allow customized reports via standard report writer software packages?
- Does the product provide earned-value fields?
- Does the program have user-definable fields?
- Does the program enable you to create custom calculations?
- Does the program create WBS diagrams?
- Does the program create organization charts from your resources?
- Does the program include weighted-average fields?
- Can the layouts (views) be shared with others?
- Can task/resource Ids be both entered and automatically generated?

GENERAL FEATURES

The questions in this section refer to the general aspects of a product including its history, its vendor, its stability, and the like. As with the advanced features, some of these general features may be more important to you than others. If so, you can assign different weights to them.

PROCEED WITH CAUTION

Because standardizing on a corporate project management software package can divide the project managers within the organization, it is best to have a representative team of project managers making the selection. While this won't eliminate disgruntled project managers, it should minimize them. When everyone understands what packages were evaluated and how the selection was made, they are more likely to comply.

Here are the general questions:

- Do the features you'll use justify the cost?
- Does the price include upgrades?
- Does the program have a solid history of success?
- Is the vendor stable and reliable?
- Does the vendor provide free product support?

- Are there user groups available?
- Is third-party training available?
- Does the product function reliably?

REVIEW SOFTWARE OPTIONS

Now that you have some idea of product capabilities and possible product requirements, we can look briefly at the various products on the market today. This section provides a general overview of some of the packages and sets the stage for the detailed package information given in subsequent sections.

JUST A MINUTE

 Remember that employee training is generally included in the cost of many of the high-end packages and suites. So, although the package price per person may seem higher, it may, in fact, be less once you factor in third-party or internal training per person.

UNDERSTAND FEATURE AND COST CLASSES

Project management packages can be divided into three main classes of low end, midrange, and high end. On the low end in both features and cost are various shareware packages, such as SureTrak 3.0. Microsoft Project 2000 is also generally considered low end because of its cost, although this current release makes it comparable in features to the midrange products.

The midrange products include CA-SuperProject 5.0, Project Scheduler/8, and Project Workbench 5.0. In general, these products contain more tracking features and better scheduling features than the lower end packages. They also cost more.

On the high end are Primavera Project Planner (P3) and Artemis View. In addition to the standard scheduling and tracking features, these packages connect to databases for resource and project information. The suite version of Workbench, known as Portfolio Manager, also has this capability.

Many of these packages now work on networks as well as in intranet environments. There are also new packages on the market that only work in a Web-based environment. While these are welcome additions to the field, many have yet to prove themselves as comparable to the more seasoned products.

Four of the most common packages—Microsoft Project, SureTrak, CA-SuperProject, and Project Workbench—will be discussed briefly in subsequent sections.

UNDERSTAND MICROSOFT PROJECT

Although a relative newcomer to the market, the highest-selling package by far is Microsoft Project, now in its sixth release as Project 2000. As the leading package, this means that one advantage of purchasing Project is that virtually all training centers provide both training and support on the product. Other major pluses include its ease of creating a plan, its Windows compliance in all selecting and printing features, and its relatively low cost. It also has good flexibility in customizing output, especially Gantt charts, and comes with standard and customizable reports.

On the minus side, Project still lacks some of the schedule-modeling features, it has limited tracking/performance capabilities, and its task ID numbers change. (Note that some project managers view this as a positive feature.)

JUST A MINUTE

If you have never used a project management software package before, you may find it easier to start with a low-end software package and upgrade to a more fully functioning package after you have practiced with the basics.

A sample Gantt chart and CPM diagram from Microsoft Project are shown in the following figures.

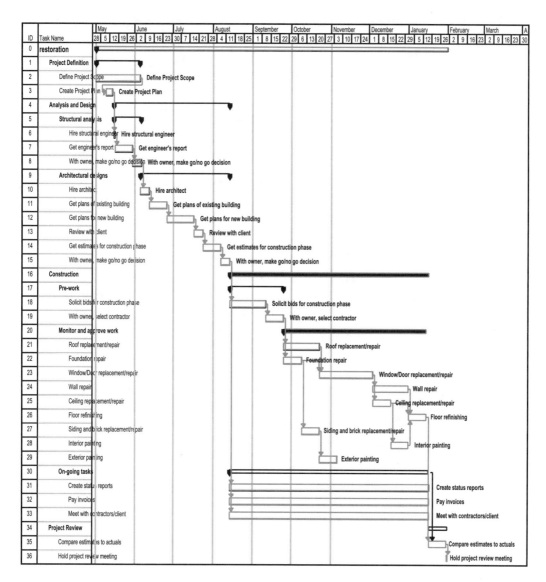

A Gantt chart created in Microsoft Project.

A CPM *diagram created in Microsoft Project*.

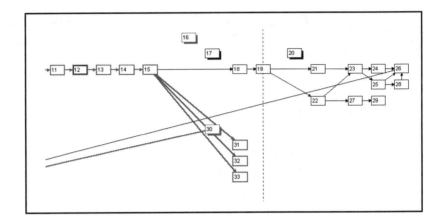

UNDERSTAND SURETRAK

SureTrak, by Primavera, is the newest of the products discussed here. Its major attraction is that it is the low-end companion to the robust, high-end Primavera Project Planner, often referred to as P3. Also, written after Windows became the standard PC operating system, it follows the Windows standards for editing, selecting, and the like.

Other advantages of the product include earned-value fields and robust view customization options, especially in organizing tasks by ways other than WBS. And for people who like the mathematical details, SureTrak calculates and displays both Free Float and Total Float, and its glossary explains the math behind each.

Disadvantages include a relatively small user base, so there are no books on the product, nor is it a standard training class, although several third-party vendors do offer training on it. It also has limited tracking capabilities and fewer scheduling options.

Samples of a Gantt chart and CPM diagram are shown in the following figures.

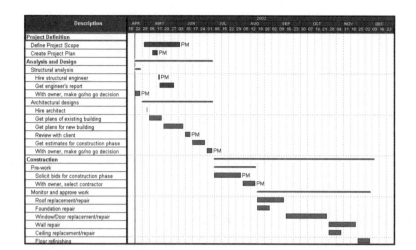

A Gantt chart created in SureTrak.

A CPM diagram created in SureTrak.

JUST A MINUTE

As with the various spreadsheet and word processing packages, project management packages continue to leapfrog one another. If you already have a standard software package, don't switch just because a new release of a different package offers features that your existing package doesn't have. Odds are that those changes are scheduled for an upcoming release of your product.

UNDERSTAND CA-SUPERPROJECT

CA-SuperProject is one of the oldest packages on the market, written originally in the early 1980s. It, too, has its pluses and minuses. On the plus side, it allows five types of tasks for accurate modeling, includes weighted average fields and skill factor fields, and contains Work Breakdown Structure and Organization charting capabilities.

It often comes with excellent programming, reporting, and time-keeping add-ins, too. An especially nice feature is the accounting code field that enables you to refer to internal account codes per task. These can then be used for extraction to your accounting package.

On the minus side, the product is difficult to learn. To be consistent with pre-Windows versions, not all the standard Windows conventions are used. As with SureTrak, it is not as large a seller, so there are no books on the product, nor is it a standard training class, although several third-party vendors do offer training on it.

Samples of a Gantt chart, CPM Diagram, and WBS diagram are shown in the following figures.

A Gantt chart created in CA-SuperProject.

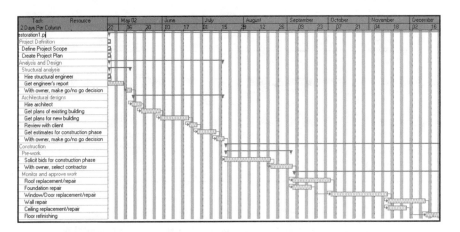

A CPM diagram created in CA-SuperProject.

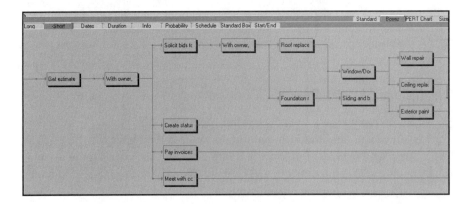

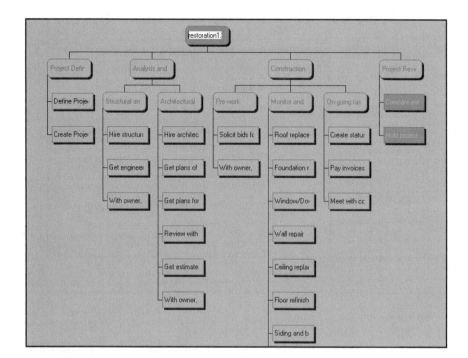

A WBS diagram created in CA-SuperProject.

TIME SAVER

Several periodicals write regular reviews of the current capabilities of project management packages. These generally include detailed product feature comparisons. Reading some of these prior to starting your own testing should help you evaluate the packages more quickly.

UNDERSTAND PROJECT WORKBENCH

Another one of the early project management packages is Project Workbench. This package is sold as a stand-alone project management package and also comes as part of the Niku Portfolio Manager suite (see the following figures). Some advantages of Project Workbench include its versatile scheduling engine, its flexibility in changing Gantt viewing scale time frames, and customizing the various views. Even as a stand-alone package, it also provides good project tracking capabilities. When used in conjunction with its time-accounting sister product, it enables you to perform extensive tracking.

A Gantt chart created in Niku Portfolio Manager, a.k.a. Project Workbench.

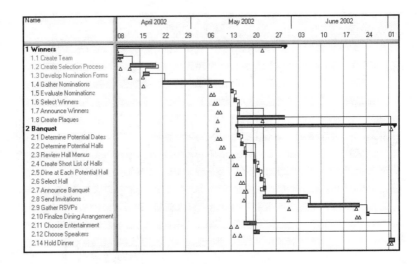

A CPM diagram created in Niku Portfolio Manager, a.k.a. Project Workbench.

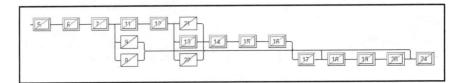

One the downside, Project Workbench is relatively expensive, especially in the stand-alone version, which is twice as much as other midrange products. It is also not 100 percent Windows-compliant in some of its functions.

Regardless of the package you choose, with a project management package you can create more than a pretty plan. You can schedule tasks, assign resources, track actual hours, durations, and costs to keep your project on time and within budget.

TIME SAVER

Today, many of the project management consultants are experts in the differences among the various tools. Hiring one to help you make the selection may speed up the process.

APPENDIX A

Sample Documents

This appendix provides the answers to the Conference Center Restoration Project exercises given throughout the book. These answers are organized sequentially by the Hour in which they are introduced.

HOUR 2 ANSWERS

ANSWER TO PROJECT NEEDS

The case study did not provide a lot of detail on the business motivation for Leetle Toy Company on this project, but one need might be the following:

- To increase the company visibility by participating in a worthwhile public project

Although not stated in the case, it may be that the Leetle Toy Company needs additional meeting and training space, and that by helping in this project they would get free or low-cost rentals in the completed facility. Stated as a need, this would read as follows:

- To obtain additional, low-cost meeting and training space

The business needs of the nonprofit organization are a little clearer. They would include the following:

- To stabilize the building to prevent continued deterioration

- To restore the meeting house to useable condition
- To restore the building in a manner compatible with its historic character

ANSWER TO PROJECT FEASIBILITY

Feasibility:

As with the awards project, we'll look at feasibility based on the constraint categories we discussed.

Technical Feasibility:

This building was already built once and restorations are frequently performed, so the project is technically feasible.

Financial Feasibility:

The main financial issue is cost/benefit, which we will evaluate in the next section. There are, however, many ongoing costs to consider. In addition to the utilities, which could be very high on such a large structure, there will be taxes to pay and continual maintenance required. These ongoing costs will need to be evaluated in the cost/benefit in the next section.

Operational Feasibility:

There are no internal operational issues that would make the project infeasible, but the interface between the nonprofit and Leetle Toy Company may be awkward. This shouldn't be so bad as to make the project operationally infeasible, however.

Geographic Feasibility:

All the employees of the Leetle Toy Company are local, as is the building and the nonprofit preservation group. There may not be local experts in the trade skills needed for the restoration, but this would increase the cost and not be a geographic deterrent, so the project is geographically feasible.

Time Feasibility:

No time limit has been set for this restoration, so the project is time feasible.

Resource Feasibility:

The project would require the time of an administrative assistant, the project manager, architects, and contractors. The Leetle Toy Company has offered your project management services, and the nonprofit has an administrative assistant, but will need to consider the hiring of the tradespeople in the cost/benefit analysis. Still, at this point, the project is resource feasible.

Legal Feasibility:

The building is a contributing building in a National Historic District and as such, all exterior modifications will have to be approved by the local and state historic preservation offices. Both offices have approved similar projects in other districts in the city, so it is legally feasible, although the approval process will no doubt slow down the restoration progress.

Political Feasibility:

No one in senior management opposes the project, and the local residents and politicians appear to be in favor of removing a neighborhood eyesore, so it is politically feasible.

COST/BENEFIT ANALYSIS—SUPPLEMENTAL DATA

Before you can provide any type of cost/benefit analysis on this project, even at a high level, you need to investigate the costs of both the restoration and the upkeep. You also need some idea of the monetary benefits the project could accrue and where the funding for both the restoration and the upkeep will come from.

Here's what you've found:

- Architects charge from $3,000 to $6,000 for plans for similar-sized buildings.
- Roof repairs cost approximately $1,000, and a complete roof job on a building that size costs anywhere from $20,000 to $50,000, depending on the materials selected.
- New furnaces run $5,000 to $10,000.
- If an elevator is required for ADA compliance, it will cost $100,000.
- Window repairs would cost approximately $500 per window, and there are 64 windows.

- Door repair would also be about $500 per door, and there are three exterior and 14 interior doors.
- If needed, new electric will cost about $10,000.
- If needed, new plumbing for the kitchen and baths and hot water heat would cost $15,000.
- New ceilings and walls in each room would cost around $20,000.
- If done, it would cost $2,000 each to restore the two fireplaces.
- If used, carpeting averages $35 per square yard.
- Refinishing of the hardwood floor in the auditorium would cost approximately $6,000.
- Utilities on similar-sized buildings average $1,000 per month.
- Rental on similar sized conference facilities averages $350 per day.
- Apartments in the area rent for $750 per month.
- Taxes will be around $4,000 per year.
- The nonprofit group is currently paying $500 per month for rent.
- The nonprofit group has $100,000 in the bank, only $25,000 of which can be spent toward this project.
- The net annual income from memberships and other fundraising activities averages $20,000.
- The nonprofit has applied for a restoration grant of $35,000, which it is likely to receive.
- Donations from the Leetle Toy Company and other corporate sponsors average $35,000, which is included in the net income. The toy company has created a special matching grant program; however, it will match up to $50,000 in donations from other sources toward the restoration.

Based on this information, create the Cost/Benefit statement in a format similar to that used in the awards banquet.

BENEFIT ANALYSIS ANSWER

This restoration project has both tangible and intangible benefits. The tangible benefits include the following:

- Elimination of monthly rent, saving $6,000 per year
- Income-producing meeting space
- Income-producing apartment space

The intangible benefits include the following:

- Restoration of an historic building to its former grandeur
- Improved community by removing a neighborhood eyesore

COST ANALYSIS ANSWER

The costs of this project are divided into the actual costs of the improvements in the building and the ongoing maintenance costs. The costs of the restoration would be as follows:

Architect	$3,000 to $6,000
Roof repairs	$1,000
Roof replacement	$20,000 to $50,000
New furnace	$5,000 to $10,000
Elevator	$0 to $100,000
Window repairs	$32,000
Door repairs	$8,500
New electric	$10,000
New plumbing	$15,000
New ceilings and walls	$20,000
Fireplace repairs	$4,000
Carpeting	$0 to $16,000
Refinishing floor	$6,000
Total	$118,500 to $272,500

The recurring annual costs would be as follows:

Utilities	$12,000
Taxes	$4,000
Maintenance	$6,000
Total	$22,000
Less rent savings	$6,000
Net increase	$16,000

The expected project funding sources are as follows:

Cash on hand	$25,000
Grant	$0–$35,000
Corporate Donations	$0–$100,000
Total	$25,000–$160,000

The expected operating income is as follows:

Net annual income	$20,000
Conference rentals (at 10%)	$12,600
Apartment (10 months)	$7,500
Total	$41,100

RECOMMENDATION STATEMENT

Based on the estimated costs investigated to date, the entire restoration of the conference center would cost somewhere between $118,500 and $272,500. The anticipated funding for the restoration is between $25,000 and $160,000 if the Leetle Toy Company is successful in raising $50,000, which it will then match. This leaves a potential shortfall of $112,500, most of which would be eliminated if the building will not require an elevator.

Unexpected expenses during restoration may be able to be covered with some of the organization's net $20,000 per year until the building is completed and operational.

The anticipated annual cost of operating the building is $22,000, with the annual savings of $6,000 currently going toward office rent. The projected annual income of the building itself, even at only 10 percent use, is $20,100, which would nearly cover the upkeep all by itself. With the continued net income of $20,000, the organization could cover the operational expenses.

Based on the above figures, it appears that the project is financially feasible as long as the grant funding comes through and the donations meet exceptions. It is recommended that the project proceed into the planning phase to better detail both the work that will be involved and its corresponding cost.

PROJECT SPONSOR ANSWER

The Leetle Toy Company project sponsor is Sam Parker, Senior Vice-President of Human Resources.

HOUR 3 ANSWERS

PROJECT GOAL ANSWER

To sympathetically restore the 1884 meeting hall building, turning it into corporate headquarters for the preservation group and also into rentable conference and apartment space.

OBJECTIVES ANSWER

- To create a third-floor three-bedroom apartment
- To create third-floor corporate office space
- To create rentable conference center space on the first and second floors capable of handling 200 attendees
- To restore the meeting hall according to the secretary of the interior's standards

SCOPE ANSWER

The project manager will oversee the entire restoration project, which will include hiring the structural engineer, the project architect, and the general contractor and approving the final designs, the hiring of any subcontractors, the use of materials, and finished products. The project manager will submit monthly progress reports to the owner, with more frequent contact as needed. The project manager will also be responsible for paying any bills within budget and getting approval from the client before approving any cost or schedule overruns.

SCOPE EXCLUSIONS ANSWER

Procuring building permits, certificates of appropriateness, zoning variances, and so on.

DELIVERABLES ANSWER

End Deliverables:

- Restored building including conference-center facilities, corporate office space, and third-floor apartment

Intermediary Deliverables:

- Monthly status reports
- Structural engineer's report
- Architect plans of existing building
- Architect plans for restored building
- Architect elevations for restored building
- RFPs for contractors
- Contractor evaluation reports

CONSTRAINTS ANSWER

- All plans for external changes will have to be approved by the local and state preservation offices. This will affect the timeline as well as the cost of the options chosen.
- Only $25,000 of the actual funding needed is available for the project at this time.
- The layout for the rentable apartment will limit the remaining available office space.
- Appropriate craftsperson may not be available when needed.

HOUR 4 ANSWERS

APPROACH ANSWER

- Ensure owner approval of all plans
- Use owner go/no go decision points at critical junctures
- Use qualified architect to also act as supervisor of contractor work
- Encourage preservation group board of directors to actively solicit appropriate funding

REQUIRED RESOURCES ANSWER

Internal Resources:

- Project Manager
- Administrative Assistant

Contract Resources:

- Architect
- Structural Engineer
- General Contractor
- Roofing Crew
- Drywall Crew
- Floor Finishers
- Plumbers
- Electricians
- HVAC Specialist

PROJECT STAKEHOLDERS ANSWER

- Project Sponsor, Sam Parker
- Project Manager
- Project team members
- Contractors
- Board of the preservation group
- Members of the preservation group
- Senior executives at Leetle Toy Company
- Employees of Leetle Toy Company
- Donators to the preservation group

PROJECT ASSUMPTIONS ANSWER

- The President of the preservation group is responsible for obtaining all appropriate permits
- The donations and grant for the funding will come through, and in a timely manner
- The building is structurally sound
- The local and state preservation offices will approve the restorations and do so in a timely manner
- Appropriately skilled tradespeople will be located

Critical Success Factors Answer

Project Critical Success Factors:

Note that this project has no time constraints, so it has no corresponding time success factors.

Meeting Objectives Factors:

- Restored rentable space must be comparable or superior to area apartment and conference space
- Restored office space must be comparable or superior to current rented space
- All restoration work must be approved by the appropriate preservation offices and meet the Secretary of the Interior's Standards

Note that the Happy Customer Factors would be the same as objective factors.

Cost Factors:

- Appropriate funding must be in hand or secured prior to project execution

Hour 5 Answers

Communications Plan Answer

From	To	Frequency	Format	Media
PM	Sam Parker	Monthly	Status	Meeting
PM	Owners	Monthly	Status	Hardcopy
PM	Employees	Bimonthly	Article	Corp. Newsletter
PM	Members	Bimonthly	Article	Association Newsletter
Sup. Arch.	PM	Weekly	Status	Hardcopy
Owners	PM	As Needed	Approvals	Hardcopy
Owners	Hist. Pres. Office	As Needed	Plans	Hardcopy
Hist. Pres. Office	Owners	As Needed	Approvals	Hardcopy

CHANGE CONTROL PLAN ANSWER

- Changes must be requested on form CC-1, Change Control Request Form.
- The project manager can approve any changes to delivery dates.
- No increases to the budget can be made without owner approval.

QUALITY MANAGEMENT PLAN ANSWER

- All work will conform to the Secretary of the Interior's Standards for restoration
- All work will comply with appropriate state and local building, fire, and preservation codes
- The appropriate state and local building, fire, and preservation inspectors will inspect all work

PROCUREMENT PLAN ANSWER

- The project manager and owners will identify at least three potential candidates for each of the trade skills needed and get references and bids from each.
- Selection will be made based on price as well as quality measures noted above.
- Materials will be included in the bids of each contractor/subcontractor, but donations of appropriate materials from vendors will also be considered.
- All vendors will submit invoices after rendering of services to be paid within 30 days.

COMPLETION PLAN ANSWER

The project will be considered complete after the certificate of occupancy has been issued and all outstanding invoices have been received and paid.

Hour 6 Answer

Restoration WBS

ID	Name
1000	Project Definition
1100	Define project scope
1200	Create project plan
2000	Analysis and Design
2100	Structural analysis
2110	Hire structural engineer
2120	Get engineer's report
2130	With owner, make go/no go decision
2200	Architectural designs
2210	Hire architect
2220	Get plans of existing building
2230	Get plans for new building
2240	Review with client
2250	Get estimates for construction phase
2260	With owner, make go/no go decision
3000	Construction
3100	Prework
3110	Solicit bids for construction phase
3120	With owner, select contractor
3200	Monitor and approve work
3210	Roof replacement/repair
3220	Foundation repair
3230	Window replacement/repair
3240	Wall repair
3250	Ceiling replacement/repair
3260	Floor refinishing
3270	Siding and brick replacement/repair
3280	Interior painting
3290	Exterior painting
3300	Ongoing tasks
3310	Create status reports
3320	Pay invoices
3330	Meet with contractors/client
4000	Project Review
4100	Compare estimates to actuals
4200	Hold project review meeting

WBS chart answer.

HOUR 7 ANSWER

RESOURCE AVAILABILITY ANSWER

The only internal resources on this project are the project manager and administrative assistant. The project manager is available quarter-time to the project as is the administrative assistant. Contractor availability will vary, depending on the contractor selected.

RESOURCE WORK STYLE ANSWER

Because there are only two internal resources on this project and they were preassigned to the project, the work styles are not really relevant. The other key team member would be the architect, who has yet to be identified, but as the project manager you would want to consider his or her style and its compatibility with yours when making the selection.

ORGANIZATIONAL PLAN ANSWER

Organization Chart:

The project manager reports directly to Sam Parker, the Leetle Toy Company sponsor of the project, and indirectly to the president of the preservation group. The supervising architect will report directly to the project manager and the contractors to the architect.

Roles and Responsibilities Matrix: D = Do, A = Approve, R = Receive

ID	Name	PM	Owners	Sponsor	Contractors
1000	Project Definition				
1100	Define project scope	D	A	A	
1200	Create project plan	D	A	A	
2000	Analysis and Design				
2100	Structural analysis				
2110	Hire engineer	D	A		
2120	Get report	R			D
2130	Go/no go decision	D	D	D	
2200	Architectural designs				
2210	Hire architect	D			
2220	Get existing plans	R			D
2230	Get new plans	R			D
2240	Review with client	D	D		D
2250	Get estimates	D			
2260	Go/no go decision	D	D	D	
3000	Construction				
3100	Prework				
3110	Solicit bids	D			
3120	Select contractors	D	D	D	
3200	Monitor/approve work				
3210	Roof	R			D
3220	Foundation repair	R			D
3230	Window	R			D
3240	Wall repair	R			D
3250	Ceiling	R			D

ID	Name	PM	Owners	Sponsor	Contractors
3260	Floor refinishing	R			D
3270	Siding and brick	R			D
3280	Interior painting	R			D
3290	Exterior painting	R			D
3300	Ongoing tasks				
3310	Create status	D			
3320	Pay invoices	D			
3330	Meetings	D	D	D	D
4000	Project Review				
4100	Compare estimates	D			
4200	Hold project review	D			

ACQUISITION PLAN ANSWER

As noted, the internal resources are assigned, and all external resources will be acquired via the procurement plan.

HOUR 8 ANSWERS

EFFORT AND DURATION ESTIMATE ANSWERS

ID	Name	Effort/Duration
1000	Project Definition	
1100	Define project scope	2 hours
1200	Create project plan	10 hours
2000	Analysis and Design	
2100	Structural analysis	
2110	Hire structural engineer	3 hours
2120	Get engineer's report	2 weeks
2130	With owner, make go/no go decision	1 week
2200	Architectural designs	
2210	Hire architect	4 hours
2220	Get plans of existing building	2 week

continues

continued

ID	Name	Effort/Duration
2230	Get plans for new building	3 weeks
2240	Review with client	1 week
2250	Get estimates for construction phase	2 weeks
2260	With owner, make go/no go decision	1 week
3000	Construction	
3100	Prework	
3110	Solicit bids for construction phase	4 weeks
3120	With owner, select contractor	2 weeks
3200	Monitor and approve work	
3210	Roof replacement/repair	4 weeks
3220	Foundation repair	2 weeks
3230	Window/door replacement/repair	6 weeks
3240	Wall repair	4 weeks
3250	Ceiling replacement/repair	2 weeks
3260	Floor refinishing	2 weeks
3270	Siding and brick replacement/repair	2 weeks
3280	Interior painting	2 weeks
3290	Exterior painting	2 weeks
3300	Ongoing tasks	
3310	Create status reports	4 hours/week
3320	Pay invoices	4 hours/week
3330	Meet with contractors/client	6 hours/week
4000	Project Review	
4100	Compare estimates to actuals	20 hours
4200	Hold project review meeting	2 hours

EFFORT COST ESTIMATE ANSWERS

ID	Name	Effort Cost
1000	Project Definition	
1100	Define project scope	144
1200	Create project plan	720

ID	Name	Effort Cost
2000	Analysis and Design	
2100	Structural analysis	
2110	Hire structural engineer	216
2120	Get engineer's report	
2130	With owner, make go/no go decision	72
2200	Architectural designs	
2210	Hire architect	288
2220	Get plans of existing building	
2230	Get plans for new building	
2240	Review with client	72
2250	Get estimates for construction phase	
2260	With owner, make go/no go decision	72
3000	Construction	
3100	Prework	
3110	Solicit bids for construction phase	144
3120	With owner, select contractor	72
3200	Monitor and approve work	
3210	Roof replacement/repair	
3220	Foundation repair	
3230	Window/door replacement/repair	
3240	Wall repair	
3250	Ceiling replacement/repair	
3260	Floor refinishing	
3270	Siding and brick replacement/repair	
3280	Interior painting	
3290	Exterior painting	
3300	Ongoing tasks	
3310	Create status reports	288/week
3320	Pay invoices	288/week
3330	Meet with contractors/client	432/week
4000	Project Review	
4100	Compare estimates to actuals	1440
4200	Hold project review meeting	144

Hour 9

Task Relationship Answer

ID	Name	Depends On
1000	Project Definition	
1100	Define project scope	
1200	Create project plan	1100
2000	Analysis and Design	
2100	Structural analysis	
2110	Hire structural engineer	1200
2120	Get engineer's report	2110
2130	With owner, make go/no go decision	2120
2200	Architectural designs	
2210	Hire architect	2130
2220	Get plans of existing building	2210
2230	Get plans for new building	2220
2240	Review with client	2220, 2230
2250	Get estimates for construction phase	2240
2260	With owner, make go/no go decision	2250
3000	Construction	
3100	Prework	
3110	Solicit bids for construction phase	2260
3120	With owner, select contractor	3110
3200	Monitor and approve work	
3210	Roof replacement/repair	3120
3220	Foundation repair	3120
3230	Window replacement/repair	3120
3240	Wall repair	3210, 3220, 3230
3250	Ceiling replacement/repair	3210, 3220, 3230
3260	Floor refinishing	3240, 3250
3270	Siding and brick replacement/repair	3210, 3220, 3230
3280	Interior painting	3260
3290	Exterior painting	3270
3300	Ongoing tasks	
3310	Create status reports	3120

ID	Name	Depends On
3320	Pay invoices	3120
3330	Meet with contractors/client	3120
4000	Project Review	
4100	Compare estimates to actuals	3280, 3290, 3310–3330
4200	Hold project review meeting	4100

CPM DIAGRAM ANSWER

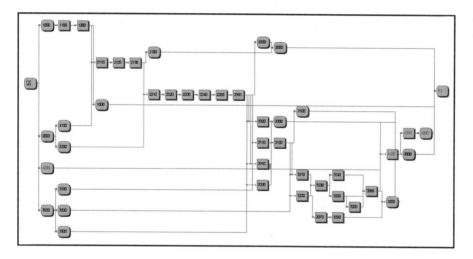

CPM *diagram answer.*

HOUR 10

DURATION ANSWER

ID	Name	Effort/Duration
1000	Project Definition	
1100	Define project scope	1 day
1200	Create project plan	1 week
2000	Analysis and Design	
2100	Structural analysis	
2110	Hire structural engineer	1 week
2120	Get engineer's report	2 weeks

continues

continued

ID	Name	Effort/Duration
2130	With owner, make go/no go decision	1 week
2200	Architectural designs	
2210	Hire architect	1 week
2220	Get plans of existing building	2 week
2230	Get plans for new building	3 weeks
2240	Review with client	1 week
2250	Get estimates for construction phase	2 weeks
2260	With owner, make go/no go decision	1 week
3000	Construction	
3100	Prework	
3110	Solicit bids for construction phase	4 weeks
3120	With owner, select contractor	2 weeks
3200	Monitor and approve work	
3210	Roof replacement/repair	4 weeks
3220	Foundation repair	2 weeks
3230	Window/door replacement/repair	6 weeks
3240	Wall repair	4 weeks
3250	Ceiling replacement/repair	2 weeks
3260	Floor refinishing	2 weeks
3270	Siding and brick replacement/repair	2 weeks
3280	Interior painting	2 weeks
3290	Exterior painting	2 weeks
3300	Ongoing tasks	
3310	Create status reports	Ongoing
3320	Pay invoices	Ongoing
3330	Meet with contractors/client	Ongoing
4000	Project Review	
4100	Compare estimates to actuals	2 weeks
4200	Hold project review meeting	1 day

FORWARD PASS ANSWER

ID	Name	Early Start	Early Finish
1000	Project Definition	4/8/02	4/19/02
1100	Define project scope	4/8/02	4/12/02
1200	Create project plan	4/15/02	4/19/02
2000	Analysis and Design	4/22/02	7/26/02
2100	Structural analysis	4/22/02	5/17/02
2110	Hire structural engineer	4/22/02	4/26/02
2120	Get engineer's report	4/29/02	5/10/02
2130	Make go/no go decision	5/13/02	5/17/02
2200	Architectural designs	5/20/02	7/26/02
2210	Hire architect	5/20/02	5/24/02
2220	Get plans of existing	5/27/02	6/7/02
2230	Get plans for new building	6/10/02	6/28/02
2240	Review with client	7/1/02	7/5/02
2250	Get construction estimates	7/8/02	7/19/02
2260	Make go/no go decision	7/22/02	7/26/02
3000	Construction	7/29/02	12/27/02
3100	Prework	7/29/02	9/6/02
3110	Solicit bids for construction	7/29/02	8/23/02
3120	With owner, select contractor	8/26/02	9/6/02
3200	Monitor and approve work	9/9/02	12/27/02
3210	Roof replacement/repair	9/9/02	10/4/02
3220	Foundation repair	9/9/02	9/20/02
3230	Window/door replacement	10/7/02	11/15/02
3240	Wall repair	11/18/02	12/13/02
3250	Ceiling replacement/repair	11/18/02	11/29/02
3260	Floor refinishing	12/16/02	12/27/02
3270	Siding and brick replacement	9/23/02	10/4/02
3280	Interior painting	12/2/02	12/13/02
3290	Exterior painting	10/7/02	10/18/02
3300	Ongoing tasks	7/29/02	11/29/02
3310	Create status reports	7/29/02	11/29/02

continues

continued

ID	Name	Early Start	Early Finish
3320	Pay invoices	7/29/02	11/29/02
3330	Meet with contractors/client	7/29/02	11/29/02
4000	Project Review	12/30/02	1/13/03
4100	Compare estimates to actuals	12/30/02	1/10/03
4200	Hold project review meeting	1/13/03	1/13/03

BACKGROUND PASS ANSWER

ID	Name	Late Start	Late Finish	Float
1000	Project Definition	4/8/02	4/19/02	0 days
1100	Define project scope	4/8/02	4/12/02	0 wks
1200	Create project plan	4/15/02	4/19/02	0 wks
2000	Analysis and Design	4/22/02	7/26/02	0 days
2100	Structural analysis	4/22/02	5/17/02	0 days
2110	Hire structural engineer	4/22/02	4/26/02	0 wks
2120	Get engineer's report	4/29/02	5/10/02	0 wks
2130	Make go/no go decision	5/13/02	5/17/02	0 wks
2200	Architectural designs	5/20/02	7/26/02	0 days
2210	Hire architect	5/20/02	5/24/02	0 wks
2220	Get plans of existing	5/27/02	6/7/02	0 wks
2230	Get plans for new building	6/10/02	6/28/02	0 wks
2240	Review with client	7/1/02	7/5/02	0 wks
2250	Get construction estimates	7/8/02	7/19/02	0 wks
2260	Make go/no go decision	7/22/02	7/26/02	0 wks
3000	Construction	7/29/02	1/13/03	0 days
3100	Prework	7/29/02	9/6/02	0 days
3110	Solicit bids for construction	7/29/02	8/23/02	0 wks
3120	With owner, select contractor	8/26/02	9/6/02	0 wks
3200	Monitor and approve work	9/9/02	1/13/03	0 days
3210	Roof replacement/repair	9/9/02	10/4/02	0 wks
3220	Foundation repair	9/23/02	10/4/02	2 wks
3230	Window/door replacement	10/7/02	11/15/02	0 wks
3240	Wall repair	11/18/02	12/13/02	0 wks

ID	Name	Late Start	Late Finish	Float
3250	Ceiling replacement/repair	11/18/02	11/29/02	0 wks
3260	Floor refinishing	12/16/02	12/27/02	0 wks
3270	Siding and brick replacement	12/17/02	12/30/02	12.2 wks
3280	Interior painting	12/2/02	12/13/02	0 wks
3290	Exterior painting	12/31/02	1/13/03	12.2 wks
3300	Ongoing tasks	8/26/02	12/27/02	
3310	Create status reports	8/26/02	12/27/02	
3320	Pay invoices	8/26/02	12/27/02	
3330	Meet with contractors/client	8/26/02	12/27/02	
4000	Project Review	12/30/02	1/13/03	0 days
4100	Compare estimates to actuals	12/30/02	1/10/03	0 wks
4200	Hold project review meeting	1/13/03	1/13/03	0 days

HOUR 11 ANSWER

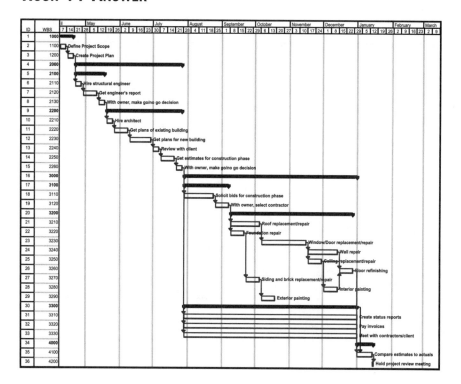

Gantt chart answer.

HOUR 12 ANSWERS

PORTFOLIO RISK ANSWER

Risk Evaluation Matrix

Section One Size Factors	Options 1	2	3	4	Weight	Choice	Score
Project Cost	<10K	10–100K	100–1M	>1M	3	3	9
Duration	<3 mon.	3–6 mon.	7–12 mon.	>12 mon.	2	3	6
Resources	1	2–5	6–10	>10	3	4	12
Departments	1	2–3	4–5	>5	2	2	4
Geographic Sites	1	2–3	4–5	>5	2	2	4
Stakeholders	1-9	10–99	100–999	>1000	3	4	12
Project Interfaces	0	1	2–4	>4	2	1	2
SECTION TOTAL							49

Section Two Stability Factors	Options 1	2	3	4	Weight	Choice	Score
Clear Requirements	High	Med.	Low	None	4	2	8
Identified Sponsor	High	Med.	Low	None	2	1	2
Dedicated Sponsor	High	Med.	Low	None	2	1	2
Influential Sponsor	High	Med.	Low	None	3	1	3
Identified Client	High	Med.	Low	None	2	1	2
Client Support	High	Med.	Low	None	3	2	6
Project Priority	High	Med.	Low	None	3	3	9
Changes Generates	None	Low	Med.	High	4	3	12
Stable Technology	High	Med.	Low	None	3	1	3
SECTION TOTAL							45

Section Two Stability Factors	1	2	Options 3	4	Weight	Choice	Score
Project Type	High	Med.	Low	None	4	4	16
Technology	High	Med.	Low	None	2	3	6
Team Makeup	High	Med.	Low	None	2	4	8
Customer	High	Med.	Low	None	3	4	12
Vendors	High	Med.	Low	None	2	4	8
Contractors	High	Med.	Low	None	3	4	12
SECTION TOTAL							62

RISK EVALUATION	Size	Stability	Experience	TOTAL
59–117 Low	49	45	62	156
118–176 Medium				
177–236 High				

The total of 156 falls into the Medium risk range, making this project a medium-risk project for the organization.

Risk Management Plan Answer

Risk	L	I	L*I	Contingency
Elements will be in worse shape than estimated	7	7	49	Build in a 20 percent time/cost factor
Craftsperson won't be available when needed	5	7	35	Find alternate craftsperson
Budget will be cut	3	8	24	Cut scope
Contractor will go bankrupt	2	10	20	Verify all contractors status
Materials will not be available	4	8	32	Have alternatives specified
Natural disaster will interrupt progress	1	9	9	Cut scope/Accept delays
Structure is not sound	2	10	20	Reevaluate feasibility
Key contractor leaves	3	8	24	Have alternatives
HVAC not sufficient	5	6	30	Evaluate prior to start
Existing plaster cannot be patched	3	8	24	Replace/Accept delays

Hour 13 Answers

Baseline Plan Answer

ID	Name	Effort	Duration	Cost	Start	End
	Restoration Proj.	564 hrs	203 days	$169,720	4/22/02	1/29/03
1000	Definition	12 hrs	10 days	$864	4/22/02	5/3/02
1100	Define scope	2 hrs	1 wk	$144	4/22/02	4/26/02
1200	Create plan	10 hrs	1 wk	$720	4/29/02	5/3/02
2000	Analysis/Design	10 hrs	70 days	$3,832	5/6/02	8/9/02
2100	Struct. analysis	4 hrs	20 days	$688	5/6/02	5/31/02
2110	Hire engineer	3 hrs	1 wk	$216	5/6/02	5/10/02
2120	Get report	0 hrs	2 wks	$400	5/13/02	5/24/02
2130	Go/no go decision	1 hr	1 wk	$72	5/27/02	5/31/02
2200	Architectural	6 hrs	50 days	$3,144	6/3/02	8/9/02
2210	Hire architect	4 hrs	1 wk	$3,000	6/3/02	6/7/02
2220	Existing plans	0 hrs	2 wks	$0	6/10/02	6/21/02
2230	New plans	0 hrs	3 wks	$0	6/24/02	7/12/02
2240	Review w/client	1 hr	1 wk	$72	7/15/02	7/19/02
2250	Get estimates	0 hrs	2 wks	$0	7/22/02	8/2/02
2260	Go/no go decision	1 hr	1 wk	$72	8/5/02	8/9/02
3000	Construction	521 hrs	112 days	$163,512	8/12/02	1/14/03
3100	Prework	3 hrs	30 days	$216	8/12/02	9/20/02
3110	Solicit bids	2 hrs	4 wks	$144	8/12/02	9/6/02
3120	Select contractor	1 hr	2 wks	$72	9/9/02	9/20/02
3200	Monitor/approve	0 hrs	80 days	$126,000	9/23/02	1/10/03
3210	Roof repair	0 hrs	4 wks	$30,000	9/23/02	10/18/02
3220	Foundation repair	0 hrs	2 wks	$15,000	9/23/02	10/4/02
3230	Window/Door	0 hrs	6 wks	$40,000	10/21/02	11/29/02
3240	Wall repair	0 hrs	4 wks	$15,000	12/2/02	12/27/02
3250	Ceiling repair	0 hrs	2 wks	$5,000	12/2/02	12/13/02
3260	Floor refinishing	0 hrs	2 wks	$6,000	12/30/02	1/10/03
3270	Siding and brick	0 hrs	2 wks	$5,000	10/7/02	10/18/02

ID	Name	Effort	Duration	Cost	Start	End
3280	Interior painting	0 hrs	2 wks	$5,000	12/16/02	12/27/02
3290	Exterior painting	0 hrs	2 wks	$5,000	10/21/02	11/1/02
3300	Ongoing tasks	518 hrs	112 days	$37,296	8/12/02	1/14/03
3310	Create status	148 hrs	112 days	$10,656	8/12/02	1/14/03
3320	Pay invoices	148 hrs	112 days	$10,656	8/12/02	1/14/03
3330	Meetings	222 hrs	112 days	$15,984	8/12/02	1/14/03
4000	Project Review	21 hrs	11 days	$1,512	1/15/03	1/29/03
4100	Compare	20 hrs	2 wks	$1,440	1/15/03	1/28/03
4200	Review meeting	1 hr	1 day	$72	1/29/03	1/29/03

Note that you would also save a copy of the entire project plan as a baseline. This just shows the schedule.

CONTACT LIST ANSWER

While we don't know the specific contact names or numbers for the people in this project, your list would include Sam Parker as sponsor, you, your administrative assistant, the architect whom you hire, and then each contractor as he or she is hired.

WORK PACKAGES ANSWER

Because you are just monitoring the work of many different subcontractors, none of whom report to you as employees, you would not create work packages for this project. Each contract, however, would need to contain the same type of information as stated in work packages.

KICK-OFF MEETINGS ANSWER

For this project, the kick-off meeting would most likely be held with Sam Parker as sponsor and the President of the preservation group. In it, you would review your approach to the project, the approvals you'll need from each of them, and how changes, status reports, and other communications will be handled.

Team Development Answer

Because this project will be performed by contractors, team development activities would not be required.

Hour 14 Answers

Use Communication Plan Answer

At this point, the only changes to the communication plan would be noting the name of the preservation group president and architect hired. As to templates, you may want to develop a template for the status reports from the architect or use a standard document that the architectural firm may already have.

Use Change Plan Answer

Because there was nothing in the original WBS or cost estimates for restoring the stairs at all, although it is obviously needed, this would be a change to the project. It would mean a cost increase, so the cost of the stair restoration would need to be priced and then approved by the preservation group president.

Use Quality Plan Answer

Following the quality plan on the staircase change, we would need to match the found balusters and restore the banister with appropriate matching wood.

Use Procurement Plan Answer

You would use the procurement plan as written. You would investigate appropriate contractors for each type of work, solicit bids, and then hire them based on examples of their work, recommendations of other clients, and price. You would make sure that the contracts specified the deliverables and the standards for those deliverables.

Use Risk Management Plan Answer

None of the risks have changed at this point, but after the HVAC is evaluated, that risk would go away. If, however, the evaluation showed you did need new heating and so on, then that would require a project change.

Hour 15 Answers

Actual Duration Answer

Actual ID	Name	Actual Start	Actual Finish	Actual Duration
1000	Project Definition	5/1/02	5/13/02	13
1100	Define project scope	5/1/02	5/9/02	8.5
1200	Create project plan	5/9/02	5/13/02	4.5
2000	Analysis and Design	5/15/02		
2100	Structural analysis	5/15/02		
2110	Hire struct. engineer	5/15/02	5/15/02	1
2120	Get engineer's report	5/16/02	5/29/02	14
2130	Make go/no go decision			
2200	Architectural designs	6/3/02		
2210	Hire architect	6/3/02		

Monitor Restoration Project Milestones Answer

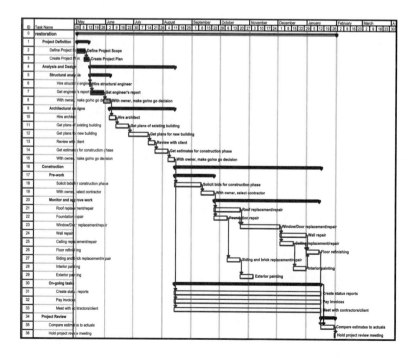

Revised restoration schedule.

Hour 16 Answers

Change Requirements Answer

At this point in the project, we haven't completed the evaluations yet, so we are not aware of any requirements changes needed. As the project progress, this will undoubtedly change.

Change WBS Answer

Comparing the WBS with the estimates given in the project initiation document, we see that several tasks are missing if subsequent evaluation says they are needed. These would include the new furnace(s), plumbing, electric, and fireplace repairs. If evaluations show these are needed, they would be added to the WBS.

Change Deliverables Answer

A new deliverable based on the change above is the restored rear stair. If the WBS is adjusted as mentioned in that section, the products of each of those tasks would also need to be added to the deliverables list.

Change Restoration Schedule

The actuals in the example earlier shows you hiring the architect before the owners have approved continuing after reading the structural engineer's report. You may have just forgotten to include the actual, but if you did go ahead without approval, you will need to change the dependency relationship between the approval task and hiring architect task.

Hour 17 Answer

Actual Cost Answer

ID	Actual Name	Actual Effort	Effort Cost	Fixed Cost
1000	Project Definition	15	$1,080	
1100	Define project scope	10	$720	
1200	Create project plan	5	$360	

ID	Actual Name	Actual Effort	Effort Cost	Fixed Cost
2000	Analysis and Design	12	$864	
2100	Structural analysis	12	$864	
2110	Hire struct. engineer	4	$288	$400
2120	Get engineer's report	8	$576	
2130	Make go/no go decision			
2200	Architectural designs	4	$288	
2210	Hire architect	4	$288	

WORK PERFORMED ANSWERS

A summary of the baseline and actual data to date is shown here:

Task	Base. Start	Base. Finish	Base. Cost	Actual Start	Actual Finish	Actual Cost
Restoration Project	4/22/02	1/29/03	$169,720	5/1/02		
1000 Definition	4/22/02	5/3/02	$864	5/1/02	5/13/02	$1,080
1100 Define Scope	4/22/02	4/26/02	$144	5/1/02	5/9/02	$720
1200 Create Plan	4/29/02	5/3/02	$720	5/9/02	5/13/02	$360
2000 Analysis/Des.	5/6/02	8/9/02	$3,832	5/15/02		$864
2100 Str. analysis	5/6/02	5/31/02	$688	5/15/02		$864
2110 Hire engineer	5/6/02	5/10/02	$216	5/15/02	5/15/02	$688
2120 Get report	5/13/02	5/24/02	$400	5/16/02	5/29/02	$576
2130 Go/no go	5/27/02	5/31/02	$72			
2200 Architectural	6/3/02	8/9/02	$3,144	6/3/02		$288
2210 Hire architect	6/3/02	6/7/02	$3,000	6/3/02		$288

The as-of date for the calculations is 6/7/02.

Task	BCWS	BCWP	ACWP
Restoration Project			
1000 Definition	$864	$864	$1,080
1100 Define Scope	$144	$144	$720
1200 Create Plan	$720	$720	$360
2000 Analysis/Des.			

continues

continued

Task	BCWS	BCWP	ACWP
2100 Str. analysis	$688		
2110 Hire engineer	$216	$216	$688
2120 Get report	$400	$400	$576
2130 Go/no go			
2200 Architectural			
2210 Hire architect	$3,000		

EARNED VALUE ANSWER

Task	BCWS	BCWP	ACWP	SV	CV
Restoration Project					
1000 Definition	$864	$864	$1,080	$0	−$216
1100 Define Scope	$144	$144	$720	$0	−$576
1200 Create Plan	$720	$720	$360	$0	$360
2000 Analysis/Des.					
2100 Str. analysis	$688			−$688	
2110 Hire engineer	$216	$216	$688	$0	−$472
2120 Get report	$400	$400	$576	$0	−$176
2130 Go/no go					
2200 Architectural					
2210 Hire architect	$3,000			−$3,000	

At this point, the project is behind schedule and over budget.

HOUR 18 ANSWERS

COMPARE RESTORATION DELIVERABLES ANSWER

One of the seven intermediary and none of the end deliverables have been completed to date. This is the structural engineer's report.

USE PERCENT COMPLETE ANSWER

All the resource-constrained tasks that have started have also completed, so there are no outstanding tasks.

APPLY PROJECT RATIOS ANSWER

Because the majority of the tasks in this project are subcontracted tasks, this process has little or no value in this type of project.

COMPARE PROJECT SCHEDULES ANSWER

This comparison deals with durations, and where the same contractor performs tasks, would prove valuable for adjusting the project in the future. Through June 7, 2002, however, applying the ratios would not be meaningful.

HOUR 19 ANSWERS

REVIEW PROJECT DEPENDENCIES ANSWER

There do not appear to be any missing or extra dependencies at this point, nor any possible adjustments to the lead-time.

REVIEW PROJECT ESTIMATES ANSWER

With the estimates to date, there don't appear to be any changes to expedite any tasks. As the actual work progresses, however, things to consider would be to replace a contractor, ask them to use additional workers, or substitute materials that can be ordered and/or installed more quickly.

REVIEW PROJECT RESOURCES ANSWER

Because we are not directly in charge of any of the resources, we would not be able to authorize overtime and the like. We might, however, authorize the contractors to use overtime.

HOUR 20 ANSWERS

CREATE STATUS REPORTS ANSWER

MEMORANDUM
DATE: June 24, 2002
TO: City Preservation Group
FROM: Jack Dana
RE: Restoration Status

The restoration of the old meeting house started on May 1, 2002, about a month behind the original schedule and two weeks behind the baseline schedule. To date, the project plan has been completed and approved, the structural engineer has been hired, and his report gave the building a clean bill of health. Although there are minor flaws in the foundation that should be repaired, the building is in very stable condition.

Based on this positive report, an architect for the project has been retained. He has already completed the plans of the existing building and hopes to have the restoration drawings completed by next week. After I have reviewed the drawings, I will make an appointment to review them with the executive committee.

If you have any questions in the mean time, call me at 555-6321.

CREATE PRESENTATION ANSWER

1. Project Description
   - Business Need—From plan—1 minute
   - Project Goal—From plan—1 minute
   - Project Sponsor—From plan—1 minute
   - Project Approval—How handled and date—2 minutes
   - Project Team—From plan—2 minutes
   - Project Approach—From plan—2 minutes

2. Project Review
   - Start Date—From schedule—1 minute
   - How Contractors were/will be considered—From plan—2 minutes
   - Selection Process—From plan—2 minutes
   - Current Status—From status—2 minutes
   - Next steps—From schedule—2 minutes
   - Occupancy date—From schedule—2 minutes

3. Interesting Notes
   - Cache of balusters under stage—2 minutes
   - Evidence of fire under dressing rooms—2 minutes
   - Hidden pocket doors—architect plans—2 minutes

- Sketches of restored exterior—architect plans—2 minutes
- Sketches of restored first floor—architect plans—2 minutes
- Sketches of restored second floor—architect plans—2 minutes
- Sketches of restored third floor—architect plans—2 minutes
- Questions?

NEWSLETTER ARTICLE ANSWER

For the last few months, we have been involved in the restoration of the old meeting house on Main. When completed in early spring 2003, this facility will bring a much-needed conference and meeting space to our section of town. We will be using the space at a significantly discounted rate, and it will also be rented as a means of income to the preservation group.

To date, the project is moving smoothly, albeit somewhat behind the original schedule. The building has been rated in very stable condition, and the architect renditions of the restored building are complete. The search for contractors will most likely begin next week.

If you have any questions in the meantime, call me at 555-6321.

HOUR 21 ANSWERS

USE COMPLETION PLAN ANSWER

You would follow the completion plan as noted in the original, although you may want to discuss the warranty/support aspects with each individual tradesperson. In fact, this should have been included in the original contract with each.

The actuals versus baselines for the entire project were as follows:

Task	Base. Start	Base. Finish	Base. Cost	Actual Start	Actual Finish	Actual Cost
Restoration Proj.	4/22/02	1/29/03	$169,720	5/1/02	1/29/03	$149,867
1000 Definition	4/22/02	5/3/02	$864	5/1/02	5/13/02	$1,080
1100 Define Scope	4/22/02	4/26/02	$144	5/1/02	5/9/02	$720
1200 Create Plan	4/29/02	5/3/02	$720	5/9/02	5/13/02	$360
2000 Analysis/Des.	5/6/02	8/9/02	$3,832	5/15/02	8/5/02	$5,416
2100 Str. analysis	5/6/02	5/31/02	$688	5/15/02	6/03/02	$1,336
2110 Hire engin.	5/6/02	5/10/02	$216	5/15/02	5/15/02	$688
2120 Get report	5/13/02	5/24/02	$400	5/16/02	5/29/02	$576
2130 Go/no go	5/27/02	5/31/02	$72	6/3/02	6/03/02	$72
2200 Architecture	6/3/02	8/9/02	$3,144	6/3/02	8/5/02	$4,080
2210 Hire arch.	6/3/02	6/7/02	$3,000	6/3/02	6/6/02	$3,288
2220 Exist. plans	6/10/02	6/21/02	$0	6/7/02	6/14/02	$0
2230 New plans	6/24/02	7/12/02	$0	6/17/02	7/3/02	$72
2240 Rev.w/client	7/15/02	7/19/02	$72	7/8/02	7/10/02	$144
2250 Get estimat	7/22/02	8/2/02	$0	7/15/02	8/2/02	$576
2260 Go/no go	8/5/02	8/9/02	$72	8/5/02	8/5/02	$72
3000 Construction	8/12/02	1/14/03	$163,512	8/7/02	1/28/03	$124,899
3100 Prework	8/12/02	9/20/02	$216	8/7/02	9/23/02	$720
3110 Solicit bids	8/12/02	9/6/02	$144	8/7/02	9/10/02	$576
3120 Select contr	9/9/02	9/20/02	$72	9/11/02	9/23/02	$144
3200 Monitor/appr	9/23/02	1/10/03	$126,000	9/30/02	1/28/03	$124,179
3210 Roof repair	9/23/02	10/18/02	$30,000	9/30/02	10/18/02	$26,543
3220 Foundation	9/23/02	10/4/02	$15,000	9/30/02	10/18/02	$10,600
3230 Window/Door	10/21/02	11/29/02	$40,000	9/30/02	12/20/02	$35,732
3240 Wall repair	12/2/02	12/27/02	$15,000	11/7/02	12/27/02	$18,950
3250 Ceiling rep.	12/2/02	12/13/02	$5,000	11/7/02	12/27/02	$4,536
3260 Floor ref.	12/30/02	1/10/03	$6,000	1/8/03	1/17/03	$6,563
3270 Siding/brick	10/7/02	10/18/02	$5,000	10/7/02	10/18/02	$6,745
3280 Interior pt	12/16/02	12/27/02	$5,000	1/17/03	1/28/03	$6,910
3290 Exterior pt	10/21/02	11/1/02	$5,000	11/1/02	11/8/02	$7,500
3300 Ongoing	8/12/02	1/14/03	$37,296	8/7/02	1/28/03	$18,256
3310 Status	8/12/02	1/14/03	$10,656	8/7/02	1/28/03	$10,944

Task	Base. Start	Base. Finish	Base. Cost	Actual Start	Actual Finish	Actual Cost
3320 Pay invoices	8/12/02	1/14/03	$10,656	8/7/02	1/28/03	$1,152
3330 Meetings	8/12/02	1/14/03	$15,984	8/7/02	1/28/03	$6,160
4000 Proj. Review	1/15/03	1/29/03	$1,512	1/28/03	1/29/03	$216
4100 Compare	1/15/03	1/28/03	$1,440	1/28/03	1/28/03	$144
4200 Rev. meeting	1/29/03	1/29/03	$72	1/29/03	1/29/03	$72

Obtain Project Signoffs Answer

The restoration signoff document should be signed by you, the project manager, as well as by Sam Parker, the sponsor, and the president of the preservation group. It might be easiest to gather the signatures in a brief closeout meeting.

The special account for building donations and invoice payments will be closed at project end, as would the Leetle Toy Company account that you charged your time to.

An appropriate restoration project celebration would be to have the entire preservation group, all the employees of the Leetle Toy Company, and representatives of all the other major donors attend an open house in the new conference facility.

Hour 22 Answers

Conduct Restoration Surveys Answer

Client surveys should go to the sponsor and the president of the preservation group. These could be conducted during the signoff meeting if the sponsor and president would be honest with one another in the room. The team surveys would not be appropriate because external subcontractors did the work.

Conduct Lessons-Learned Answer

Again, because of the fact that there wasn't a true "team" performing this project, a lessons-learned session might not be practical. What you would do, though, is analyze the actuals on your own and note what went well and what didn't.

Write Summary Report Answer

The conference center restoration project was designed to turn an old neighborhood eyesore into productive meeting, office, and living space for the city nonprofit preservation group. The building was to be restored following the standards set by the Secretary of the Interior and the state and local preservation offices.

The project was scheduled to start on April 8, 2002, and complete in early January. Despite starting nearly a month late, on May 1, 2002, the project still ended up finishing in late January.

The baseline budget for the project was $169,720, and the actual cost was $149,867, so the project came in under budget. Most of the reduction in cost was due to time-savings in the ongoing tasks of the project manager. Both the Leetle Toy Company management and the preservation group were very pleased with the restoration.

Attached is a table listing the baseline start, baseline finish, baseline effort, and baseline cost columns as well as the actual start, actual finish, actual effort, and actual cost columns.

Hour 23 Answers

Review Lessons Answer

The lessons-learned based on the actuals would have been that the project manager's time on ongoing tasks was overestimated.

Adjust Future Projects Answer

Applying this to future projects, you may want to lower the estimates of hours to pay invoices and attend meetings.

Appendix B
Glossary

Actual Cost of Work Performed (ACWP)   An earned-value field, calculated as the actual cost of the work performed to date.

As Late As Possible (ALAP) Dependency relationship where the finish of the predecessor will be scheduled as late in the schedule as possible.

As Soon As Possible (ASAP) Dependency relationship where the start of the successor task will be scheduled as close to the finish of the predecessor task as possible.

baseline   A stored copy of your original plan used to compare to your actual plan as the project progresses.

bottom-up estimating   Estimating per task, and then totaling the individual estimates to get a total project time and cost estimate.

Budgeted Cost of Work Performed (BCWP)   An earned-value field, calculated as the baseline cost of the work performed to date.

Budgeted Cost of Work Scheduled (BCWS)   An earned-value field, calculated as the baseline cost of what, according to the baseline schedule, should have been performed to date.

co-location   Placing all the key team members in close physical proximity to one another.

communication channel   The communication line between two people or two groups of people. To calculate the channels of communication in a project, use the following formula:

> $C = n(n–1) \div 2$, where n represents the number of people on the project team.

constraint Something that limits a project. Common constraint categories include time, cost, resources, technology, geography, and the like.

contingency plan A plan to cope with uncertain events and uncertain event outcomes.

critical path The longest path through the project network. By definition, all tasks on the critical path have no float, which means that any increase in the duration on any critical tasks will increase the schedules.

dependency A relationship between two tasks in which the start or finish of one is somehow dependent on the start or finish of the other.

dependency violation An error in the schedule where an actual date or hours entered causes the early start dates calculated in the schedule to miss the dependency conditions coded.

duration The elapsed number of days, weeks, and so on that a project task will take.

early finish The earliest a task can finish based on its duration and early start.

early start The earliest a task can start based on dependencies and other project constraints.

earned value A cost and schedule analysis tool designed to help you evaluate whether or not your project is on schedule and within budget.

effort The actual amount of work, usually expressed in resource hours.

Estimate At Completion (EAC) The estimate for both effort and cost at the finish of a task. It is the sum of the actuals to date, plus the new estimate to complete.

Estimate To Complete (ETC) The effort and/or cost left remaining on a task.

float The amount of time that a task can slip without delaying the project. Another term for float is *slack*.

Joint Requirements Planning (JRP) session A technique for gathering and agreeing to system requirements more quickly.

late finish The latest a task can finish without delaying the project.

late start The latest a task can start without delaying the project.

lessons-learned session A postproject meeting with the entire team to review various aspects of the recently completed project. The purpose of this meeting is to document lessons so that subsequent projects can benefit from that knowledge. This meeting may also be called a project-review meeting.

methodology   A set of standards and guidelines, often with templates, used for performing any process.

milestone   A specific point in time tied to a significant project accomplishment.

network diagram   A special type of chart showing the interrelationships between project tasks.

portfolio risk management Evaluating the chances of an individual project's success, based on a variety of factors, including how the project fits with the mix of other projects currently underway.

predecessor   Task on which another task depends.

project   According to the Project Management Institute, a project is a temporary endeavor undertaken to create a unique product or service.

project charter   A document signed by the sponsor and/or client agreeing to the definition of the project and authorizing the continuation of the project.

project management   The planning, scheduling, and controlling of a project to meet the project's goals.

project plan   A formal document with many components. It is not just the project schedule as created in a software package, but includes project goals, objectives, assumptions, and the like.

project quality   Defined as the ability to meet the project's requirements. It does not mean meeting a client's expectations, but properly managed, a project can still do both.

resource leveling   The adjusting of task schedules to eliminate resource overallocation.

resource-constrained task   A task whose duration depends on the number of resources assigned to it, the hours in which they work, and so on.

risk   Any potential event that might delay a project, increase its cost, or otherwise harm the project.

role   The type of work the resource will be performing on the project. In smaller organizations, a single person may perform multiple project roles.

scope   The amount of work to be done in a project.

scope creep   The continual addition of unplanned work to the project.

slack   The amount of time that a task can slip without delaying the project. Another term for slack is *float*.

stakeholder   Anyone who will be affected by a project.

steering committee   A small group of senior executives who approve, prioritize, and monitor projects.

successor   Task whose start and/or finish is somehow dependent on another task.

symbology   The term used for the graphic symbols expressing the durations of tasks in the project schedule.

template   A specially formatted document with a standard layout for the required sections. It may also contain instructions for use. Project management templates are usually word-processing documents for forms and reports, spreadsheet documents for risk and cost/benefit analysis, or scheduling software files for work-breakdown structures.

time-constrained task   A task whose duration is fixed. Adding more resources will not decrease the duration.

top-down (analogous) estimating   Estimating total current projects based on actuals from similar past projects. If a project took 20 percent of its hours in the planning phase, then this project should, also. While some organizations use this method as the primary estimation method, it is generally better used as a reality check for a bottom-up method.

WBS Code   The numeric scheme describing a task's relative position in the hierarchy. The traditional scheme of 1.1.1 would mean the first task, under the first activity, under the first phase. Some organizations use four to eight digit numbers (with 1 equaling 1000, 2.3.1 equaling 2310, and so on) or alphanumeric schemes (A.1 for Analysis.1, and so on).

Weighted AVErage (WAVE) estimating   Creating three estimates for each detail task in your project. Optimistic is the estimate if everything goes perfectly. Pessimistic is the estimate is nothing goes right and is how long a task will most likely take. These three estimates are then averaged, with a weight of four on most likely. The formula is WAVE = [Optimistic + 4(Most Likely) + Pessimistic] ÷ 6.

work package   The collective name given to a project task and all its relevant work information. Generally included in this package are the task name, scheduled start and end date, duration, effort estimate, deliverable, completion measurements, quality measurements, and standards.

Work-Breakdown Structure (WBS)   A hierarchical arrangement of a project's tasks in levels similar to a company's organization chart.

Index

Q–R